D1612843

The
Land of Opportunity

JOSEPH HAYDN
AND BRITAIN

The Land of Opportunity

JOSEPH HAYDN AND BRITAIN

EDITED BY RICHARD CHESSER
AND DAVID WYN JONES

THE BRITISH LIBRARY

First published 2013 by
The British Library
96 Euston Road
London NW1 2DB

Text © 2013 The Contributors
Illustrations © 2013 The British Library Board and other named copyright owners

A catalogue record for this book is available from The British Library

ISBN 978 0 7123 5848 4

Designed and typeset by Geoff Green Book Design, Cambridge CB24 4RA
Printed in England by T J International

Contents

Preface

T EN OF THE ELEVEN ESSAYS in this volume originated as papers given
at an international conference held in the British Library in March 2009 to
mark the 200th anniversary of Haydn's death. Presented in conjunction with the
Haydn Society of Great Britain, the conference took as its theme the relationship
between the composer and the wider commercial, political and social world. While
Haydn's international reputation at the end of the eighteenth century has long been
documented, the enabling characteristics of that relationship have not been subjected
to sustained scrutiny. On more than one occasion the composer remarked that he
became well known in his own country only after he had made his two visits to
London in the 1790s. Very appropriately – particularly for a conference organized
by the British Library – a number of the papers focused on the British environment
and Haydn's response to it.

Revised as a set of complementary essays, most of this volume, *The Land of Opportunity: Joseph Haydn and Britain*, is not, therefore, primarily concerned with
Haydn as a long-standing servant of the Esterházy court, over forty years from 1761
to 1803 (the year he effectively retired from composition), but on the period from
the 1780s onwards when the composer began to engage consistently and decisively
with musical life elsewhere: in Austria, especially Vienna, and in Britain, especially
London. London was to be the only European city, apart from Vienna, to welcome
the composer in person. He engaged fully with its musical life during his two visits
in the 1790s and responded readily to its commercial vitality, later telling his

biographer, Albert Christoph Dies, that it was his 'land of opportunity'. The essays by Alan Davison, Caroline Grigson and Thomas Tolley deal with particular features of Haydn's experience in London.

Although very different, the London period was not to be a self-contained episode in Haydn's life, followed by a retreat into his former existence in Austria. On the contrary, Haydn and London, Austria and Britain remained a constant thread in the composer's life through to his retirement and beyond. Indeed the interaction between the two is key to understanding the unparalleled popularity that the composer and his music enjoyed at the turn of the century. The essays by David Wyn Jones, Balázs Mikusi and David Rowland deal with various aspects of this dual relationship, while those by Ingrid Fuchs, Otto Biba and Rupert Ridgewell focus on the Austrian dimension. Within a year of Haydn's death in May 1809, two biographies of the composer written in German had appeared, by Georg Griesinger and Albert Christoph Dies; prompted by multiple conversations in Vienna with the composer, both reported in detail on the London experience. Christopher Wiley examines some of their features and how they evolved into defining tropes of Haydn biography through to the present day, in English and in German. The final essay, by Arthur Searle, was especially written for this volume and documents another aspect of the Haydn legacy: the holdings of the British Library – manuscripts, printed editions, letters and other material – one of the richest in the world and in its particulars constantly reflecting the Austrian and the British dimensions.

The editors are pleased to record their thanks first and foremost to the authors who have allowed their contributions to be published here. Thanks are also due to Denis McCaldin and his colleagues in the Haydn Society of Great Britain who worked jointly with staff from the British Library in the organization of the bicentennial conference of 2009 in which the original papers were given; we are grateful too to Cambridge University Press for permission to publish Alan Davison's article here in a revised form of the original publication in *Eighteenth-Century Music*. Additional thanks are gratefully given to Stephen Parkin for his assistance with translations from Italian, and to Oliver Neighbour who made countless helpful suggestions in the preparation of the final texts. Finally, the editors owe a debt of gratitude to David Way and his colleagues in British Library Publishing, whose support and guidance have been much appreciated in bringing this work to the press.

Richard Chesser
David Wyn Jones

Illustrations

In addition, various musical examples from printed and manuscript sources relating to Haydn's Piano Trios Hob.XV:5–8, the Keyboard Concerto Hob.XVIII:11, and Giuseppe Sarti's *Sonata caracteristica* are reproduced in Rupert Ridgewell's article (pp. 163–194).

For permission to reproduce the above illustrations, thanks are gratefully given to the relevant authorities at the British Library, London (pp. 19, 94, 165, 171, 172, 186, 187, 199, 222, 223, 224); British Museum, London (pp. 26, 27, 30, 32, 36, 44, 45, 48, 49, 75, 93); National Portrait Gallery, London (p. 37); Royal College of Music, London (pp. 60, 61, 70, 74); Music Collection of the National Széchényi Library, Budapest (pp. 118, 122, 124); Gesellschaft der Musikfreunde in Wien (pp. 139, 141, 142, 148, 153, 161, 203); Bibliothèque nationale de France, Département de la Musique (pp. 168, 181, 182, 183, 184, 185); Universiteitsbibliotheek Utrecht (p. 189).

Abbreviations

Landon, *Haydn: Chronicle and Works*, I	H. C. Robbins Landon, *Haydn: Chronicle and Works*, I: *The Early Years, 1732–1765* (London: Thames and Hudson, 1980)
Landon, *Haydn: Chronicle and Works*, II	H. C. Robbins Landon, *Haydn: Chronicle and Works*, II: *Haydn at Eszterháza, 1766–1790* (London: Thames and Hudson, 1978)
Landon, *Haydn: Chronicle and Works*, III	H. C. Robbins Landon, *Haydn: Chronicle and Works*, III: *Haydn in England, 1791–1795* (London: Thames and Hudson, 1976)
Landon, *Haydn: Chronicle and Works*, IV	H. C. Robbins Landon, *Haydn: Chronicle and Works*, IV: *The Years of 'The Creation', 1796–1800* (London: Thames and Hudson, 1977)
Landon, *Haydn: Chronicle and Works*, V	H. C. Robbins Landon, *Haydn: Chronicle and Works*, V: *The Late Years, 1801–1809* (London: Thames and Hudson, 1977)

Hoboken, *Werkverzeichnis*, I — Anthony van Hoboken, *Joseph Haydn: Thematisch-bibliographisches Werkverzeichnis*, I: *Instrumentalwerke* (Mainz: Schott, 1957)

Hoboken, *Werkverzeichnis*, II — Anthony van Hoboken, *Joseph Haydn: Thematisch-Bibliographisches Werkverzeichnis*, II: *Vokalwerke* (Mainz: Schott, 1971)

Hoboken, *Werkverzeichnis*, III — Anthony van Hoboken, *Joseph Haydn: Thematisch-Bibliographisches Werkverzeichnis*, III: *Register, Addenda und Corrigenda* (Mainz: Schott, 1978)

Collected Correspondence and London Notebooks — *The Collected Correspondence and London Notebooks of Joseph Haydn*, ed. by H. C. Robbins Landon (London: Barrie and Rockcliff, 1959)

Gesammelte Briefe und Aufzeichnungen — *Gesammelte Briefe und Aufzeichnungen*, ed. by Dénes Bartha (Kassel: Bärenreiter, 1965)

Contributors

OTTO BIBA is Director of the Archive, Library and Collections of the Gesellschaft der Musikfreunde in Vienna, a position he has held for over thirty years. He has written extensively on musical life in Vienna from the seventeenth to the twentieth century and has prepared scholarly editions of works by over fifty composers including Brahms, Dittersdorf, Joseph Haydn, Michael Haydn, Mozart and Salieri. He has also curated several exhibitions in the Musikverein, drawing on the rich resources of the Gesellschaft der Musikfreunde.

RICHARD CHESSER joined the British Library as a music curator and became head of the Music department in 2007. His research interests range from the eighteenth to the twentieth centuries and he is active in many bodies in the field of music research, bibliography and copyright. He was President of the UK and Ireland Branch of the International Association of Music Libraries 2010–13, is Chair of the RISM (UK) Trust, and a member of the Commission Mixte of RILM.

ALAN DAVISON is Senior Lecturer in the School of Arts, University of New England, Australia. His specific area of research is in music iconography in European portraiture from the eighteenth and nineteenth centuries, including studies of Dussek, Haydn, Liszt and Mozart. A co-edited volume entitled *Late Eighteenth-Century Music and Visual Culture* will appear in 2013.

INGRID FUCHS was born in Vienna and undertook university studies there in musicology and cello. From 1981 to 1999 she served on the staff of the Committee for Musicological Research at the Austrian Academy of Sciences, Vienna, and from 1986 to 1996 as general secretary of the Austrian Musicological Society. Since September 1999, she has been vice-director of the Archives of the Gesellschaft der Musikfreunde in Wien. She has collaborated on numerous international musicological projects, conferences and exhibitions, and is a regular speaker at musicological conferences in Europe, USA, Canada and Japan. She publishes on the music of the eighteenth, nineteenth and twentieth centuries, especially that of Haydn, Mozart, Beethoven, Brahms, Bruckner and Gottfried von Einem.

CAROLINE GRIGSON's interest in the words of Haydn's songs began when she was researching the composer's relationship with the poet Anne Hunter for her *Life and Poems of Anne Hunter: Haydn's Tuneful Voice* (2009). The manuscripts of Anne's poems, housed in the Royal College of Surgeons in London, where Caroline was the Curator of the College's museums, were the original inspiration for the book. Although trained as a zoologist Caroline has always been fascinated by the relationship between art and science, especially in eighteenth-century England.

DAVID WYN JONES is Professor of Music at Cardiff University. He has written extensively on music and musical life in the classical period. His book on Haydn in the Oxford Composer Companion series is a major reference work which appeared in 2002 and *The Life of Haydn*, published by Cambridge University in 2009, was the first biography of the composer to have appeared in quarter of a century. He is currently in receipt of a major research fellowship from the Leverhulme Trust to write a cultural history of music in Vienna. He is Chair of the Music Libraries Trust and a trustee of the RISM (UK) Trust.

BALÁZS MIKUSI holds a PhD from Cornell University and has been Head of Music at the National Széchényi Library, Budapest, since 2009. A recipient of grants by the Fulbright Commission and the German Academic Exchange Service (DAAD), he has published numerous articles on the music of Haydn (*Eighteenth-Century Music, Journal of Musicological Research, Ad Parnassum, Studia Musicologica*) and Mozart (*The Musical Times, Mozart-Jahrbuch*), as well as studies of musical exoticism in the works of Mendelssohn (*Nineteenth-Century Music*) and Schumann (*The Musical Times*). His monograph entitled *The Secular Partsong in Germany 1780–1815* is forthcoming in the Eastman Studies in Music series of the University of Rochester Press.

RUPERT RIDGEWELL is Curator of Printed Music at the British Library and Honorary Lecturer in Music at Cardiff University. His research interests embrace music printing and publishing, especially in the eighteenth century, Mozart biography and reception, and music bibliography. His publications have appeared in such journals as *Music & Letters*, the *Journal of the Royal Musical Association*, and *Early Music*. In 2010, he was awarded the Richard S. Hill Award by the Music Library Association for the article 'Artaria Plate Numbers and the Publication Process, 1778–87'. He is also Chair of the IAML Bibliography Commission.

DAVID ROWLAND is Professor of Music and Dean of Arts at the Open University. He is the author of three books and numerous chapters and articles on the performance practice and history of the piano and early keyboard instruments. His most significant contribution to Clementi scholarship is the first scholarly edition of the composer's correspondence, which provided the impetus for a much broader investigation of the London music trade during the French Revolution and Napoleonic wars. He has published widely on the relationship between key figures such as Clementi and Dussek and their European counterparts. In addition to his academic work, he is a performer on early keyboard instruments and Director of Music at Christ's College, Cambridge.

ARTHUR SEARLE is Honorary Librarian to the Royal Philharmonic Society, and was formerly Curator of Music Manuscripts at the British Library.

THOMAS TOLLEY is Senior Lecturer in the History of Art in Edinburgh University. He has two distinct specialist areas of expertise: Netherlandish painting in the fifteenth century, and the relationship between music and culture and the practice and theory of music in all periods. A widely acclaimed pioneering study focused on Haydn, *Painting the Canon's Roar: Music, the Visual Arts and the Rise of Attentive Public in the Age of Haydn* (2001). From this he has developed a particular interest in popular prints of the later eighteenth century.

CHRISTOPHER WILEY is Senior Lecturer in Music and Director of Undergraduate Studies at City University London, UK. He is the author of journal articles appearing in *Musical Quarterly*, *Music & Letters*, *Comparative Criticism*, *Biography*, *Musical Stages* and *Journal for Eighteenth-Century Studies*, as well as various book chapters, on subjects as wide-ranging as Ethel Smyth, Michael Jackson, and Buffy the Vampire Slayer. His doctoral dissertation, 'Re-writing Composers' Lives: Critical Historiography and Musical Biography', undertaken at the University of London, provides a critical examination of musical biography through comparative studies of texts on several canonical composers. He is currently preparing a monograph on the earliest volumes of the celebrated Master Musicians series. Other research interests include music and gender studies, popular music studies and music for television.

Haydn, Austria and Britain: Music, Culture and Politics in the 1790s

DAVID WYN JONES

'Such a thing is possible only in England'

During an eight-week period at the end of the 1795 musical season in London, the concert room in the King's Theatre was the venue for five benefit concerts for some of the leading participants in the only subscription series to be held that year, the Opera Concert. The violinist Madame Gillberg was the first, on Thursday 23 April, followed by Wilhelm Cramer, the leader of the orchestra, on 1 May; Haydn's concert took place three days later, 4 May; a concert for the double bass player Domenico Dragonetti occurred on 8 May; and, finally, on 8 June, there was a concert for Andrew Ashe, the flute player.[1] Haydn participated in all five, directing one of his latest symphonies from the keyboard on each occasion. The Opera Concert had been set up as a loose, rather uncomfortable alliance between leading figures from the concert world in London and members of the opera company in the King's Theatre, and Haydn, nominally, was one of four featured composers alongside Clementi, Martin y Soler and Francesco Bianchi. But he was undoubtedly the main attraction, not only as a composer but also as a revered musical figure in general. For the composer's own benefit concert, on 4 May, the most frequently performed of his London symphonies, the 'Military' Symphony (no. 100), was an inevitable choice and was presented alongside two entirely new works, a concert aria for Brigida Banti, 'Berenice

1.   Landon, *Haydn: Chronicle and Works*, III, 304–13.

che fai', and what was to be his last symphony, no. 104. Haydn wrote in one of his London Notebooks: 'The whole company was thoroughly pleased and so was I. I made four thousand Gulden on this evening. Such a thing is possible only in England.'[2]

The particular aspect that prompted Haydn's appreciation was money. Since it was the composer's benefit concert one would expect some indication of how successful it had been, but the remark does also reveal a certain consistent, mercenary, streak in his personality, and there is no disguising his delight at this figure: 4000 gulden was the amount deposited at the Fries banking house in Vienna. The exchange rate in 1795 was nine gulden to a pound,[3] which gives a figure of £450, a considerable sum. Elsewhere in the London Notebooks Haydn writes that a chicken for roasting cost seven shillings; a pair of scissors, three shillings; six shirts, eight guineas; and a gold watch, thirty guineas; if a gold chain was needed to go with the watch, that was another guinea.[4] Haydn could easily afford all these and much more. More relevant to music, a subscription ticket for the 1795 Opera Concert (nine evenings) cost four guineas,[5] a ticket for a single public concert was usually ten shillings and sixpence. Half a guinea was also the standard price for a set of six quartets, such as John Bland's publication in 1792 of the op. 64 set; and seven shillings and sixpence would buy a collection of six songs, such as the first and second set of Canzonettas by Haydn.[6] These random prices were part of an entrepreunerial commercialism that characterized British economic life in general and governed much of its musical life in particular and, although Haydn himself never wrote at length about this, it is this wider economic vibrancy that prompted the many details recorded in his Notebooks and informed the admiring comment 'Such a thing is possible only in England.'

Implicit in this remark is Haydn's recognition of the many differences between musical life in London in the 1790s and that in Austria, whether at the Esterházy court or in Vienna. Haydn's benefit concert was his reward for being a leading participant in the Opera Concert of 1795. Subscription concerts followed by several benefit concerts for the leading figures had been a well-established pattern in

---

2. *Collected Correspondence and London Notebooks*, p. 306; *Gesammelte Briefe und Aufzeichnungen*, p. 553.

3. Exchange rate as recorded by Ignaz de Luca, *Topographie von Wien* (Vienna, 1794); facsimile edn (Vienna: Promedia, 2003), p. 219. Taking ten shillings and sixpence as the price of a ticket for Haydn's benefit concert and the composer's income of £450 this produces a notional audience of *c.* 850, close to the reported capacity of the Concert Room in the King's Theatre of 800.

4. *Collected Correspondence and London Notebooks*, pp. 259, 277, 251; *Gesammelte Briefe und Aufzeichnungen*, pp. 492, 515, 481.

5. Landon, *Haydn: Chronicle and Works*, III, 286.

6. See title-pages transcribed in Hoboken, *Werkverzeichnis*, I, 418; II, 254, 262.

London for over thirty years – notably the Bach-Abel concerts from 1765 to 1781, the Pantheon Concerts between 1774 and 1785, the Professional Concerts between 1785 and 1793, and the Salomon Concerts in 1786 and 1791–94 – making the city one of the leading centres for public concerts in the whole of Europe.[7] This was in stark contrast to Vienna, where there was no equivalent organization that promoted subscription concerts over a sustained period of time; the last attempt at a public subscription series had been that of Mozart in 1788, and it is not certain that it took place.[8] There were benefit concerts in Vienna but these were one-off occasions, usually for the benefit of a performer, especially singers, rather than for a composer.[9] Apart from the public theatres, musical life in Vienna was at its most active in private, in the palaces of the aristocrats and the salons of the slowly emerging professional class. As Kapellmeister at the Esterházy court, Haydn composed symphonies as part of his formal duties; in London he composed symphonies as part of a commercial contract negotiated with an impresario, Salomon, in 1791, 1792 and 1794, and the Opera Concert in 1795. If the performances went well, which they always did, there was then a gathering momentum towards a successful benefit concert at the end of the season.

It is worth unpicking the role that the symphony played in concerts in London and refining the still familiar narrative, that Haydn was invited to London by Salomon as a composer of symphonies. As Ian Woodfield's work on Salomon and on the music publisher John Bland has shown,[10] it was rather more complex than that. In 1790 Salomon and Bland (who already knew the composer in person) were working alongside a third individual, Sir John Gallini, trying to organize the musical programme for the re-opening of the King's Theatre in the Haymarket, splendidly re-built after a fire. Gallini made himself responsible for the season of Italian opera, Salomon was going to be the leader of the opera orchestra and the organizer of a parallel concert series, and any composer or performer–composer could be directed

7. Simon McVeigh, *Concert Life in London from Mozart to Haydn* (Cambridge: Cambridge University Press, 1993); Simon McVeigh, 'The Professional Concert and Rival Subscription Series in London, 1783–1793', *RMA Research Chronicle*, 22 (1989), 1–135.

8. In a letter to Michael Puchberg, apparently written in June 1788, Mozart refers to his Casino concerts that begin in a few weeks (that is in the Trattnerhof), but there is no other record of them. See *The Letters of Mozart and his Family*, ed. by Emily Anderson, 3rd edn revised by Stanley Sadie and Fiona Smart (London: Macmillan, 1985), pp. 914–15; *Mozart: Briefe und Aufzeichnungen* ed. by Wilhelm A. Bauer and Otto Erich Deutsch, 7 vols (Kassel: Bärenreiter, 1962–75), IV (1962), 65.

9. Mary Sue Morrow, *Concert Life in Haydn's Vienna: Aspects of a Developing Musical and Social Institution* (Stuyvesant, NY: Pendragon Press, 1989), pp. 50–51.

10. Ian Woodfield, 'John Bland: London Retailer of the Music of Haydn and Mozart', *Music & Letters*, 81 (2000), 210–44; Ian Woodfield, *Salomon and the Burneys: Private Patronage and a Public Career* (Aldershot: Ashgate, 2003), pp. 72–76.

to Bland as a would-be publisher. Haydn's hurriedly arranged first visit to London was negotiated by Salomon in Vienna in December 1790 but he was acting directly on behalf of Gallini, while simultaneously cementing the existing relationship with Bland. Accordingly, Haydn agreed to compose an opera for Gallini and symphonies for Salomon. As is well known, the opera, *L'anima del filosofo*, was more or less completed by Haydn but because Gallini had failed to secure a licence for theatrical performances in his new theatre it was never performed. In those altered circumstances, Haydn was able to concentrate on the second element of the contract – the composition of symphonies.

Given this wider background to the invitation, it is worth asking two related questions: how central was the symphony to musical life in London and what were Haydn's views on the relative importance of the genre as he anticipated his journey to London? From the time of Bach and Abel in the 1760s, public concerts in London had always featured at least one symphony; in the 1780s it was more often or not a work by Haydn, especially in the Professional Concert.[11] It is safe to assume that Haydn knew this, but it is doubtful that he shared the perception of the English of the wider status of his symphonies. Haydn's daily existence at Eszterháza was dominated by Italian opera, not symphonies, and it had been like that for fourteen years. Next in importance for Haydn in the 1780s was the music he was able to compose because of the priorities of Artaria, his publisher in Vienna: quartets, piano trios, piano sonatas, variations and songs. It took the two visits to London and the initial, potentially humiliating non-performance of an Italian opera to convince the composer of something the London public already knew: the primacy of the composer's symphonies. Two days after Haydn's benefit concert in May 1795 the *Morning Chronicle* included the following on the composer's last symphony, the one posterity was to call the 'London' Symphony; the sense of Haydn and the symphony becoming central to an unfolding historical narrative is clear.[12]

> He rewarded the good intentions of his friends by writing a new Overture [symphony] for the occasion which, for full, richness and majesty in all its parts, is thought by some of the best judges to surpass all his other compositions. A Gentleman, eminent for his musical knowledge, taste and sound criticism, declared this to be his opinion, that, for fifty years to come Musical Composers would be no better than imitators of Haydn; and would do little more than pour water on his leaves. We hope the prophecy may prove false; but probability seems to confirm the prediction.

This newspaper criticism is typical of its kind: a considered assessment of the impact of the music in descriptive terms, but with some hints of wider aesthetic

11. See the programmes detailed in McVeigh, 'The Professional Concert', 27–79.
12. Landon, *Haydn: Chronicle and Works*, III, 308.

concerns, followed by acclaim of its creator, the composer himself. Again all this was something new for Haydn. Whereas London had several newspapers that regularly reported on musical life (*Morning Chronicle, Oracle, Sun* and *Times*), Vienna had one, the *Wiener Zeitung*, the court newspaper, which hardly ever did. From this culture of reporting and debating emerged the public figure of the creative artist; as soon as he set foot in London in January 1791, Haydn was the centre of attraction; he was constantly surprised by this adulation, sometimes wearied, but in the end gratified. A natural extension of this celebrity status was that Haydn sat for his portrait six times while in London: there were paintings by Thomas Hardy, John Hoppner, Ludwig Guttenbrunn and A. M. Ott, a pencil drawing by George Dance, and a wax profile by James Tassie.[13]

It was in this thriving civic culture that Haydn, always a naturally curious man, acquired a new layer of intellectual curiosity, materially promoted by the award of an honorary doctorate from Oxford University. By the end of 1795, his English was reasonably fluent, if somewhat erratic, but certainly good enough to purchase, or receive as appropriate gifts, a ten-volume edition of the plays of Shakespeare, a book on Captain Cook's voyages, a guide to the Isle of Wight, as well as Charles Burney's four-volume history of music. In addition to books, Haydn acquired a substantial collection of music in Britain and had a distinctive taste for British engravings too.[14] Dr Haydn, as he liked to be called, was now a connoisseur and a gentleman, as well as an artist.

As well as regular performances of his music from the mid-1780s onwards, Haydn's reputation in London was sustained and promoted by an active music publishing industry. As a result of his meeting with Haydn in Eisenstadt in 1788–89, John Bland became the London publisher of the op. 64 Quartets (duly played in the first season of Salomon's concerts), and also of the popular cantata *Arianna a Naxos*. Nearly a decade earlier, William Forster had secured an agreement with the composer that led to a regular supply of symphonies and quartets.[15] During his four years in London, Haydn responded enthusiastically to the musical marketplace: he

13. On the Thomas Hardy painting, see Alan Davison's article at pp. 59–76 below. The wax profile by James Tassie was discovered in 1979: see H. C. Robbins Landon, 'A New Haydn Portrait', *Soundings*, 9 (1979–80), 2–5. The miniature by A. M. Ott was discovered in 1996: see Otto Biba, 'Ein verschollen gewesenes Haydn-Portrait', *Musikblätter der Wiener Philharmoniker*, 50/7 (Vienna, 1996), 219–22.

14. The music acquired by Haydn in London is discussed in Balázs Mikusi's article, at pp. 112–136 below; Haydn's collection of British engravings is the subject of Thomas Tolley's article, pp. 22–58 below.

15. Full details are given in William Sandys and Simon Andrew Forster, *The History of the Violin and other Instruments Played on with the bow from the remotest times to the present* (London: J. R. Smith, 1864), pp. 300–14.

set over 150 Scottish folk songs for William Napier, part of the wider fashion for all things Caledonian, composed English canzonettas for Corri, Dussek and Co. and entrusted the same company with the publication of the Quartets opp. 71 and 74. The most important publisher, however, was Longman & Broderip and its successors. From the 1780s, they had acted as Artaria's agents in London, importing most of Haydn's music published in Vienna by the firm; in the 1790s, they were the authorized publisher in London of several sets of piano trios and the op. 76 Quartets, and then, with Clementi on board, attempted to strengthen further the relationship at the turn of the century. In various intertwining combinations – Haydn and Artaria, Haydn and Longman & Broderip, and Artaria and Longman & Broderip – this is a complex narrative that spreads over fifteen years.[16] It also characterized a wider musical relationship between Britain and Austria.

German culture and 'Music of the Austrian school'

The foregoing emphasizes the differences in musical culture between Haydn's Britain and Haydn's Austria, and the enthusiasm with which the composer embraced them with immediate and enduring effect on his creativity. But Haydn was not a lone figure in London, and certainly not an outsider. There was a wider receptivity to German culture – the term is used in the sense that Haydn would have used it, culture from German-speaking countries – in London in the 1790s that nurtured this particular enthusiasm for the composer.

To begin at the top of society, the ruling Hanoverian dynasty was German, and that language was still regularly heard at court. When Haydn was invited to Windsor Castle in 1795, he and George III conversed in German, and the composer sang a German version, 'Ich bin der verliebteste', of his English canzonetta 'Content'.[17] He had been a much more frequent guest of the Prince of Wales, a notable enthusiast for music, in Carlton House; again the language of conversation was German. His brother, the Duke of York, invited Haydn to his country estate, Oatlands, near Weybridge in Surrey, in November 1791; the Duke had recently married the daughter of Friedrich Wilhelm II, Friedericke Charlotte Ulricke. An accomplished musician, at the age of seventeen she was rather homesick and sat next to Haydn

16. Rupert Ridgewell's article at pp. 163–193 below investigates the unusual history of Artaria's publication of three piano trios in the mid-1780s (Hob.XV:6–8); David Rowland's article at pp. 92–111 below documents the relationship between Artaria in Vienna and Longman & Broderip in London in the late 1790s.

17. *Haydn: Two Contemporary Portraits*, trans. and ed. by Vernon Gotwals (Madison: University of Wisconsin Press, 1968), p. 34; Georg August Griesinger, *Biographische Notizen über Joseph Haydn* (Leipzig: Breitkopf & Härtel, 1810), p. 58.

for four hours at a music party during which the composer played the piano and sang, probably in German.[18]

A substantial number of London's instrumentalists were German. Born in Bonn, Salomon had lived in the city since 1781, his principal rival as a violinist and leader, Wilhelm Cramer, even longer, from 1772; other resident Germans included Karl Friedrich Baumgartner, Johann Ludwig Dussek, Joseph Diettenhofer, Friedrich Hartmann Graff, Nicholas Joseph Hüllmandel and Franz Tomich. Haydn was not the only visiting German composer in London in the early 1790s: Gyrowetz was in London from 1790 to 1792, and Pleyel, a former pupil of Haydn, was resident composer in the Professional Concert during the 1792 season. Salomon, with Haydn's approval, had vague plans to invite Mozart and, later, the young Beethoven to London.[19] Both would have felt at home. An inspiring model to everybody, including Haydn, was the earlier but omnipresent example of the German composer Georg Friedrich Händel, who had become a treasured Englishman, George Frederic Handel.

Modern commentators on Salomon's concerts in London in 1791, 1792 and 1794 have quite understandably concentrated on Haydn's contribution, but he was not the only German who figured as a composer of symphonies. While he dominated the concerts certainly, with fifty-two performances in three seasons, there were also seven performances of symphonies by Gyrowetz, two by Hoffmeister, eight by Kozeluch, one by Mozart, four by Pichl, five by Pleyel, six by Reichardt and six by Rosetti;[20] all but the last two – that is Gyrowetz, Hoffmeister, Kozeluch, Mozart, Pichl and Pleyel – had associations with Vienna. The Viennese Classical School is a problematic term. Not the least of its problems is that there was a Viennese Classical School in London in the early 1790s, with Haydn at its head and at a particularly significant time in the development of a key genre, the symphony. In the fourth volume of his *General History of Music*, published in 1789, Charles Burney, a persuasive advocate of German music, had incorporated Haydn, Kozeluch, Mozart and others into the chapter entitled 'Music in Germany during the XVIII century'; a very short penultimate

---

18. Letter from Haydn to Maria von Genzinger, 20 December 1791: *Collected Correspondence and London Notebooks*, p. 123; *Gesammelte Briefe und Aufzeichnungen*, p. 268.

19. Salomon's attempt to invite Mozart to London is mentioned in *A Mozart Pilgrimage, Being the Travel Diaries of Vincent & Mary Novello in the year 1829*, trans. by Nerina Medici di Marignano and ed. by Rosemary Hughes (London: Novello, 1955), p. 92. That a visit for the 1792 season was planned is given some credence by a remark in a letter dated 13 October 1791 from Haydn to Maria von Genzinger: he asks her to inform Mozart that if he has queries about Haydn's remuneration in London he should ask his banker (Fries) and Prince Esterházy. See *Collected Correspondence and London Notebooks*, p. 120; *Gesammelte Briefe und Aufzeichnungen*, p. 264. For Beethoven's proposed visit see Landon, *Haydn: Chronicle and Works*, III, 192–93.

20. Statistics compiled from the programmes given in Landon, *Haydn: Chronicle and Works*, III, 45–83, 133–72, 233–52.

paragraph in the chapter is devoted to the publisher Artaria who, Burney notes, has 'opened an extensive commerce in the sale of the Music of the Austrian school'.[21] This formulation, 'Austrian school', was never to catch on but it was obviously a characteristic that Burney recognized as early as the 1780s. In the following decade, this incipient focus on Austria, rather than Germany in general, was to gain real presence, as contemporary political events unfolded and the music of one Austrian composer in particular, Haydn, became intertwined with them.

Austria and Britain: a political and musical alliance

The influence of Britain on Haydn remained long after he left the country in 1795. He stayed in contact with Salomon, Burney and the firm of Longman & Broderip amongst others, and two of his largest works, *The Creation* and *The Seasons*, were fundamentally determined by an English heritage, both literary and musical. *The Creation* was conceived as a bilingual work and published in 1800 with parallel texts in German and English. The score was preceded by a lengthy subscription list,[22] conspicuously headed by members of the Austrian imperial court (the empress Marie Therese, the court secretary Heinrich Joseph von Collin, the Grand Duke and Duchess of Tuscany, Archduke Joseph, Archduke Ferdinand and Duke Albert of Sachsen-Teschen), followed by members of the British royal family (Queen Charlotte, King George, Prince of Wales, Princess of Wales, Duchess of York, and five princesses, Augusta, Elizabeth, Maria, Sophia and Amalia). This is a very striking expression of Haydn's esteem in his native country and in the country that had embraced him so enthusiastically. Yet, it is only one such representation of Haydn's twin affections and needs to be projected against the stormy historical events of the 1790s, the immediate aftermath of the French Revolution, the French Revolutionary Wars and the early course of the Napoleonic Wars.

For much of that decade, and through to 1814, Austria and Britain were formal coalition partners in the struggle against the common enemy, France.[23] Formed in 1792, the so-called First Coalition also included Holland, Prussia and Spain but by the summer of 1795 Austria and Britain stood alone; following Napoleon's aggressive Italian campaign and fearing an invasion of their heartlands, Austria and

21. Charles Burney, *A General History of Music, from the Earliest Ages to the Present Period*, 4 vols (London: author, 1776–89), with critical and historical notes by Frank Mercer (New York: Dover, 1957), II, 963.

22. David Wyn Jones, *The Life of Haydn* (Cambridge: Cambridge University Press, 2009), pp. 198–200. Haydn's manuscript list of subscribers is transcribed in Landon, *Haydn: Chronicle and Works*, IV, 619–32.

23. For a concise history, especially useful for the Austrian perspective, see Charles Ingrao, *The Habsburg Monarchy 1618–1815* (Cambridge: Cambridge University Press, 1994), pp. 226–39.

France signed the Peace of Campo Formio, leaving Britain and France as the sole combatants for months. A similar pattern then began to unfold once more: the formation of a Second Coalition in January 1799 (Austria, Britain, Italian states, Papal states, Russia, Turkey and Portugal), the withdrawal of a major power, Russia, later in 1799, a signing of a peace treaty between Austria and France in 1801, and Britain as the sole protagonist until it, too, signed a peace treaty, the Treaty of Amiens, in 1802. These events are summarized in the first column of Table 1, where they are placed alongside salient aspects of Haydn's career and reputation in Britain and in Austria up to 1802, when the composer had all but retired from composition.

Table 1 does not provide a complete list of Haydn's music composed in the last twelve years of his working life, much less a complete list of music by the composer that was published in London and Vienna during the period. It focuses on those works that, to a greater or lesser extent, reflected national pride in Austria and Britain, or, for instance, in the case of the two oratorios, *The Creation* and *The Seasons*, promoted a dual national heritage.

The number of works that evoke nationalist pride – British, Austrian – or mutual national solidarity, is significant: over fifteen, covering a wide range of genres, including a canzonetta (the 'Sailor's Song'), a full-scale vocal cantata (*The Battle of the Nile*), a patriotic ode (*Invocation of Neptune*), incidental music (the *Alfred* music), two masses (*Missa in tempore belli* and *Missa in angustiis*), several marches, symphonies, and a quartet featuring the new Austrian national anthem, 'Gott erhalte Franz den Kaiser', itself composed by Haydn.

Any number of detailed narratives could be teased from this material: the particular popularity of the 'Military' Symphony in England throughout the period, the role of the march in general in Haydn's output, and the cultural as well as political symbolism represented by the separate visits of Admiral Nelson and Count Starhemberg, the Austrian ambassador in London, to Eisenstadt. Many of the mentioned works feature prominently in an article by Nicholas Mathew that argues strongly for a developing heroic aesthetic in Haydn's music and, consequently, a heroic status for its creator too.[24] This essay focuses on the composition and early reception of two works, 'Gott erhalte' and the 'Sailor's Song', that illuminate the linked political and cultural histories of Austria and Britain in the 1790s.

Two national anthems and an Anglican hymn

The most overtly patriotic work in Table 1 is the national anthem, or 'Volkslied' as Haydn called it, commissioned by the Austrian authorities from the composer

24. Nicholas Mathew, 'Heroic Haydn, the Occasional Work and "Modern" Political Music', *Eighteenth-Century Music*, 4 (2007), 7–25.

Date	European Conflict	Haydn in London	Haydn in Vienna/Eisenstadt
1789	Outbreak of French Revolution.		
1790			
1791	End of Austro-Turkish war. Austria and Prussia threaten military support for Louis XVI.	January: Haydn arrives in London.	
1792	First Coalition formed: Austria, Britain, Holland, Prussia, Spain. France declares war on Austria. Prussia declares war on France.	Notes the anecdote of hearing 'God save the King' played during a snowstorm on the express order of Lord Claremont. Principal motif of slow movement of Symphony no. 98 alludes to 'God save the King'. Composes the chorus 'The Storm'. Composes march for the Prince of Wales.	July: Haydn returns to Vienna.
1793	Louis XVI and Marie Antoinette guillotined. Reign of Terror. France declares war on Britain, Holland and Spain.		'The Storm' performed in German translation.
1794	Jacobin sympathizers ruthlessly suppressed in Austria.	February: Haydn arrives. Symphony no. 100 ('Military') performed six times in just over three months, including Haydn's benefit concert in May. Begins composition of patriotic ode, *Invocation of Neptune*; two out of five/six movements completed. Following the 'Glorious First of June', Haydn visits Portsmouth and boards a captured, heavily damaged French ship in the harbour but is denied access to the dockyard because he is a foreigner. Writes in one of his Notebooks about the failed attempt to assassinate George III.	Unidentified Haydn symphony performed at two benefit concerts for war widows and orphans.

Date	European Conflict	Haydn in London	Haydn in Vienna/Eisenstadt
1795	France signs peace treaties with Holland, Prussia and Spain, leaving Austria and Britain as the sole enemy states.	'Military' Symphony performed three times between February and May. 'Sailor's Song' published as first song in second set of Canzonettas. Composes two marches for the Derbyshire Regiment. At some point during the second visit Haydn makes an arrangement of 'God save the King' (lost).	August: Haydn's return journey is via Hamburg and Dresden in order to avoid Rhine war zone. Three symphonies (from nos 99–104) performed in Kleiner Redoutensaal.
1796	France initiates pincer movement on Austria, from west and south.	'Military' Symphony performed twice in Salomon's concerts.	First performance of incidental music to *Alfred, King of Saxons*. Symphony no. 94 ('Surprise'), and possibly others, performed at five concerts for the benefit of the Vienna Volunteer Corps. *Missa in tempore belli* first performed in Vienna.
1797	Napoleon's troops occupy Carinthia. Austria and France sign armistice at Leoben, confirmed by Peace of Campo Formio, leaving Britain as sole enemy state.	Piano trio arrangement of 'Military' Symphony published by Salomon.	Volkslied 'Gott erhalte Franz den Kaiser' performed throughout Austrian territories. Quartet op. 76 no. 3 includes it as a theme for a set of variations. *Missa in tempore belli* performed in Eisenstadt.
1798	Tricolour provocatively raised outside French embassy in Vienna. Britain and France fight for supremacy in the Mediterranean; Battle of the Nile.	Quintet arrangement of 'Military' Symphony published by Salomon.	First, semi-public performances of *Die Schöpfung*. 'Sailor's song/Matrosenlied' issued in a bilingual publication of the second set of Canzonettas by Artaria. *Missa in angustiis* ('Nelson' Mass) first performed in Eisenstadt. 'Military' Symphony performed at the two Christmas concerts of the Tonkünstler Societät.

Date	European Conflict	Haydn in London	Haydn in Vienna/Eisenstadt
1799	Second Coalition formed: Austria, Britain, Italian states, Papal states, Russia, Turkey and Portugal. Austria declares war on France; achieves major victories in Italy. Russia withdraws from Second Coalition	Op. 76 Quartets published by Longman, Clementi & Co. Charles Burney translates text of 'Volkslied' as 'Hymn for the Emperor Francis'.	Op. 76 Quartets published by Artaria. First public performances of *Die Schöpfung*. Unidentified Haydn symphony performed at benefit concert for the fallen of the Tyrol.
1800	Napoleon achieves strategic victories at Marengo and Hohenlinden.	First performances of *The Creation* in London.	Haydn directs performances of two unidentified symphonies at a benefit concert for wounded soldiers. Directs *Die Schöpfung* in a benefit concert for wounded soldiers. Publishes *Die Schöpfung* / *The Creation* as a bilingual score, with a list of subscribers headed by the Austrian imperial and British royal families. Nelson, Lady Hamilton and others visit Eisenstadt; Haydn composes *Battle of the Nile* for Emma Hamilton; possible performance of 'Nelson' Mass.
1801	Austria and France sign Treaty of Luneville.	'Military' Symphony performed at Salomon's benefit concert. 'Volkslied' published as an Anglican hymn, 'Praise the Lord, ye Heav'ns adore Him'; tune later often named 'Austria'.	First, semi-private and public performances of *Die Jahreszeiten* in Vienna.
1802	Britain and France sign Treaty of Amiens.		Composes Hungarian National March. Austrian Ambassador in London, Count Ludwig Starhemberg, visits Eisenstadt and meets Haydn. *Die Jahreszeiten* / *The Seasons* published bilingually by Breitkopf & Härtel.

Sources
Oesterreich 1790–1848: Das Tagebuch einer Epoche ed. by Peter Csendes (Vienna: Christian Brandstätter, 1987). Anthony van Hoboken, *Joseph Haydn: Thematisch-bibliographisches Werkverzeichnis*, 3 vols (Mainz: Schott, 1957–78). Charles Ingrao, *The Habsburg Monarchy 1618–1815* (Cambridge: Cambridge University Press, 1994). David Wyn Jones, 'Haydn, Hoffmeister, Beethoven and Mozart. Salomon's 1801 concert series', *Festschrift Otto Biba zum 60. Geburtstag*, ed. by Ingrid Fuchs (Tutzing: Schneider, 2006), pp. 29–37. Landon, Haydn: *Chronicle and Works*, III and IV. Ian Taylor, *Music in London and the Myth of Decline: From Haydn to the Philharmonic* (Cambridge: Cambridge University Press, 2010).

in the winter of 1796–97.[25] Their stated motivation was to have a national song – hence 'Volkslied' – that equalled the patriotic fervour that 'God save the King' produced in Britain at a time (the winter of 1796–97) when Austria and Britain were the only two remaining European powers from the First Coalition still at war with France. The text is clearly modelled on that of the British anthem, including the climactic repetition of 'God save' as 'Gott erhalte'. It might be thought that the Austrian authorities would have turned to a court composer in this time of national crisis, Salieri, Kozeluch or Teyber; instead, they turned to Haydn, an Austrian who had achieved unprecedented success in London and who personified that sense of international solidarity that the anthem was meant to promote. Performances of Haydn's music in Vienna had recently become strongly associated with the Austrian war effort; in the autumn of 1796 five benefit concerts were held in the Grosser Redoutensaal and the Kärntnertor Theater to raise money for the Vienna Volunteer Corps that was to defend the city in the event of invasion. The precise content of these benefit concerts is not known but the 'Surprise' Symphony, no. 94, composed in London in 1794, was given several times.[26] From performing one of the 'London' Symphonies in order to foster national resolve to composing an Austrian national anthem to match the British one was an entirely natural progression.

Table 1 allows the relationship between 'God save the King' and 'Gott erhalte', Haydn the committed Anglophile and the proud Austrian, to be traced through the 1790s. Haydn, who was more than once alarmed by the excessive drinking of the British aristocracy, noted the following eccentric performance of 'God save the King' in one of the London Notebooks:[27]

> Lord Claremont recently gave a large *Soupé*, and when the King's health was drunk, he ordered the wind band to play the well-known song, 'God save the King' during a wild snowstorm. This occurred on 19 February 1792, so madly do they drink in England.

Also in 1792 the slow movement of Symphony no. 98 seems to allude to the opening of 'God save the King', constructing a four-note motif that figures throughout the slow movement, differently harmonized on each occasion. At some point during Haydn's two visits, the composer made an arrangement of the anthem, now lost. The only reference to the work is its inclusion in a list of compositions for London contained in the fourth London Notebook and subsequently transcribed by

25. Otto Biba, *God Preserve: Joseph Haydn's Imperial Anthem: Facsimile of the First Edition, 1797* (Vienna: Doblinger, 1982); Landon, *Haydn: Chronicle and Works*, IV, 241–49.

26. Morrow, *Concert Life*, 292; Landon, *Haydn: Chronicle and Works*, IV, 110–11.

27. *Collected Correspondence and London Notebooks*, p. 276; *Gesammelte Briefe und Aufzeichnungen*, p. 513.

Griesinger;[28] described as occupying two sheets of manuscript paper it could either have been for voice and orchestra or, perhaps more likely, a setting for smaller domestic forces.

Haydn's op. 76 Quartets, including no. 3 in C with 'Gott erhalte' as the theme for a set of variations, were published simultaneously in Vienna and London in 1799, by Artaria and by Longman, Clementi & Co. respectively. Neither publication identifies the source of the melody in the set of variations. Austrian players and listeners, of course, would have done so with immediate delight. In London, Charles Burney seems to have determined to make British audiences aware of its origins by publishing the Austrian anthem with an English translation of the text within a few months of the publication of op. 76.[29] In a letter to Haydn, Charles Burney writes enthusiastically about the op. 76 Quartets and goes on to mention his English translation of 'Gott erhalte'. The letter is written in English rather than the Italian the correspondents had previously used, partly because Burney wanted to flatter Haydn, but more particularly because he is keen to encourage the composer to compare the original German text with the English translation.[30]

> The Divine Hymn, written for your imperial master, in imitation of our loyal song, 'God save great George our King', and set so admirably to music by yourself, I have translated and adapted to your melody, which is simple, grave, applicating, and pleasing [...] in comparing my version with the original, you will perceive that it is rather a paraphrase than a close translation; but the liberties I have taken were in consequence of the supposed treachery of some of his Imperial Majesty's generals and subjects, during the unfortunate campaign of Italy, of 1797, which the English all thought was the consequence, not of Buonaparte's heroism, but of Austrian and Italian treachery.

Burney's 'paraphrase' was not just a convenient solution to the usual problem of rendering, with minimum adjustment to the music, a poetic text into another language. Very deliberately, as the author frankly indicates to Haydn, he wanted to adjust the text to reflect residual sensitivity in Britain about Austria's capitulation in 1797, the effective end of the First Coalition. The original German has four verses

28. *Collected Correspondence and London Notebooks*, pp. 309–10; *Gesammelte Briefe und Aufzeichnungen*, pp. 555–56; *Haydn: Two Contemporary Portraits*, trans. and ed. by Gotwals, pp. 31–32; Griesinger, *Biographische Notizen*, pp. 53–55.

29. *Hymn for the Emperor. Translated by Dr. Burney. Composed by Doctor Haydn* (London: printed by Broderip and Wilkinson, [n. d.]). It is set for two sopranos, bass and piano, with the climactic section marked 'Chorus'.

30. Letter is dated 19 August 1799: *Collected Correspondence and London Notebooks*, p. 164; *Gesammelte Briefe und Aufzeichnungen*, p. 335.

of eight lines each; Burney's translation has four verses of ten lines each. The sensitive lines are at the end of the first two verses.[31]

Gott! erhalte Franz den Kaiser	God preserve the Emp'ror Francis!
Unsern guten Kaiser Franz!	Sov'reign ever good and great;
Lange lebe Franz der Kaiser	Save, o save him from mischances
In des Glückes hellstem Glanz!	In Prosperity and State!
Ihm erblühen Lorbeer-Reiser,	May his Laurels ever blooming
Wo er geht, zum Ehren-Kranz!	Be by Patriot Virtue fed;
Gott! erhalte Franz den Kaiser,	May his worth the world illumine
Unsern guten Kaiser Franz!	And bring back the Sheep misled!
	God, preserve our Emp'ror Francis!
	Sov'reign ever good and great.
Lass von seiner Fahnen Spitzen	From his glorious Banners streaming,
Strahlen Sieg und Fruchtbarkeit!	May success and plenty grow!
Lass in seinem Rate sitzen	In his Councils brightly beaming.
Weisheit, Klugheit, Redlichkeit;	O may wisdom, prudence flow!
Und mit seiner Hoheit Blitzen	Fill the hearts of his Commanders
Schalten nur Gerechtigkeit!	With integrity and zeal;
Gott! erhalte Franz den Kaiser,	Be they deaf to lies and slander
Unsern guten Kaiser Franz!	Gainst their Prince and public weal
	God, preserve our Emp'ror Francis!
	Sov'reign ever good and great.

'May his worth the world illumine / And bring back the Sheep misled' is a reference to the perception in Britain that the Austrian army in Italy combined with some voices of authority in Hapsburg Vienna had surrendered prematurely in 1797, signing a preliminary treaty in April (Leoben) even as the British foreign minister, Lord Grenville, was travelling to Vienna to persuade the Habsburg authorities to maintain the First Coalition.[32] Two years on, and with the Second Coalition formed and achieving some notable victories against the French, Burney is anxious to promote the authority of the Austrian emperor; at the end of the second verse he pointedly encourages the loyalty of 'his Commanders', a sentiment entirely absent in the German original. With Haydn surreptitiously implicated, Charles Burney had managed to incorporate a British perspective into the most overt musical manifestation of the Austro-British alliance, the Austrian national anthem.

Burney's description of 'Gott erhalte' as a 'Hymn' and a 'Divine Hymn' was unwittingly prophetic of its later reception in Britain. By the end of the Victorian

---

31. The complete German text and English translation are given in Otto Erich Deutsch, 'Haydn's Hymn and Burney's Translation', *Music Review*, 4 (1943), 157–62 (pp. 160–61).

32. William Hague, *William Pitt the Younger* (London: Harper Collins, 2004), pp. 399–400.

era, the melody was widely known as a hymn tune, variously titled 'Austria', 'Vienna' and 'Haydn', with two standard texts, 'Glorious things of Thee are spoken' and 'Praise the Lord, ye Heav'ns adore him'.[33] The appropriation of the national anthem of a staunchly Catholic country as a Protestant hymn had begun as early as 1801, when the London publisher Joseph Dale issued it as a single vocal line with piano accompaniment, setting the four verses of 'Praise the Lord, ye Heav'ns adore him', a metrical version of Psalm 148.[34] Dale may well have been capitalizing on the increasing number of performance of Haydn's *Creation* in England, in particular the many choruses of praise in the work that derive their text from the psalms.

The 'Sailor's Song' and the 'Matrosenlied'

While the history of 'Gott erhalte' is of an Austrian work that was modified by British environment, the history of 'The Sailor's Song' is the reverse, a British work that had to be adapted to suit the Austrian environment. It was composed in the winter of 1794–95 and published by Corri, Dussek & Co. in August 1795 as the first song in the second set of six Canzonettas. The two verses, by an unknown poet, paint a stirring image of a fearless sailor on the high seas whose sole duty is to maintain 'Britain's glory' in the face of the 'hostile foe'. It was clearly meant to tap into the rampant jingoism that followed the Reign of Terror and at a time when the First Coalition was becoming increasingly disunited. In the summer of 1794, the British navy had achieved a notable victory over the French fleet at Cape La Hogue, the celebrated 'Glorious First of June'. The damaged French ships and their captured sailors were taken to Portsmouth, where they soon became a prize attraction for visitors, including Haydn. In one of his Notebooks he wrote all kinds of detail about his visit, clearly drawing on conversations as well as personal observation: he comments on the damaged ships, the differences between an English man-of-war, a frigate, a brig, a cutter and a fire-ship (he sketches a crude drawing of the last), gives details of how enemy ships are torched and the role of a cockswain.[35] When it came to writing 'The Sailor's Song' a few months later, Haydn could not have been a more enthusiastic patriot.

Haydn took the six Canzonettas back to Vienna with him and began to interest

33. For details of the origins of the two texts and the publication of the hymn tune in the nineteenth century see J. Julian, *A Dictionary of Hymnology*, rev. ed. (London: John Murray, 1907), pp. 903–04; and *An Annotated Anthology of Hymns* ed. by J. R. Watson (Oxford: Oxford University Press, 2002), pp. 216–18.
34. No title-page. The music is headed 'Praise the Lord, ye Heaven's adore him, Adapted to Dr. Haydn's celebrated Hymn'. It was entered at Stationers' Hall on 21 August 1801; *Music Entries at Stationers' Hall 1710–1818* [compiled by] Michael Kassler (Aldershot: Ashgate, 2004), p. 457.
35. *Collected Correspondence and London Notebooks*, pp. 289–91; *Gesammelte Briefe und Aufzeichnungen*, pp. 532–33.

Artaria in a German version. Artaria had already published three collections of songs by the composer: two sets of German songs in the 1780s (Hob.XXVIa:1–24) and a German translation of the first set of English Canzonettas in 1794. Publishing the next set of Canzonettas was a natural continuation and it duly appeared in July 1798.[36] What is unusual about this publication is that it is a bilingual one, with the German translation, credited to one Daniel Jäger, running in parallel above the English original; previously all Artaria's publications of Haydn's songs had been in German only. Artaria's customers were predominantly local and though there was a small English-speaking community in Vienna, it was hardly large enough to warrant the effort of providing the English text as well as the German translation. It seems that Artaria and Haydn between them wished to make a wider statement about the composer and his music, to suggest a sense of shared values between Austria and Britain; in addition to featuring Haydn, the set includes a setting of words from Shakespeare's *Twelfth Night*, 'She never told her love', rendered as 'Stets barg sie ihre Liebe'. If that was the intention, it was severely compromised in the German translation of the 'Sailor's Song'. The complete bilingual text is given below; Fig. 1 reproduces two pages of the song.

'Sailor's Song'
High on the giddy Mast
The seaman ferles the rending sail.
And fearless of the rushing blast

He careless whistles to the Gale.
Rattling ropes and rolling Seas.
Hurly Burly! Hurly Burly!
War nor Death can him displease.

The Hostile Foe his Vessel seeks
High bounding o'er the Raging Main!
The Roaring Cannon loudly speaks
Tis BRITAIN'S Glory we maintain.
Rattling ropes and rolling Seas.
Hurly Burly! Hurly Burly!
War nor Death can him displease.

'Matrosen Lied'
Hoch klimmt der Seeman auf den Mast
Und fragt nicht ober wankt und kracht.
Der Sturmwind heult, ihn kümmerts
    nicht,
Er singet sorgenfrey sein Lied.
Rollt, ihr wogenpfeife Wind.
Hurli Burli! Hurli Burli!
Krieg und Tod ich kenn' euch schon von
    langem her.
Krieg und Tod, ihr schreckt mich nicht,
Ihr schreckt mich keinen Augenblick

O Schade dass die Feinde nicht
Sich jetzt zu kommen unterstehn!
Zum Donner der Kanonen klingt
Ein muntres Liedchen wunderschön.
Rollt ihr wogenpfeife Wind.
Hurli Burli! Hurli Burli!
Krieg und Tod ich kenn' euch schon von
    langem her.
Krieg und Tod ihr schreckt mich nicht,
Ihr schreckt mich keinen Augenblick.

36. *Sechs Lieder beym Clavier zu singen mit deutschem und Englischen Texte. Die Musik vom Herrn Joseph Haydn. 4ter Theil.*

The translation is a reasonably close one for much of the first verse except for some minor changes, ones that ultimately assume greater significance. Whereas the English has the sailor whistling, in the German the sailor 'sings without care his song'. The final single line 'War nor Death can him displease' is rendered as three lines: 'Krieg und Tod ich kenn' euch schon von langem her / Krieg und Tod ihr schreckt mich nicht / Ihr schreckt mich keinen Augenblick' ('War and Death I've known you already for some time / War and Death you don't frighten me, / You don't frighten me for a moment'). This expanded translation seems entirely unnecessary since the German version could easily have used the second line only, 'Krieg und Tod ihr schreckt mich nicht', repeating the last four words to mirror the several repetitions of 'can him displease' in the English original. The added first line, 'Krieg und Tod ich kenn' euch schon von langem her', hints at a weary familiarity with war and death, a sentiment not evident in the English, which bravely welcomes both. In the second verse the changes are even more obvious, comically so: the climactic middle lines in the English 'The Roaring Cannon loudly speaks, tis Britain's Glory we maintain' are given as 'Zum Donner der Kanonen klingt ein muntres Liedchen wunderschön', literally 'To the roar of cannons beautifully sounds a lively little song', linking back to the singing sailor, rather than the whistling sailor, of the first verse and, conveniently, to the title of the song. Evidently the sailor's bravery is just something to sing about; it is not associated explicitly with the British cause. This jars fundamentally with Haydn's music, particularly for the immediate repetition of the text in which a held note on 'Glory' is accompanied by an outburst of martial figuration in the piano; in the German that outburst underpins the words 'little song', blatantly avoiding at least one German word that would have fitted, 'Ehre'. In this bilingual edition, therefore, Haydn's responsive British jingoism is toned down for the German-speaking Viennese. Why?

The only explanation is censorship, promoted by particular anxieties in 1797–98. All published texts in Vienna, from playing cards to plays, had to be scrutinized by the imperial censors to ensure that they did not contain anything that unsettled the population.[37] Even though Britain was a long-standing ally, tub-thumping nationalism of any kind was obviously thought potentially dangerous. The date of publication, July 1798, is of crucial significance. Since the previous October, following the signing of the Peace of Campo Formio with France, Austria had not been an active participant in the war and the First Coalition had finally unravelled. For much of 1798 the sensitive authorities were painfully anxious to maintain the appearance

---

37. Franz Hadamowsky, 'Ein Jahrhundert Literatur- und Theaterzensur in Österreich', *Die österreichische Literatur: Ihr Profil an der Wende vom 18. zum 19. Jahrhundert (1750–1830)*, 2 vols, ed. by H. Zeman (Graz: Akademische Druck- und Verlaganstalt, 1979), I, 289–306.

Fig. 1. Joseph Haydn, 'Matrosen Lied' ('Sailor's Song') from *Sechs Lieder beym Clavier zu singen mit deutschem und englischen Texte* (Vienna: Artaria, 1798).

of neutrality, even as they were preparing for the resumption of hostilities.[38] This febrile atmosphere was evidenced in the provocative display of the French Tricolour outside the home of the French Ambassador in April 1798; the public became alarmed and attacked the house before the anxious Austrian authorities acted quickly to restore law and order.[39] It was during this period that Artaria would have submitted Haydn's text to the imperial censors; he may, of course, have already anticipated difficulties by submitting a German text that did not overtly praise the now former coalition partner. But, as often with censorship (or the fear of censorship), there was an element of futility: anybody who could read English or even spot the word 'Britain's' in capital letters would immediately have responded to the sense of Austro-British identity in Haydn's song.

The greatest living Austrian and the greatest living Briton

Haydn told his first biographer, Griesinger, that some of the happiest days of his life had been spent in England, and that he had become famous in his native country only after becoming famous in England.[40] These seemingly casual remarks hide some fundamental truths. As Kapellmeister at the Esterházy court for nearly thirty years before his first visit to London, Haydn lived in a social environment that could not have been more different from that which he experienced in Britain. And both environments were different again from that of Vienna, a city the composer visited for only a few weeks of the year in the 1770s and 1780s, typically either side of Christmas, and which had not always readily embraced him as a composer. Only in the last phase of his life, after the second visit to London, did the composer identify himself wholeheartedly with Vienna, and Vienna with him; much of that new identity has a strong British element to it, not merely as a natural consequence of Haydn's two hugely successful visits but as a product of contemporary European politics.

Music historians have always celebrated the part that London played in Haydn's musical development, notably that of the symphony, but the composer was also an active agent in a much broader historical process at this time, one in which culture interacted with new economic forces, social change and political turmoil. In partic-

38. C. A. Macartney, *The Habsburg Empire, 1790–1918* (London: Weidenfeld & Nicolson, 1969), p. 155.

39. The incident is recounted in Thayer's biography of Beethoven as background to Anton Schindler's claim, now thoroughly discredited, that the idea of the 'Eroica' Symphony originated at this time. See *Thayer's Life of Beethoven*, rev. and ed. by Elliot Forbes, 2 vols (Princeton, NJ: Princeton University Press, 1964), I, 203–04.

40. *Haydn: Two Contemporary Portraits*, trans. and ed. by Gotwals, pp. 23, 36; Griesinger, *Biographische Notizen*, pp. 36, 62.

ular, through his music Haydn symbolized the most potent political alliance of the time, that between Austria and Britain, one that was eventually to triumph five years after the composer's death, in 1814. Fourteen years earlier, in September 1800, Admiral Nelson together with Lady Hamilton visited the Esterházy court in Eisenstadt, an occasion that encapsulated and celebrated that relationship.[41] Haydn, who owned an engraving of Nelson, spent some time with the guests. Since the admiral spoke only English, the composer, ever the diplomat, presumably revived his fractured knowledge of the language. He composed a cantata, *The Battle of the Nile*, that was duly performed by the composer and Emma Hamilton. The greatest living Briton gave Haydn a watch. At Nelson's request, the greatest living Austrian had given him something infinitely more meaningful: a used quill.

41. Otto Erich Deutsch, *Admiral Nelson und Joseph Haydn. Ein britisch-österreichisches Gipfeltreffen*, ed. by Gitta Deutsch and Rudolf Klein (Vienna: Österreichischer Bundesverlag, 1982). Landon, *Haydn: Chronicle and Works*, IV, 558–62.

Caricatures by
Henry William Bunbury in the
Collection of Joseph Haydn

THOMAS TOLLEY

T HE DISCOVERY, discussed here for the first time, that six prints after drawings by the celebrated amateur artist Henry William Bunbury (1750–1811)
formed part of the print collection of Joseph Haydn presents an opportunity to re-
assess Bunbury's artistic production from the early 1790s, when the prints were first
published, in light of the composer's interest in it. All six prints were probably acquired by Haydn during this period, when the composer was in London, where the
prints were issued. Bunbury enjoyed a reputation at this time matched only by professional caricaturists such as Rowlandson and Gillray.[1] Horace Walpole, who collected everything he could of Bunbury's, called him 'the second Hogarth; and the
first imitator who ever fully equaled his original', an opinion shared by Garrick.[2]

1.   For Bunbury, see in particular: John C. Riely, *Henry William Bunbury: The Amateur as Caricaturist*,
     exh. cat. (Sudbury: Gainsborough House, 1983); Peter de Voogd, *Henry William Bunbury 1750–
     1811: 'De Raphaël der Carricatuurteekenaars'*, exh. cat. (Amsterdam: Rijksmuseum, 1996); *A Talent
     to Amuse: The Eighteenth-Century Caricaturist Henry William Bunbury, 1750–1811*, exh. cat. (Nor-
     wich: Norwich Castle Museum, 1998).
2.   George Paston, *Social Caricature in the Eighteenth Century* (London: Methuen, 1905), p. 83;
     John C. Riely, 'Horace Walpole and *the Second Hogarth*', *Eighteenth-Century Studies*, 9 (1975),
     28–44. For Garrick on Bunbury, see letter no. 1128 (8 September 1776) in *The Letters of David
     Garrick*, ed. by David Mason Little and George Morrow Kahrl (London: Oxford University
     Press, 1963).

As late as 1823, a Dutch visitor to England expressed the view that he was 'the Raphael of caricaturists'.[3]

Contemporary accounts point to two aspects of Bunbury's work on which his reputation in England was chiefly founded: first, a capacity to make any audience laugh; and, second, an ability to entertain without giving offence. Unlike the creations of many contemporary caricaturists, Bunbury's prints, it was felt, could be safely viewed by anyone, their 'exquisite humour' containing 'no ribaldry, no profaneness, no ill-natured censure'.[4] Even members of the royal family, targets of so much visual satire in late eighteenth-century England, are known to have relished his designs.[5] According to the poet Cowper, Bunbury's 'expressive figures' were so 'immeasurably droll' that the world might 'die of Laughing' were they to be complemented by verse and set to music.[6] Indeed, one of Bunbury's most popular prints actually became the basis of a *tableau vivant* on the London stage, performed with music in the late 1780s and 1790s.[7] It seems likely that this musical aspect to contemporary appreciation of Bunbury encouraged Haydn in his own regard for the artist.

Like other admirers of Bunbury's work, Haydn would also have relished the artist's singular ability to identify and capture through his pencil comic situations, a talent that led to the name Bunbury being frequently invoked by writers during the last two decades of the eighteenth century to draw attention to a scene, the visual aspects of which contained the potential for humour.[8] For example, in 1781 Fanny Burney, the literary daughter of Haydn's friend the music historian Charles Burney, instinctively identified a particular situation – and its comic potential – as of the kind on which Bunbury built his reputation. Recalling an evening spent with Dr Johnson, she recorded how the great man had[9]

3. De Voogd, *Bunbury*, p. 47.
4. From an obituary notice of 1811, reprinted in Joseph Grego, *Rowlandson the Caricaturist*, 2 vols (London: Chatto & Windus, 1880), I, 79.
5. Fanny Burney reports how members of the royal family enjoyed Bunbury's work: *Diary and Letters of Madame d'Arblay as edited by her niece Charlotte Barrett*, with preface and notes by Austin Dobson, 6 vols (London: Macmillan, 1904–05), III (1905), 304, 308, 316, 323–24, 331, 481.
6. *The Letters and Prose Writings of William Cowper*, ed. by James King and Charles Ryskamp, 5 vols (Oxford: Clarendon Press, 1979–86), III (1982), 87–88, quoted in Diana Donald, *The Age of Caricature: Satirical Prints in the Reign of George III* (New Haven: Yale University Press, 1996), p. 75.
7. The print in question was *A Long Minuet as Danced at Bath* (1787). There are documented performances (acting as an after-piece) in 1789 and 1795, though there were presumably others between: *The London Stage 1660–1800*, ed. by Charles Beecher Hogan, 5 parts (Carbondale: Southern Illinois University Press, 1968), V, ii (1164); iii (1805, 1807).
8. For examples see: *A Tour from London to the Lakes, containing Natural, Economical, and Literary Observations, Made in the Summer of 1791* (London: [n. p.], 1792), p. 59; Mary Elizabeth Robinson, *The Shrine of Bertha: A Novel in a Series of Letters*, 2 vols (London: printed for the author, 1794), II, 69.
9. *Diary and Letters of Madame D'Arblay*, I (1904), 497.

forced me to sit on a very small sofa with him, which was hardly large enough for himself; and which would have made a subject for a print by Harry Bunbury that would have diverted all London; *ergo*, it rejoiceth me that he [Bunbury] was not present.

Shortly after this Bunbury did indeed feature Dr Johnson in a print, the doctor's corpulent frame – and how he maintained it – providing the basis of its satire.[10]

The collection formed by Haydn which included the Bunbury prints is no longer extant, having been dispersed shortly after his death in 1809. However, an inventory of the composer's possessions drawn up in Vienna with a view to their sale permits a reasonably comprehensive reconstruction of its contents.[11] The collection consisted of over two hundred prints, mostly kept in a portfolio, with a small number framed and glazed, presumably so that they might be displayed on the walls of his house in the Viennese suburb of Gumpendorf.[12] The precise number of printed items in the collection cannot now be established with certainty since the cataloguer did not always distinguish clearly between prints and other items (such as the occasional drawing) kept with them. Several prints were sometimes also included in the catalogue under a single item and accounted for rather vaguely.[13] But for many items, the cataloguer provided sufficient details (titles, names of designers and engravers) to identify the prints unambiguously. Although little care was taken in transcribing words – Bunbury's name, for example, consistently appears as 'Bunburg' – it is clear that the bulk of the collection consisted of English prints, the majority of which (judging from their dates of publication) are likely to have been acquired when Haydn was in England.[14]

10. *A Chop-House* (1781). For the identification with Dr Johnson, see *Catalogue of Political and Personal Satires Preserved in the Department of Prints and Drawings in the British Museum*, 11 vols (London: British Museum, 1870–1954), VI, ed. by Mary Dorothy George (1938), no. 5922.

11. The inventory recording the collection of engravings belonging to Haydn, drawn up after his death, was published without comment by Landon, *Haydn: Chronicle and Works*, V, 392–403. For discussion of Haydn's print collection, see: Thomas Tolley, *Painting the Cannon's Roar: Music, the Visual Arts and the Rise of an Attentive Public in the Age of Haydn, c. 1750 to c. 1810* (Aldershot: Ashgate, 2001), pp. 207–57, 324–26; Otto Biba, 'Joseph Haydn: Kunst-Freund, -Kenner und -Sammler', *Musikblätter der Wiener Philharmoniker*, 63/9 (2009), 337–50.

12. The portfolio was seen by Haydn's early biographer, the painter Albert Christoph Dies, during a visit to the composer on 9 June 1806: 'Haydn showed me a portfolio of copper engravings, some of them purchased in London, some received as gifts.' Albert Christoph Dies, *Biographische Nachrichten von Joseph Haydn*, ed. by Horst Seeger (Berlin: Henschelverlag, [1959]), p. 131.

13. Item 609, which is discussed later in this article, is one example of this.

14. Correspondence between Haydn and one of his publishers, however, indicates that Haydn was starting to form a collection with a special interest in English prints by 1789 at the latest, two years before his first London visit: *Gesammelte Briefe und Aufzeichnungen*, p. 203; *Collected*

Haydn's motivation for collecting perhaps stemmed in part from knowledge of the extensive print collections assembled in Vienna in the second half of the eighteenth century, such as the one amassed by Prince Nicolaus Esterházy, his patron.[15] Another patron connected with Haydn before he arrived in London, Prince Kraft Ernst von Oettingen-Wallerstein, is known to have taken copies of many prints published in London, including those also subsequently collected by Haydn. Knowledge of these collections perhaps influenced Haydn's thinking.[16] By the time that Haydn was sufficiently secure financially to devote funds to a print or two, such collecting was recognized as a valuable pastime for the well-to-do in German-speaking countries.[17] During the last quarter of the eighteenth century, English prints in particular claimed the attention of collectors throughout the German-speaking world.[18] By the time Haydn came to England, Bunbury's reputation had certainly already reached German-speaking countries. One account published in Germany in 1790 describes how crowds would gather around caricature shops in London 'where they stare at the latest inventions of Bunbury, perhaps or Gillray' with 'merriment and pleasure'.[19] According to Johann Wilhelm von Archenholz, whose account this is, the hilarity provoked by such caricatures charmed those who came to them with preconceived moral objections, since the joy they inspired ensured the whole population took a healthy interest in the political process.

Haydn's specific interest in Bunbury, however, requires special explanation since

14. *Cont.*
  Correspondence and London Notebooks, p. 83. Although the Bunbury prints were probably acquired during Haydn's first visit to London in 1791–92, he continued to add to it during his second visit of 1794–95.
15. For an account of these collections, see Antony Griffiths and Frances Carey, *German Printmaking in the Age of Goethe*, exh. cat. (London: British Museum, 1994), p. 18.
16. Haydn visited the Oettingen-Wallerstein court at Wallerstein Castle in southern Germany on his way to England at the end of 1790.
17. Johann Georg Sulzer's *Allgemeine Theorie der schönen Künste*, the popular and influential encyclopedia first published 1771–74, promoted the study and collecting of prints as a critical factor in the formation of good taste, in itself a matter, Sulzer claimed, of (German) national significance. Print collecting was also especially recommended in verses about various hobbies and pastimes by Anna Louise Karshin, published in the *Lauenburger Genealogischer-Kalender* for 1781 and illustrated with a set of engravings by her friend, the engraver Daniel Niklaus Chodowiecki under the title *Steckenpferdreiterei* ('Hobbyhorse Riders'). Among several hobbies discussed, only print-collecting, it is claimed, may be practised with total approbation: Griffiths and Carey, *German Printmaking*, p. 62.
18. Timothy Clayton, 'Reviews of English Prints in German Journals 1750–1800', *Print Quarterly*, 10 (1993), 123–37.
19. *Annalen der Brittischen Geschichte des Jahrs 1789*, 3 (1790), pp. 189–90; translation from Christiane Banerji and Diane Donald, *Gillray Observed: The Earliest Account of his Caricatures in London and Paris* (Cambridge: Cambridge University Press, 1999), p. 22, n. 62.

Fig. 1. *Patience in a Punt*, by Henry Bunbury, engraved and published by
W. Dickinson, 1 May 1792.

Bunbury was one English artist who seems to have baffled many Germans. In England, Bunbury's talent for humour was usually understood as a vehicle for ridiculing
whole social groupings and their behaviour, rather than prominent individuals or
their political views. In Germany and elsewhere, however, this distinction seems to
have been made much less readily, Bunbury's name often being coupled with that
of the most biting of English personal and political caricaturists, Gillray, as though
there were little to distinguish them.[20]

Haydn's distinct interest in Bunbury is evident from the fact that he selected three
of his six Bunbury prints for framing and display at Gumpendorf. No other artist
represented in the collection was singled out in this way. The prints in question were
catalogued after his death as 'Patience in a punt, dann Bethnal Green und ein
anderes nach Drawing von Bunburg.'[21] *Patience in a Punt* was published on 1 May
1792 and *Bethnal Green* on 11 June of the same year. Both were issued by W.
Dickinson, the engraver, who had a print shop at 24 Old Bond Street. The unnamed
print can reasonably be identified as *Patience in a Punt No 2*, also published by

20. For contemporary texts by foreign visitors to England, commenting on the practice and reception
    of English caricature, which discuss Bunbury and Gillray as though they were apparently
    indistinguishable, see Banerji and Donald, *Gillray Observed*, pp. 26, 204 (with comment in n. 2).
21. Item 55, catalogued immediately after the heading 'Kupferstich unter Glas und Rahme': Landon,
    Haydn: Chronicle and Works, V, 393.

Fig. 2. *Patience in a Punt No 2*, by Henry Bunbury, engraved and published by
W. Dickinson, 1 May 1792.

Dickinson on 1 May 1792.[22] Probably haste in cataloguing the collection led the
compiler of the inventory to ignore a title which he had already just written down
in referring to its companion. Haydn's selection of these three prints for display suggests either that they held a particular appeal for him, or that they represented some
kind of special significance which he wished to recall through regular viewing.

Patience in a Punt (Fig. 1) shows two men, oblivious to the world, solemnly fishing
on a punt. One of them, his poor vision apparently unimproved by the pair of spectacles he wears, has caught a small dog in the river, looked on in amazement by the
boy who propels the boat. A third man, smoking a pipe, sits with his back to the
others, uninterested in their enterprise. He seems merely to have come along for
the ride. The whole situation, especially the idea of fishing from a moving punt, is
clearly intended to be seen as ludicrous. The visual joke takes on further resonance
when it is recognized as a parody of George Morland's *Party Angling*, a favourite
work by a popular artist of the time.[23]

22. *Patience in a Punt No 2* features the inscription 'Engraved from an Original *Drawing* by H.
 Bunbury Esqʳ', the wording of which fits the entry by the cataloguer. Haydn also possessed *A
 Smoking Club*, a further print after Bunbury published on 1 May 1792, suggesting that he probably
 acquired all three prints published on this date at the same time. For descriptions of these prints,
 see *Catalogue of Political and Personal Satires*, nos 8205–08.
23. Engraved in mezzotint by William Ward and published by J. R. Smith in 1780; reissued in colour
 in 1789.

Patience in a Punt No 2 (Fig. 2) is a variant of the same theme. This time the punt is, appropriately enough for a fishing party, moored to a pole close to the riverbank. The four men on board are all starting to show their age: one appears to be asleep, his bait dangling in mid-air, eyed by a duck beneath; the second, his rod leaning on his shoulder, yawns widely, expressing boredom; the third, probably the boatman, is trying to hook a worm onto the line of the yawning man, who has evidently lost interest; the fourth man, having taken off his coat and wig, which is suspended on the back of a chair, has caught his line on some foliage on the bank and is trying to free it. Both prints, with their amusing details, were clearly intended to provoke laughter from their audience; but the premise on which Bunbury based his humour had more far-reaching consequences for his contemporaries.

In the later eighteenth century, patience was a topical theme in literature and the visual arts in England, with memorable consequences for foreign visitors. For example, Mozart, who had only been to England as a child, associated the idea of patience with the English, as is evident from some jottings he made in a visitors' book belonging to a Viennese teacher of English, at a time when he was contemplating a visit to London in 1787.[24] Haydn, who found himself in tune with and sensitive to most aspects of English culture, is likely to have understood and relished this English preoccupation of the time. One of his English canzonettas is a setting of part of Viola's moving speech from Shakespeare's *Twelfth Night*, which includes the lines 'like *patience* on a monument smiling at grief'.[25] At the time Haydn was in London, these lines were well known through the portrayal of Viola by the actress Dorothea (Dora), whom Haydn is known to have particularly admired.[26] Bunbury, one of Mrs Jordan's most ardent fans, actually depicted her in this role.[27] Haydn

24. 'Patience and tranquillity of mind contribute more to cure our distempers as the whole art of medecine [*sic*].' Signed and dated by Mozart, 30 March 1787: Otto Erich Deutsch, *Mozart: A Documentary Biography*, trans. by Eric Blom, Peter Branscombe, and Jeremy Noble (London: Black, 1965), p. 287.

25. As a female personification, associated with sorrow, suffering and adversity, Patience had long been known to educated audiences from Cesare Ripa's *Iconologia*, three editions of which in English appeared in 1785: Mario Praz, *Studies in Seventeenth-Century Imagery*, 2nd edn (Rome: Edizioni di Storia e Letteratura, 1964), p. 474. Haydn's Canzonetta (Hob.XXVIa:34) is part of a set of songs first published in 1795.

26. *Gesammelte Briefe und Aufzeichnungen*, pp. 390–91, 516; *Collected Correspondence and London Notebooks*, pp. 198–99, 278. For Haydn's interest in Mrs Jordan, see Thomas Tolley, '"Exemplary patience": Haydn, Hoppner and Mrs Jordan', *Imago musicae*, 20 (2003), 109–41.

27. *The Duel Scene between Sir Andrew Aguecheek and Viola (Twelfth Night, III.iv)*: see *Shakespeare in Art*, ed. by Jane Martineau, exh. cat. (London: Merrell, 2003), pp. 136–37, no. 39. It is suggested later in this article that Haydn owned the print made after this representation. For a literary tribute to Mrs Jordan by Bunbury, see James Boaden, *The Life of Mrs Jordan, including Original Private Correspondence and Numerous Anecdotes of Her Contemporaries*, 2 vols (London: Edward Bull, 1831), I, 184–86.

may also have known Maria Cosway's painting, first exhibited in 1781, illustrating the 'Patience on a monument' speech from *Twelfth Night*, or the print after it.[28] The artist, however, who most consistently explored the theme of patience in later eighteenth-century England was Angelika Kauffman. Her subjects often illustrate the theme of wifely obedience and devotion in the face of long-term adversity. *Gualtherius and Griselda* (Iveagh Bequest, Kenwood House), based on a famous tale found in Boccaccio and Chaucer, is one example portrayed by Kauffman which extols the exceptional patience of the heroine, presenting it as worthy of imitation by the artist's female contemporaries.[29] One woman Haydn knew in England who certainly would have valued this sentiment was Mary Boydell, wife of John Boydell, the famous publisher of popular prints.[30] Her personal collection of publications issued by her husband, assembled in 1790, includes an inscription addressed to artists, impressing on them 'the truth […] that Industry, *Patience* and Perseverance, united to Talents, are certain to surmount all Difficulties'.[31] Her husband had previously issued a print after a painting by Kauffman, inscribed 'Industry, attended by Patience and assisted by Perseverance …'.[32] Patience was therefore an issue for women in England in the later eighteenth century.

In fact, so deeply was the theme of patience and its association with women

28. Stephen Lloyd, *Richard & Maria Cosway: Regency Artists of Taste and Fashion*, exh. cat. (Edinburgh: National Libraries of Scotland, 1995), p. 134 (no. 235). Mrs Cosway was an artist whom Haydn certainly admired. He acquired for his own collection a print after one of her paintings made for the fifth exhibition of Thomas Macklin's Poets' Gallery in 1792. This was *Lodona*, illustrating a passage in Pope's *Windsor Forest*, engraved by Haydn's friend Francesco Bartolozzi: Landon, *Haydn: Chronicle and Works*, V, 392 (no. 28). For the engraving, see Lloyd, *Richard & Maria Cosway*, p. 134 (no. 233). The admiration seems to have been mutual; Mrs Cosway's attempts to obtain a score of Haydn's *The Creation* in later life are well documented. Not only does her name appear on the list of subscribers to *The Creation* (see Landon, *Haydn: Chronicle and Works*, IV, 624), but also her determination to acquire a copy of *The Creation* at the time of publication is referred to in a letter from Fanny Burney to Charles Wesley written in 1821: see *The Journals and Letters of Fanny Burney (Madam d'Arblay)*, ed. by Joyce Hemlow and others, 12 vols (Oxford: Clarendon Press, 1972–82), XI (1982) 232, n. 1252.

29. Another favourite 'patience' theme with Kauffman was the story of Penelope endlessly waiting for the return of her husband, Ulysses: see figs 12, 23, 33, 47, 48 in *Angelica Kauffman: A Continental Artist in Georgian England*, ed. by Wendy Wassyng Roworth (London: Reaktion Books for the Royal Pavilion, Brighton: 1992). The story of Griselda was a particular favourite in the eighteenth century forming, for example, the basis of a number of operas, including the *Griselda* of Bononcini, popular in London in the 1720s.

30. Haydn refers to Mary Boydell in his first London Notebook (1791–92). He wrote that 'she is Mylady and remains so': *Gesammelte Briefe und Aufzeichnungen*, p. 483; *Collected Correspondence and London Notebooks*, p. 253.

31. Winifred H. Friedman, *Boydell's Shakespeare Gallery* (New York: Garland, 1976), p. 31.

32. *Kauffman*, ed. by Roworth, p. 182.

Fig. 3. *Patience on a Monument*, by James Gillray, published by
H. Humphrey, 19 September 1791.

etched on the consciousness of genteel English society that by the time of Haydn's
first visit to London it had become the object of satire. An especially bitter comment
on patience as a convention is Gillray's *Patience on a Monument* (Fig. 3), published
in September 1791, which mocks the social pretensions of one of the leading so-
cialites of the period by implying that fashions associated with female youth and
beauty, including the pretense of patience, become ridiculous when exhibited by
older women.[33] The starting-point for the theme of this print is the same speech in
Twelfth Night, spoken by Viola, a young and beautiful woman, part of which was

33. *Catalogue of Political and Personal Satires*, no. 7971. This caricature shows a pyramid monument
    in relief in front of which appears the wizened figure of Lady Cecilia Johnston. For Gillray, Lady
    Cecilia (known in royal circles as 'the divine') personified pretentious and outmoded coquetry,

set by Haydn. This is also the inspiration for the humour in Bunbury's pair of prints. Viola makes the 'patience on a monument' speech disguised as a man, a situation which presented Bunbury with an opportunity to subvert patience's traditional associations and undermine its premise, the very notion of patience on a punt being altogether less secure (than patience on a monument). Both of Bunbury's patience prints show men mindlessly engaged in a time-consuming pursuit, thus parodying the convention of female patience advocated by Kauffman and mocked by Gillray. In drawing attention to a favourite *male* pastime, especially of the retired, requiring considerable patience for success, Bunbury derides both the convention of patience itself and a certain kind of individual, apparently considered inept and self-absorbed, associated with the pastime.[34]

Although these prints may be enjoyed for their visual humour alone, the situations they portray presenting hilarious spectacles of men of advanced years at recreation, the appeal of the prints for many collectors, perhaps including Haydn, would also have stemmed from the sense of instability they convey. This may have had wider ramifications for the alert viewer in 1792. If Viola's famous speech was a reminder that the appropriate place for representing patience was on a monument, a permanent form of commemoration to the great and the good, then Bunbury's alternative image, of patience 'in a punt', implies an altogether less stable, perhaps slightly risky, aspect to the venture of the protagonists, whose antics clearly merit no form of commemoration. The most prominent of these figures is sufficiently reminiscent of the standard caricatured appearance of one of the best known Whig politicians of the time, Edmund Burke, to suggest that the artist expected viewers attuned to popular print culture to perceive a reference to his political outlook.[35] It seems possible,

33. *Cont.*
   the subject of a number of his prints. In 1760 Horace Walpole had referred to Lady Cecilia as 'an absolute original', but by the 1790s he could write that 'her narrow mind [...] never cultivated any seed but that of wormwood!' (quoted in Nicholas Penny, *Reynolds*, exh. cat. (London: Weidenfeld and Nicolson for the Royal Academy of Arts, 1986), p. 390, no. 204). Gillray took a similar view, and used the conventions of female patience and of society ladies having themselves portrayed in the guise of St Cecilia (patron saint of music), conventions usually associated with the young and beautiful, in order to mock Lady Cecilia's intention of remaining a leader of fashion at a relatively advanced age (she was sixty-four years old in 1791).

34. *Catalogue of Political and Personal Satires*, no. 8206; Riely, *Bunbury*, p. 14, no. 65.

35. It is not suggested here that a portrait of Burke was intended, only that certain features of the figure (especially his spectacles, his elongated nose and his wig) were close enough to the image of Burke developed by caricaturists during the 1780s to put viewers in mind of him. The figure in the print is slightly more reminiscent of the standard caricatured image of Burke than the one in Bunbury's original drawing: Riely, *Bunbury*, p. 14, no. 65. For caricaturists' portrayals of Burke, see Nicholas K. Robinson, *Edmund Burke: A Life in Caricature* (New Haven: Yale University Press, 1996).

Fig. 4. *Bethnal Green*, by Henry Bunbury, engraved and published by
W. Dickinson, 11 June 1792.

therefore, that Bunbury's patience prints were in part intended to act as satirical
comment on the predicament of the Whig Party at the time that they were first
published, a possibility strengthened through a consideration of the remaining Bunbury prints owned by Haydn.

A further aspect of the amusement originally generated by Bunbury's pair of patience prints lies in the implication that the men he depicted, no longer young,
though hardly infirm, relish as much being away from their wives as engaging in
their chosen sport. *Bethnal Green* (Fig. 4), the remaining print Haydn displayed at
Gumpendorf, may also be interpreted as a comment on the relationship of men of
this age and class with their spouses.[36] It depicts a well-to-do, portly man and his
dumpy wife standing beside the fence of their country residence. The entrance has
a warning labelled 'Men Traps', presumably to deter poachers. Such traps were a
matter of public interest in the later 1780s. George III had been publicly criticized
for making use of them on his estates and was caricatured in this connection.[37] In
Bethnal Green the residence itself is a Chinese pagoda, not dissimilar to the one by

36. *Catalogue of Political and Personal Satires*, no. 8208; M. D. George, *Hogarth to Cruickshank: Social
Change in Graphic Satire* (London: Allen Lane, 1967), p. 78, Fig. 62.

37. See *Catalogue of Political and Personal Satires*, no. 6947.

Sir William Chambers at Kew, dating from the early 1760s, a probable indication of the couple's pretentious, though out-moded, tastes.[38] The man is preparing for a shooting expedition by loading his gun, posing in the manner of a figure in a shooting painting by Stubbs, though without the poise, the size of the gun emphasizing his diminutive stature. Beside him is his dog, probably a foxhound bitch, carrying only a bone, hinting perhaps at the emptiness of the expedition. Bethnal Green was a pleasant London suburb at this time with a fast-rising population, though it seems to have had no reputation for being an advantageous place for blood sports.

The main butt of the humour of the print is reserved for the wife, who wears a riding habit. Her role in the outing is unclear. She is undoubtedly bored; and her indifference to standards of fashion and bearing are suggested by her bad posture and the carrying of her husband's wig in her right hand. An upside-down umbrella is held in her left hand. The brim of her extravagant hat casts its shadow over her eyes, a motif borrowed from Bunbury's friend Reynolds, though used here to suggest her lack of vision.[39] This point is stressed by a horse with blinkers shown immediately behind, and by contrast with the far-seeing man at the top of the pagoda, viewing the landscape through a telescope. The horse is pulling a trap, which was probably intended not only as a pun on the woman's own trappings, but also on her role in the couple's marriage. Bunbury draws clear attention to this theme because the sign warning of 'Men Traps' sticks up immediately behind her. A pretty woman was sometimes called during this period 'a man-trap', the title of one popular print showing a coy beauty.[40] Viewing the woman in Bunbury's print in these terms was presumably a huge joke for purchasers such as Haydn. Its subtitle, *Hie away Juno*, serves to complete the ridicule: exertion seems to be the last thing on the woman's mind. Moreover, she cannot be said to have much in common with the reputed stately beauty of Jupiter's jealous wife.

Bethnal Green seems to have been aimed primarily at amusing men who longed to escape their wives' control, such as Haydn.[41] This helps to account for Haydn's decision to display this print at Gumpendorf, where his wife may have seen it, though probably with little idea of its gist. Haydn's fondness for hunting would also

---

38. Chambers's *Designs of Chinese Buildings* was published in 1757. A view of the pagoda at Kew was included in *Plans [...] of the Gardens and Buildings at Kew* which appeared in 1763.

39. For the motif of a shadow cast over the eyes in Reynolds, see (for examples) Penny, *Reynolds*, nos 13, 120. The motif probably derives from Rembrandt.

40. Published 6 January 1780 by Carington Bowles (*Catalogue of Political and Personal Satires*, no. 5814).

41. Haydn's wife remained in Austria during the period of his London visits. But it was an open secret that their relationship was antagonistic. Several artists with whom Haydn may have come into contact in London were well known to have left their spouses or been on bad terms with them, including Loutherbourg, Romney and Fuseli.

have drawn him to it. The transparently exaggerated stories about his supposed shooting skills he later related to his credulous biographer, Griesinger, shows the composer developing his own verbal wit along the lines seen in Bunbury's prints.[42]

Haydn was probably sufficiently familiar with English popular culture to recognize that part of the humour in *Bethnal Green* was drawn from subverting a story long associated with this suburb, that of the blind beggar and his beautiful daughter. This had become well known through several musical settings and artistic depictions in various media, some of which were labelled 'Bethnal Green'.[43] Bunbury illustrated the story in 1790.[44] Its humour lies in the father's inability to see that his success in begging depends on his daughter's comeliness, of which he is ignorant. By the time *Bethnal Green* was published, drawing attention to an inability to see would also have encouraged some viewers to perceive a political dimension to the print. Caricaturists at this time frequently made use, for example, of the spectacles of Edmund Burke to suggest the politician's foresight – or more often lack of it – and similar motifs were applied more widely to hint at the ineptitude of politicians in general.[45] The bespectacled man in *Patience on a Punt*, who as already mentioned bears some resemblance to the image of Burke developed by caricaturists, was possibly intended to call to mind this preoccupation of the time.[46] Bunbury further encourages a political reading of *Bethnal Green* with other strategically placed motifs. The wig, which the husband has discarded, clearly refers to the Whigs, and perhaps in particular to leading members of the party falling out over their responses to the French Revolution. *A Barber's Shop* (1785), Bunbury's lampoon on the intense Westminster election campaign of 1784, provides clear evidence, were it needed, that prominent

---

42. *Haydn: Two Contemporary Portraits*, trans. and ed. by Vernon Gotwals (Madison: University of Wisconsin Press, 1968), pp. 20, 220–21.

43. One example is Thomas Arne's *Blind Beggar of Bethnal Green* (first performed 1741), based on a seventeenth-century play by John Day: Roger Fiske, *English Theatre Music in the Eighteenth Century* (London: Oxford University Press, 1973), p. 207. For the painting by Opie (he apparently made more than one version, all dating from the early 1780s), see Ada Earland, *John Opie and His Circle* (London, Hutchinson, 1911), p. 339.

44. *The Blind Beggar and his Daughter of Bethnal Green*, published 20 August 1790 by Thomas Macklin.

45. A good example is *Mr Burke's Pair of Spectacles for short sighted politicians*, published 12 May 1791 (*Catalogue of Political and Personal Satires*, no. 7858). For discussion of this and other themes connected with seeing in caricature of the period, see Robinson, *Burke*, esp. pp. 23, 152–53.

46. It has frequently been claimed that Bunbury did not caricature known personalities in his published prints. But this is not so. It was only claimed at the time that he did not divulge who his models were. An allusion to Burke in *Patience on a Punt* seems possible though not certain. The important point, however, is that the spectacles on this figure would at the time have suggested a political reference.

wigs in English caricatures of this date refer to Whigs.[47] A wig set aside, as in *Bethnal Green*, may have had the sense of political disillusionment, suggesting a hardening of attitude on the part of some Whigs along the lines set out by Burke, whose fierce denunciation of the French Revolution had caused a recent rift in his party.[48] The dog's bone may also have brought to mind contemporary contention among Whigs.[49] The woman's yawn, a favourite Bunbury motif, also had a political origin in English caricature. George Bickham's *Great Britain and Ireland's Yawn* (1743), depicting a yawning head, refers to the long administration of Sir Robert Walpole, as is evident in lines quoted from Pope's satirical *Dunciad* placed beneath: 'And Chief-less Armies doz'd out the Campaign; And Navies yawn'd for Orders on the Main.'[50] In *Bethnal Green*, the yawning woman holding her husband's wig may comment on the tedium of Whig infighting at the time it was published. Many of these features of the print are likely to have appealed to Haydn. The emptiness of the relationship between the man and his wife in *Bethnal Green* may have reminded him of his own unsuccessful marriage. Haydn's wife is known to have been indifferent to her husband's activities. She, herself, was the daughter of a wig-maker, and Haydn might well have been put in mind of her by the bored wife carrying a wig in Bunbury's print.

Bunbury had numerous family connections with Charles James Fox, the Whig leader, so it is not surprising that oblique comments on Whig fortunes are part of the fun of many of his caricatures during the early 1790s.[51] Another of the Bunbury prints owned by Haydn, *A Smoking Club* (Fig. 5), first published on 1 May 1792, presents a further example.[52] In this caricature the artist mocks another pleasurable

47. In the foreground two dogs, labelled with the names of the candidates, pull at either side of a wig. The original drawing for this print, exhibited at the Royal Academy in 1785, was in the collection of Reynolds, who reportedly called it 'one of the best drawings he had ever seen […] it would be admired in every age and country': Reva Wolf, *Goya and the Satirical Print in England and on the Continent, 1730 to 1850* (Boston: Godine, for Boston College Museum of Art, 1991), pp. 46–49, Fig. 19.

48. A print published in February 1790 (*Catalogue of Political and Personal Satires*, no. 7627), for example, shows Sheridan snatching off Burke's wig, exposing the label 'Tory' on his head. Another of March 1793 (*Catalogue of Political and Personal Satires*, no. 8315) portrays Burke and other Whigs discarding their wigs on a pile to the dismay of Fox and Sheridan.

49. See, for example, *Bone of Contention* [*Different Sensations*], published 26 February 1790 (*Catalogue of Political and Personal Satires*, no. 7631): Robinson, *Burke*, pp. 137–39.

50. *Catalogue of Political and Personal Satires*, no. 2607; [Lionel Lambourne] *English Caricature 1620 to the Present: Caricaturists and Satirists, Their Art, Their Purpose and Influence*, exh. cat. (London: Victoria & Albert Museum 1984), pp. 50–51, no. 41, pl. 16.

51. For a resumé of these complicated family connections, see H. Ewart 'Henry Bunbury, Caricaturist', *Connoisseur*, 6 (1903), 156–57.

52. *Catalogue of Political and Personal Satires*, no. 8205. Roy Porter, *Enlightenment: Britain and the Making of the Modern World* (London: Allen Lane, 2000), p. 473.

Fig. 5. *A Smoking Club*, by Henry Bunbury, engraved and published by
W. Dickinson, 1 May 1792

pastime involving minimal effort, one particularly known to have been forbidden
to many husbands in the comfort of their own homes by disapproving wives. The
print depicts four men, seated facing each other in a circle, as if to suggest that they
might engage one another in conversation. The arrangement perhaps appealed to
Haydn since the four seated figures and their gestures correspond closely with the
traditional grouping of members of a string quartet in performance. Bunbury contrasts two fat men with two thin men to comic effect. The only activity in which
they indulge, however, is smoking which, judging from the expressions on their faces,
provides considerable satisfaction. Great clouds of smoke rise from their mouths
and from the bulbs of the pipes held by all four men. The smoke is so considerable
that it obscures most of the pictures hanging on the wall behind. Only one picture
remains visible through the haze, immediately behind the peg-legged smoker on
the left of the group. This may be identified as a popular print of Fox by the artist
James Sayers, an associate of the prime minister, William Pitt, Fox's chief political
opponent.[53] Published in 1782, Sayers' print (Fig. 6) depicts the Whig leader

53. *Catalogue of Political and Personal Satires*, no. 6054; Donald, *Age of Caricature*, p. 62.

Fig. 6. *Vox populi*, by James Sayers, published by
Charles Bretherton, 1782.

delivering a speech, his right arm raised in an exaggerated gesture of defiance, fists clenched. Although Sayers' uncharitable portrayal of Fox is reproduced on a small scale in Bunbury's *Smoking Club*, there can be little doubt that Bunbury expected his own audience to recognize this reference to the politician. The peg-legged smoker seated in front of the print hanging on the wall was possibly intended to allude to the well known one-legged actor Moses Kean, who at this time was celebrated as 'a very extraordinary mimic, particularly in his imitations of Charles James Fox'.[54] The proximity of the peg-legged figure to the image of Fox in Bunbury's

54. John Thomas Smith, *Nollekens and his Times* (London: Colbourn, 1829), p. 202. For a representation of Kean as an actor, see *Moses Kean Imitating Henderson's Hamlet*, which was engraved in 1786: Hogan, *The London Stage*, V, ii, p. 690.

print is likely therefore to have suggested to early purchasers of the print a mocking reference to the Whig leader, especially since the smoke billowing from his mouth partly obscures the picture itself, implying perhaps that impersonators (and doubtless caricaturists) had served to cloud Fox's reputation through their portrayals of him. The smoker's disability was possibly even intended as a visual metaphor for Fox's standing at the time that the caricature was first published, when he began to be undermined by the attacks of Burke and others.

Sayers labelled his 1782 caricature of Fox *Vox Populi*, an allusion to Fox's own identification of himself with the voice of the people, a means of distinguishing himself and his supporters from the Tories, the party of king and country, which from 1783 to 1801 formed the government under Pitt's premiership. The play on words between Fox and *vox* made the connection irresistible to caricaturists, many of whom were in the pocket of Pitt's followers. It seems probable that in *A Smoking Club*, the reproduction of Sayers' *Vox Populi* was introduced by Bunbury to remind his audience of Fox as the voice of the people. The fact that Bunbury depicted all four smokers in obvious silence suggests perhaps an ironic visual comment on the way Fox had tried to present himself. Haydn is likely to have understood this. The composer's London journals record a number of anecdotes he had heard concerning Fox and his electioneering tactics, indicating his interest in the man himself and how he was generally perceived.[55] Moreover, Haydn's earliest biographer records the composer's use of the adage 'vox populi, vox Dei' ('the voice of the people is the voice of God') in discussing the popularity of his own music.[56] Since the dictum had been long established in England, though it seems to have been rarely used on the Continent before Haydn's time, the possiblity exists that the composer first heard it in connection with Fox.[57] *Vox populi, vox Dei*, for example, is the title of an anonymous print featuring the electioneering Fox, the publication of which coincided with the Westminster election of 1784, an important test of public opinion followed nationwide and with phenomenal popular enthusiasm in the capital.[58]

55. *Gesammelte Briefe und Aufzeichnungen*, pp. 493, 509; *Collected Correspondence and London Notebooks*, pp. 260, 273.
56. *Haydn: Two Contemporary Portraits*, trans. and ed. by Gotwals, p. 44. For a detailed discussion of the phrase 'Vox populi, vox dei' used by, and in relation to, Haydn, see Tolley, *Painting the Cannon's Roar*, pp. 50–54.
57. For the use of the phrase 'Vox populi, vox dei' in England before Haydn's time, see M. P. Tilley, *A Dictionary of the Proverbs in England in the Sixteenth and Seventeenth Centuries* (Ann Arbor: University of Michigan, 1950), p. 700; *The Oxford Dictionary of English Proverbs*, 3rd edn, rev. F. P. Wilson (Oxford: Clarendon Press, 1970), p. 862. The phrase may be traced back to the time of Alcuin, in a letter to Charlemagne in the early ninth century.
58. *Catalogue of Political and Personal Satires*, no. 6594; Donald, *Age of Caricature*, pp. 126–27.

Haydn was not a smoker himself. He was perhaps drawn to Bunbury's print partly because of the fun Bunbury has at the expense of tobacco addicts, and partly because it may have again reminded him of conflicts with his own wife. One of Haydn's compositions dating from shortly after his marriage (1760) has been shown to quote *in extenso* a popular song of the time, the words of which concern the use of tobacco and how it might fuel marital strife.[59] It seems possible that Haydn was attracted to Bunbury's print because it acted as an amusing reminder of his own domestic feuds.

In common with other early collectors of Bunbury's prints, Haydn, who regularly visited print shops when he was in London, probably recognized that *A Smoking Club* belonged to a tradition of English prints featuring male smokers. Bunbury seems to have expected his audience to appreciate that the feature of tobacco smoke obscuring pictures was prompted by Hogarth's well known print *Time Smoking a Picture* (1761), a satire on the gentry's taste for 'old' paintings, or by works inspired by Hogarth's print.[60] Paintings identified as by Old Masters were sometimes artificially aged by tobacco smoke to add to their allure. It seems likely that part of the pleasure of collecting prints like *A Smoking Club* was to identify the familiar sources used by the artist. Another Hogarth print, *A Midnight Modern Conversation* (1733), showing a group of male revellers indulging in drink and tobacco, is another obvious source which Bunbury would have been confident that his audience would recognize. It was perhaps the first print by an English artist to establish smoking as a congenial activity. Moreover, *A Midnight Modern Conversation* was one of the most celebrated caricatures of the eighteenth century, often pirated and much imitated by both adherents and detractors of smoking and drinking, abroad as well as in England.[61] Hogarth made it clear from his own inscription on the print that he expected it to be understood as a general satire on overindulgence, warning in particular of the effects of drunkenness. But Hogarth's

59. The composition in question is the first movement of Symphony no. 8 (1761), quoting a song by Gluck beginning 'Je n'aimais pas le tabac beaucoup': Daniel Heartz, 'Haydn und Gluck im Burgtheater um 1760: Der neue krumme Teufel, Le Diable à quatre und die Sinfonie "Le Soir"', in *Bericht über den Internationalen Musikwissenschaftlichen Kongress, Bayreuth 1981*, ed. by Christoph-Hellmut Mahling and Sigrid Wiesmann (Kassel: Bärenreiter, 1984), 120–35. For discussion of this composition as 'a marital feud', see Richard Will, 'When God met the sinner, and other dramatic confrontations in eighteenth-century instrumental music', *Music & Letters*, 78 (1997), 175–209.

60. Ronald Paulson, *Hogarth's Graphic Works*, 2 vols (New Haven: Yale University Press, 1965), I, 241–43, pl. 229. There is an imitation of Hogarth's conception by Fuseli (1774): Gert Schiff, *Henry Fuseli 1741–1825*, exh. cat. (London: Tate Gallery), 1975, p. 53, no. 8.

61. Paulson, *Hogarth's Graphic Works*, I, 150–52, pl. 134; Wolf, *Goya and the Satirical Print*, pp. 4–10; David Bindman, *Hogarth and his Times: Serious Comedy*, exh. cat (London: British Museum, 1997), pp. 71–73.

design was soon appropriated to act as a celebration of the pleasures of wine, spirits and tobacco; it was featured on items such as snuffboxes and punchbowls. Indeed, Hogarth himself did much to encourage such a reading since the announcement for the print's subscription coincided with a major attack by the vintners of London on Walpole's proposed excise bill on wine and tobacco, aimed at prohibiting common fraudulent practices on the part of importers, but perceived in the public sphere as an attack on pleasure and liberty.[62] Such was the strength of feeling against Walpole's bill that it had to be withdrawn. Bunbury's *Smoking Club* may in part have been inspired by similar issues. Pitt introduced a similar excise bill for tobacco in 1789 which, unlike Walpole's, was indeed enacted.[63] In the years following it there may well have been a certain strength of feeling concerning tobacco, manifested by conspicuous displays of indulgence.

Although *A Midnight Modern Conversation* was not one of the prints in Haydn's collection, it seems quite likely that he knew it. A novel published during his second London visit, which he acquired at the time, includes a description of Hogarth's print forming the centrepiece of an arrangement of pictures, the remainder of which consisted, with obvious irony, of various portraits of English archbishops.[64] The print was also the subject of an extensive commentary by the German scientist and satirist Georg Christoph Lichtenberg, who visited England on several occasions. Lichtenberg's essays on Hogarth's graphic works were well known to continental collectors of English prints. Haydn perhaps knew the edition published in Vienna in 1797. The commentary is especially useful for viewing Hogarth from a late eighteenth-century perspective. Lichtenberg found little difficulty, for example, in relating the content of *A Midnight Modern Conversation* to the world of Pitt the Younger and Charles James Fox, and contrasting the situation portrayed in the print with social trends in England at the time he was writing. In particular, Lichtenberg notes that tobacco smoking 'has much *diminished* in England now, at least in the *higher* strata of society. Nowadays it is more often dice that keep company with the bottle.'[65] Lichtenberg goes on to cite an opinion of Dr Johnson's that the rise in the

62. Stephen Dowell, *A History of Taxation and Taxes in England from the Earliest Times to the Year 1885*, 4 vols (London: Longmans, Green, 1888), IV, 255–56.

63. Compton Mackenzie, *Sublime Tobacco* (London: Chatto & Windus, 1957), p. 219.

64. The novel which Haydn possessed was Thomas Holcroft's *Adventures of Hugh Trevor*, vols 1–3 (1794): Maria Hörwarthner, 'Joseph Haydn's Library: An Attempt at a Literary-Historical Reconstruction', in *Haydn and His World*, ed. by Elaine Sisman (Princeton, NJ: Princeton University Press, 1997), p. 437, no. 85. The reference to Hogarth's print is in vol. 2, ch. VII. Haydn is known to have been on close terms with Holcroft: see the article by Caroline Grigson at pp. 85–88

65. Innes and Gustav Herdan, *Lichtenberg's Commentaries on Hogarth's Engravings* (London: Cresset, 1966), p. 184.

suicide rate among the upper classes in England could be attributed to smoking having gone out of fashion. Independent sources show that Dr Johnson did indeed connect various social trends among the nobility and gentry in the last decades of his lifetime to the phenomenon of these classes having almost completely abandoned smoking, replacing it with the rather more socially acceptable practice of snuff-taking.[66] Johnson's observation on the unacceptability of smoking is confirmed by many further accounts of the period between *c.* 1760 and *c.* 1790.[67] If smoking had become unfashionable, this raises the problem of how an audience was expected to respond to a print depicting a group of dedicated smokers published in 1791. Bunbury's *Smoking Club* is one of a number of caricatures published in the early 1790s indicating that smoking, especially viewed as a communal activity, and often divorced from its previous associations with drink and debauchery, once again emerged as an issue at this particular time.[68] What exactly was this issue?

Although smoking had become unfashionable in England during the third quarter of the eighteenth century, this did not of course coincide with any general decline in its consumption. Its popularity with the working classes (as Lichtenberg implied) was enduring, though reflections of this in the visual arts during this period are meagre. When smoking was featured in works depicting the upper classes in the 1770s and 1780s, its context often suggests moral laxity as, for example, in a series of prints conceived by Lichtenberg, *The Progress of Virtue and Vice* (1777), in which the penultimate image illustrating the progress of the dissolute male is represented by a pipe-smoking, sick old man.[69] But this association of smoking with vice, stemming from Hogarth, seems to play no part in Bunbury's *Smoking*

66. For example, see *Boswell's Life of Johnson*, ed. by George Birkbeck Hill, rev. L. F. Powell, 6 vols (Oxford: Clarendon Press, 1934–50), V (1950), 60.

67. Examples are given in *Boswell's Life of Johnson*, ed. by Hill, V, 478. Perhaps the clearest expression of the situation is found in Cowper's poem *The Pipe and the Snuff Box*, written in 1782:

> Says the Pipe to the Snuff-box, "I can't understand
> What the ladies and gentlemen see in your face
> That you are in fashion all over the land,
> And I am so much fallen into disgrace."
> (*The Poems of William Cowper*, ed. by J. C. Bailey (London: Methuen, 1905), p. 427.)

68. Despite the unfashionability of smoking between about 1760 and 1790, prints continued to be sporadically issued showing groups of revellers indulging in smoking and drinking, perpetuating the Hogarth tradition. Such prints again became plentiful in the early 1790s. But they are joined by other smoking prints, such as Bunbury's *Smoking Club*, which show the protagonists free from the influence of alcohol, suggesting that drink and tobacco as issues were no longer necessarily connected in the public mind.

69. The series was published by the *Göttinger Taschen-Calender* and etched by Chodiewiecki: Griffiths and Carey, *German Printmaking*, pp. 56–59; Bindman, *Hogarth and His Times*, pp. 78–79. This association of smoking with vice stems from Hogarth, whose prints were the subject of

Club, in which the figures, though comical and certainly genteel, convey no signs of moral impropriety. It seems likely that Bunbury expected his audience in 1791 to make a rather different kind of association with his smoking figures, political rather than moral. Smoking had, it seems, come to be perceived as an attribute of the ordinary working man, with implications for how radical thinkers from the upper classes wished to present themselves.

An indication of how smoking was especially associated with the ordinary working classes in the mind of the educated classes may be found at the very start of the period when smoking was going out of fashion in England in a short comic play by Garrick, *The Farmer's Return* (1762).[70] In this, a heavily countrified farmer, returning from a visit to London to see the 'crownation' of George III, startles his family with the story of the sighting of a ghost, topical in London at the time. Among the first things he says on arriving home is 'get me a poipe', an expression of his happiness in settling back into his own environment. This scene of the farmer telling his story, comfortably seated with his pipe in hand, was hugely popular with London audiences and is recorded in contemporary works by both Hogarth and Zoffany.[71] In devising a stereotype of the ordinary loyal countryman, Garrick (who played the farmer himself) gave his creation a pipe to smoke, not only to provide his fashionable audience with something to laugh at, but also to suggest the farmer's contentment with his lot in life.

Although Gainsborough, in his own portraiture, never depicted his fashionable sitters smoking, his so-called *Peasant Smoking at a Cottage Door* (The Wight Art Gallery, Los Angeles) of 1788 makes a clear connection between a male representative of the labouring classes, smoking, and his apparent satisfaction with his station in the world.[72] A similar sentiment was expressed in Cowper's much-admired poem *The Task* (1785), which includes a description of a woodman setting out on a frosty morning, stopping for nothing except now and then to adjust[73]

69. *Cont.*
    Lichtenberg's commentaries. The same association may be found in the work of many English artists of the same period. For example, smoking may be seen in several works by Rowlandson treating gambling and corruption.

70. *The Plays of David Garrick*, ed. by Harry William Pedicord and Fredrick Louis Bergmann, 7 vols (Carbondale: Southern Illinois University Press, 1980–82), I, 246–51, 411–12.

71. Mary Webster, *Johan Zoffany 1733–1810* (London: National Portrait Gallery, 1976), p. 25, no. 10.

72. John Hayes, *The Landscape Paintings of Thomas Gainsborough*, 2 vols (London: Sotheby Publications, 1982), II, 570–72 (no. 185); Malcolm Cormack, *The Paintings of Thomas Gainsborough* (Cambridge: Cambridge University Press, 1991), pp. 180–81.

73. *The Task*, Book V, lines 55–57.

the fragrant charge of a short tube
That fumes beneath his nose. The trailing cloud
Streams far behind him, scenting all the air.

This poetic image inspired one of the most popular paintings of the early 1790s, *The Woodman* by Thomas Barker, one of a series of pictures of country labourers, initially inspired by another late work by Gainsborough. Barker's *Woodman*,[74] which shows the countryman with a lighted pipe, was exhibited by Thomas Macklin at his Poet's Gallery in 1792, where it caused a sensation. Bartolozzi's engraving of Barker's painting (Fig. 7) was the basis of a number of further reproductions of it, on pottery and porcelain, as well as for signs for tobacconists' shops in London until well into the nineteenth century.[75] One further measure of how this painting captured the imagination of the public in London in the 1790s is that Haydn acquired Bartolozzi's print of it for his own collection.[76] What precisely in the picture appealed to Haydn and to its other admirers cannot of course today be determined with certainty; but that the combination of contentment, smoking and the rural poor was part of its success seems evident. Indeed the connection between the well-being of the working classes and tobacco-smoking was specifically made in the House of Commons by members of the Whig opposition who attacked Pitt's introduction of tobacco duty for being a tax on the poor. One of the most vociferous of Pitt's critics in this respect was John Courtenay, MP, a keen Foxite.[77] Courtenay's support for tobacco is evident from his portrayal as a smoker in a caricature by Gillray showing the MP engaged in raucous banter with a group of friends, including Fox (Fig. 8).[78] Behind him hangs a picture of a pipe-smoking monkey wearing a liberty cap, an indication that in these circles tobacco was an issue associated with freedom. It therefore connects with contemporary English notions of the rights of man inspired by the revolution in France.

Interestingly, Gillray based his composition for the Courtenay caricature on Bunbury's *Smoking Club*, a work which he used as a model on several occasions.

74. Owned by Torfaen Museum Trust; see Philippa Bishop and Victoria Burnell, *The Barkers of Bath*, exh. cat. (Bath: Bath Museums Service, 1986), p. 27, no. 10.

75. For example, the sign painter Robert Allen painted a copy of Bartolozzi's engraving of Barker's *The Woodman*, which he featured in his own painting made in 1841 of the tobacconist's shop he owned (both works now in the Museum of London): James Ayres, *Two Hundred Years of English Naïve Art, 1700–1900* (Alexandria, VI: Art Services International, 1996), p. 131.

76. Landon, *Haydn: Chronicle and Works*, V, 393, no. 39. The cataloguer mistakenly read Barker's name as 'Parker'.

77. R. G. Thorne, *The History of Parliament: The House of Commons 1790–1820*, 5 vols (London: Secker & Warburg, 1986), III, 509–13.

78. 'The feast of Reason, & the flow of Soul', published on 4 February 1797: *The Satirical Etchings of James Gillray*, ed. by Draper Hill (New York: Dover, 1976), p. 112, no. 48.

Fig. 7. *The Woodman,* by Thomas Barker, engraved by F. Bartolozzi,
published by T. Macklin, 1792.

Another example is Gillray's own *Smoking Club* (13 February 1793), in which the
proximity of the composition to its model is such that it suggests that the artist
expected his audience to identify the source. In this work, members of the government and opposition, including Pitt and Fox, sit opposite one another, blowing
smoke in each other's faces.[79] The use of tobacco smoke as a tool in the political
caricaturist's armoury is unambiguous here since the protagonists are all politicians.
However, since Gillray was compositionally indebted to Bunbury, it seems possible
that the significance he attached to smoke may also have derived from Bunbury. If

79. The use of Bunbury's print as a model in Gillray's *Smoking Club* was noted by Riely, *Bunbury,*
    p. 6.

Fig. 8. 'The feast of Reason, & the flow of Soul', by James Gillray, published
by H. Humphrey, 4 February 1797.

Fox is the voice of the people, as Bunbury reminded his audience, and tobacco is
crucial to the well-being of the ordinary people, as Courtenay and others implied,
then smoking becomes a visual means of suggesting identification with a set of
radical political objectives. It seems possible Haydn himself may have sympathized
with these at the time that he acquired the print.

The new acceptability of smoking among certain (limited) sections of the upper
classes by the early 1790s was probably in part prompted by attitudes in Britain to
the early stages of the French Revolution, which Fox and his supporters championed,
that is until the period when the position of the French royal family became seriously
precarious, following their attempted flight and consequent capture at Varennes.
Smoking among the upper classes in England during these years, as depicted for
example by Bunbury, may therefore be understood as an expression of accord with
working people, their needs and aspirations, as brought into focus for an English
public by events in France in 1789. Smoking as a sign of a radical caste of mind was
given clear expression in designs for prints published in 1793 by Richard Newton,
all depicting a number of well known radical figures, portrayed as political prisoners
(some were guilty of sedition) or prison visitors, many of whom are shown very

conspicuously smoking.[80] The connection between smoking and a radical political outlook is also manifest in a surviving tobacco paper of this period, claimed to have been found in a London tavern, which features the seditious inscription: 'I am puzzled how to live while kingcraft may abuse my rights and tax the joys of day.'[81] Many London radicals at this time would also have known that one of the most widely read journals in France during the early 1790s was *Le Père Duchesne*, the name of a popular low-life carnival character, who talked common sense to ordinary people in the language of the street, and whose most visible characteristic was his taste for tobacco.[82] Every issue was embellished with the image of 'le véritable père', defiantly portrayed bearing arms, a pipe clenched between his teeth, with smoke rising from its bulb. It is no wonder why English intellectuals at this time, sympathetic to the ideals behind recent events in France, chose to associate themselves with working people by affecting a taste for the pipe and by organizing themselves into clubs dedicated to smoking – Courtenay was chairman of one – which the Establishment continued largely to abhor, until at least the turn of the century. Perhaps the most ardent Foxite to assume a predilection for smoking was Dr Samuel Parr, occasionally identified in the 1790s as the Whigs' answer to Dr Johnson. Parr was frequently remembered for his association with the pipe and unusually, for the period, was occasionally depicted with it in hand.[83] Bunbury's *Smoking Club* may therefore be viewed as a satire, not just on the practice of smoking, but also on those of a radical disposition, mostly Whigs, who in the years after the fall of the Bastille professed an interest in tobacco and assumed the smoking habit as a means of lending a visual identity to their political philosophy. Almost certainly Haydn, a composer celebrated for his wit, would have caught many of the nuances of Bunbury's astute observations.

The two remaining Bunbury prints in Haydn's collection were literary in inspiration. Both were published by Thomas Macklin, Bunbury's original drawings having been commissioned for his Poet's Gallery. *Marian* (Fig. 9), published on 20 November 1791, illustrates an episode from *The Shepherd's Week* by John Gay, author

80. Newton's prints include *Soulagement en Prison; or, Comfort in Prison* (*Catalogue of Political and Personal Satires*, no. 8339) and *Promenade in the State side of Newgate* (*Catalogue of Political and Personal Satires*, no. 8342): David Bindman (with Aileen Dawson and Mark Jones), *The Shadow of the Guillotine: Britain and the French Revolution*, exh. cat. (London: British Museum, 1989), pp. 191–92, nos 193–94; David Alexander, *Richard Newton and English Caricature in the 1790s* (Manchester: Manchester University Press for Whitworth Art Gallery, 1998), pp. 34–41, 120–21.

81. Bindman, *The Shadow of the Guillotine*, 117–18, no. 70c.

82. *Le Père Duchesne* was the creation of Jacques René Hébert. It was published between 1790 and 1794.

83. For a list of portraits see Warren Derry, *Dr Parr: A Portrait of a Whig Dr Johnson* (Oxford: Clarendon Press, 1966), pp. 360–63.

of *The Beggar's Opera*.[84] It depicts a country-girl, whose love is unrequited, turning to gypsies to read her palm. Though the prognostication is not good, it turns out to be false. The subject of gypsy fortune-tellers commanded special interest in London at this date, since it drew attention to the credulity of young women, in both its comic and moral aspects.[85] For Haydn, the print perhaps held special interest because of his own use of thematic material associated with gypsy traditions.[86] The popularity of gypsy subjects probably affected the decision by Haydn's publishers (Longman & Broderip) to entitle the Finale of his most celebrated trio 'Rondo in the Gipsies' style' (Hob.XV:25), when it was first issued in October 1795. Haydn may have been aware that gypsies were in the public eye in the later 1780s as a result of the repeal in 1783 of a sixteenth-century Act of Parliament outlawing them in England. In the political climate in the years after 1789, when the French Revolution gave rise to notions of the rights of all men and women, the position of minorities, such as gypsies, came under closer scrutiny by those who followed politics. Haydn, who had explored Hungarian gypsy music in his own compositions, may therefore have been particularly sensitive to attitudes to gypsies at this time.

The second of Haydn's Macklin prints was *The Mouse's Petition* (Fig. 10), engraved by Bartolozzi. This illustrates Mrs Barbauld's popular poem of the same name, first published in 1773, the opening stanzas of which are quoted beneath the engraving, beginning:

Oh! Hear a pensive prisoner's prayer,
For liberty that sighs;
And never let thine heart be shut
Against a wretch's cries.

The print shows a caged mouse, set on a table in a garden, looked on by a boy, two women and an elderly man. Ostensibly, this is an example like the reading of Marian's palm of heightened sensibility, the mouse 'arguing' its own case for freedom before a varied human audience, who seemingly draw different conclusions on the

---

84. First published in 1714. The relevant part of the text is quoted beneath Bunbury's print: *The Painted Word: British History Painting 1750–1830*, exh. cat., ed. by Peter Cannon-Brookes (Woodbridge: Boydell, 1991), p. 94, no. 96 (with illustration).

85. For example, *The Gypsie Fortune Teller*, published by Sayer in 1789, is inscribed with the verse: 'The Gypsies they a Fortune telling go: The Misses they their Fortunes want to know: Credulous to believe each flattering story told, That mark on your hand will bring you much gold.' For a reproduction, see Timothy Clayton, *The English Print, 1688–1802* (New Haven: Yale University Press), p. 234 (pl. 249).

86. For 'gypsy' elements in Haydn's music, see Matthew Head, 'Haydn's exoticisms: "difference" and the Enlightenment', in *The Cambridge Companion to Haydn*, ed. by Caryl Clark (Cambridge: Cambridge University Press, 2005), pp. 77–92, esp. pp. 89–91.

Fig. 9. *Marian*, by Henry Bunbury, engraved by P. W. Tomkins, published by
T. Macklin, 20 November 1791.

matter. At this level, the theme was evidently very successful, judging from later
prints depicting trapped mice with similar titles.[87] However, Bunbury's design probably held further connotations for viewers such as Haydn, seeing it in 1791.

The poem's full title showed that *The Mouse's Petition* had originally been written
after observing the use of animals in scientific experiments conducted by Dr Joseph
Priestley, who responded to the 'petition' by releasing one intended victim.[88] Reviewers took this seriously, commending the author for providing 'this opportunity

---

87. For examples: *Muscipula*, engraved and published by John Jones after a painting by Joshua
    Reynolds; James Ward's *The Mouse's Petition*, engraved by William Ward and published in 1805:
    C. R. Grundy, *James Ward R. A. His Life and Work* (London: Otto, 1909), p. 72, no. 90 (with colour
    plate), see no. 91. The mouse is shown in a trap, looked on by three children. Another example is
    William Hamilton's *Children with Mouse-Trap*, engraved by Marcuard: Julia Frankau, *Eighteenth-
    Century Colour Prints: An Essay on Certain Stipple Engravers and Their Work*, 2nd edn (London:
    Macmillan, 1906), p. 210.
88. The poem's full title is 'The mouse's petition to Doctor Priestley found in the trap where he had
    been confined all Night'. Priestley's experiments testing gases and electrical currents using animals
    is documented in his correspondence with Benjamin Franklin and in his *History of Electricity*. For
    a resumé of this, see *The Poems of Anna Letitia Barbauld*, ed. by William McCarthy and Elizabeth
    Kraft (Athens, GA: University of Georgia Press, 1994), pp. 244–5.

Fig. 10. *The Mouse's Petition*, by Henry Bunbury, engraved by F. Bartolozzi, published by T. Macklin, 20 November 1791.

to testify our abhorrence of the cruelty practised by experimental philosophers'. By 1789, the date Mary Wollstonecraft republished the poem in the *Female Reader*, the tale of a captive seeking freedom, with its colourful images of oppression ('a tyrant's chain', 'with guiltless blood'), could be seen in light of the fall of the Bastille in July 1789.[89] Two years later, when leading radicals such as Priestley were celebrating the second anniversary of the Bastille's fall, the political tide in England was moving against them. Shortly afterwards, the reaction was such that Priestley's house and laboratory were destroyed by fire.[90] Bunbury's print, with its allusions to Priestley's humanity, was very likely conceived with these events in mind.[91] It seems probable

89. Mrs Barbauld's position in favour of the changes in France was public knowledge. A caricature ridiculing Burke's views published on 1 December 1790 (*Catalogue of Political and Personal Satires*, no. 7685), shows Mrs Barbauld being egged on to 'Cut the Jesuitical Monster in pieces': Robinson, *Burke*, p. 144.

90. For items commemorating these events, see J. Tann, S. Price and D. McCullen, *Priestley in Birmingham*, exh. cat. (Birmingham: Birmingham Museums and Art Gallery, 1980), nos, 43, 44.

91. The theme of captivity in the years leading up to 1793 would also have put people in mind of the position of the royal family in France, especially of Marie-Antoinette who, as an Austrian archduchess, would doubtless have been on Haydn's mind.

that Haydn would have grasped the political impact of such imagery at this time. He was certainly fascinated by the notion of entrapment since he owned another print based on the theme of a trapped mouse. *The Mouse Trap*, engraved by his friend Thomas Park in 1786, after a design by J. G. Huck, may allude to Shakespeare's *Hamlet* (a play Haydn saw in London), in which the prince calls the performance devised to detect Claudius's guilt 'a mousetrap'.[92] Huck, whose father ran a print shop in Düsseldorf, would certainly have known the Shakespeare reference and perhaps intended viewers of his work to have it in mind. His design, however, like Bunbury's, is entirely innocuous; it depicts a woman, her four children and three cats all gazing on the trap, with the mouse obviously inside. Cats and mice were certainly of special interest to Haydn. His scurrying keyboard Capriccio (Hob.XVII:4), published in 1789, is loosely based on the folk song 'The farmer's wife has lost the cat'.[93] In the song the cat reappears in pursuit of a mouse, a theme perhaps presented in the Capriccio by the lively interplay between the two voices, the scrambling, chasing and 'pouncing' motifs, and the ominous pauses. At the end of the piece it seems reasonably clear that the mouse has been caught. Here, as in *The Mouse's Petition* and in *Bethnal Green*, entrapment is an issue. It seems likely that during the period immediately following the fall of the Bastille, captivity as a subject for cultural consideration became something of a preoccupation. Print collectors in England certainly developed a new fascination with images concerning incarceration. Older prints, such as Huck's, took on a new resonance. Bunbury, whilst protecting his reputation for giving no cause for offence, ensured that he satisfied this interest in various ways, lending his most original prints a more searching quality, in addition to the expected humour, for those prepared to see it.

The Bunbury prints in Haydn's collection were all created during a period when political opinion in England, to a great extent dominated by events in France, was starting to shift. The general sense of optimism which had followed from the changes in the French constitutional arrangements of 1789 was starting to be replaced by more critical or sceptical opinions. The most persuasive voice articulating the view that the revolution would in the end have disastrous consequences was Burke, a Whig. His *Reflections on the Revolution in France*, published 1 November

92. Landon, *Haydn: Chronicle and Works*, V, 393, no. 40. The relevant scene from *Hamlet* was drawn by Chodiewiecki in 1778, with the title *Mausfalle*, and etched in 1780. Given Huck's background in the German print trade, he would surely have known this.
93. 'Dö Bäuren hät d'Kätz valor'n': A. Peter. Brown, *Haydn's Keyboard Music: Sources and Style* (Bloomington: Indiana University Press, 1986), pp. 220–28; Gretchen A. Wheelock, 'Mozart's Fantasy, Haydn's Caprice: What's in a Name?', in *The Century of Bach and Mozart: Perspectives on Historiography, Composition, Theory, and Performance*, ed. by Sean Gallagher, Thomas Forrest Kelly (Cambridge, MA.: Harvard University Department of Music, 2008), pp. 317–41.

1790, had a crucial impact on public opinion and led to a fracturing of relations within his party. However, Fox and his supporters continued for the time being to view the revolution as a vehicle for beneficial social change, potentially in Britain as well as in France. Given Bunbury's family connections with Fox, it is understandable why the caricaturist may have looked to Whig discomfort as a source of inspiration in the early 1790s, as indicated in most of the Bunbury prints acquired by Haydn. Whilst it is generally considered that Bunbury usually chose his targets from social types and situations, in contrast to Gillray who clearly aimed his attack at individuals and their political stances, this somewhat misrepresents the situation just before and during Haydn's first London visit. The evidence presented here suggests that Bunbury satirized the travails experienced by Whigs, especially Fox, during this period, though he did it in such a way that his long-standing reputation in England remained unimpaired. But for foreign visitors to London in the 1790s, perhaps unmindful of how Bunbury was generally perceived by English audiences, his work seemed to speak the same language as Gillray's, with an unmistakable political line.[94] Although this was in part a misreading of the situation, it was also not entirely undiscerning. The evidence of Haydn's modest collection of Bunbury caricatures not only substantiates the perception that foreigners, especially German-speaking, understood the humour in Bunbury's work, but also suggests, taking into account the particular choices made by the composer and his outlook at this time, that Haydn perceived that part of their appeal lay in the commentary they offered on issues of the day, which were as much political as social.

Evidence that Bunbury conceived his prints from the time of Haydn's first visit to London in terms of the current political situation comes from a newspaper article of December 1791 reporting on the performance of two plays at Westminster School: a tragedy and a comedy given during the same evening, in both of which the artist himself had performed.[95] The article printed the words of a special Prologue and Epilogue, both possibly written by Bunbury, though only the Epilogue was spoken by him. In the Prologue, the tragedy of *Tamerlane* (1701), traditionally performed in England to commemorate the anniversary of William III's arrival in England heralding the 'Glorious Revolution', was given a new twist by relating it to the topical concept of the 'rights of man', a clear reference to Tom Paine's *Rights of Man* (1791), which defended the French Revolution against the attack of Edmund Burke. In the Epilogue, which wrapped up the whole evening, Bunbury used the image of men angling, as he later did in the prints owned by Haydn, to poke fun at

---

94. Banerji and Donald, *Gillray Observed*, pp. 22, 204.
95. The article appeared in *The Star* for 19 December 1791 and in modified form in other newspapers at this time.

Men of much weight, who almost sink the boat,
Whenever they wipe their heads, or twitch the float;
Broil'd in the sun, what temper they display;
Their wigs blown out of curl, or blown away;
All fire exhausted at the Easter hunt;
They here exhibit *patience in a punt*.

Bunbury pursues the fishing metaphor by suggesting

That all men angle, we must agree,
For praise, preferment, flattery, or fee…
With good success, this night, our baits to throw,
And (out of season) catch our fish with Rowe.

Angling becomes a metaphor for the weaknesses of Man. By linking the instability of the punt, and the men on it, with the tragedy by Rowe that had begun the
evening, a play that had always been understood in London to celebrate the virtue
and steadfastness of the British monarchy, Bunbury injects a humorous note of cau-
tion about the development of events at the time.

The six prints by Bunbury discussed above are documented as forming part of
Haydn's collection. It seems likely, however, that Haydn's association with Bunbury
was closer than the acquisition of these prints alone might imply.

On 23 November 1791, just three days after publication of *Marian* and *The
Mouse's Petition*, the Duke of York, George III's second son, married the Prussian
Princess Friedericke Charlotte in London. In due course the new Duchess of York
proved herself the most loyal and generous of Haydn's royal patrons in England.
Throughout this period Bunbury was in attendance on the Duke in an official post
as equerry.[96] Fanny Burney, also in royal service at this time, noted in her diary 'So
now we may all be caricatured at his leisure!' on learning of Bunbury's royal appointment in 1787.[97]

The day following their wedding, the royal couple travelled to Oatlands, the Duke
of York's Surrey residence, where according to Haydn's own journal the composer
also spent the next two days, enjoying 'many marks of graciousness and honour, not
only from the Prince of Wales but also from the Duchess, daughter of the King of
Prussia'.[98] Although Haydn's journal makes no mention of Bunbury, it seems clear

96. For the role taken by Bunbury in the ceremonial surrounding the marriage of the Duke and
Duchess of York, see *The Annual Register, or a View of the History, Politics and Literature for the
Year 1791* (London, 1795), pp. 48–50. Bunbury's position in the royal household is noted in *The
London Kalendar; or Court and City Register for England, Scotland, Ireland, and America, for the Year
1795* (London: [n. pub.], 1795), p. 100.

97. *Diary and Letters of Madame d'Arblay*, III (1905), 304.

98. *Collected Correspondence and London Notebooks*, p. 272.

that the two men would have come into contact at this time. Within a week of his visit to Oatlands, Haydn spent three days at Langham in Suffolk, the country estate of Sir Patrick Blake. Sir Patrick was Harry Bunbury's nephew.[99] Had Haydn never heard of Bunbury before November 1791, it seems reasonable to infer from these associations that by the end of this month the composer certainly knew of him.

Within a year of this both Haydn and Bunbury had taken prominent positions in cultural enterprises to which the new Duchess of York lent her name. She was dedicatee of a collection of a hundred Scottish songs, all arranged by Haydn, published by William Napier in London in June 1792.[100] Concurrently Bunbury created a series of drawings for the Duchess illustrating favourite scenes from Shakespeare's plays, mostly comic. The following year the publisher Thomas Macklin started issuing engravings of these scenes. Macklin's prospectus for what he called *Bunbury's Shakespeare* shows that he intended the whole series, which was dedicated to the Duchess of York, to amount to forty-eight prints to be published by subscription in twelve 'Numbers', each containing four prints. Unfortunately, like other illustrated publishing schemes of the late eighteenth century, the series was never completed because of deteriorating economic circumstances caused by the war with France, only five complete instalments having been realized.

Macklin conceived *Bunbury's Shakespeare* partly as an alternative, or rival, to another publishing venture, Boydell's much weightier and more comprehensive *Shakespeare Gallery*, and partly as a venture complementing his own Poet's Gallery, founded in Fleet Street in 1787 with the purpose of displaying paintings by leading artists of the day illustrating famous poems in the English language. Macklin's gallery generated income by charging for admission and selling prints reproducing the paintings. Haydn may be identified as one client since a significant proportion of the prints published by Macklin may be identified in his collection. Among these were Barker's *Woodman* and Bunbury's pair of prints *Marian* and the *Mouse's Petition*; and there were many more.[101]

99. Haydn visited Sir Patrick Blake (b. 1768), who was the son of Sir Patrick Blake (d. 1784) and Annabella Bunbury (b. 1745), elder sister of the artist Henry Bunbury. The younger Sir Patrick's parents divorced in 1773 following a celebrated case concerning Annabella's adultery with a Mr Boscowen. For the continuing legal disputes ensuing from this during the time that Haydn was in England, see William Brown, *Reports of Cases Argued and Determined in the High Court of Chancery [...] from 1778 to 1794* (London: E. Brooke, 1785–94), IV (1794), 21–28.

100. *A Selection of the most Favourite Scots-Songs*, 3 vols (London: Napier, [1790–95]), II: *A Selection of Original Scots Songs in Three Parts, the Harmony by Haydn* ([1792]).

101. Of the prints listed in Macklin's 1794 catalogue (*Poetic Description of Choice and Valuable Prints published by Mr Macklin at the Poets' Gallery, Fleet Street*), excluding the Shakespeare series, eighteen were certainly in Haydn's collection; a further nine may tentatively be identified in Haydn's collection; and three had the same titles as Macklin prints, though they were in fact

Although none of Macklin's Shakespeare prints appears unambiguously in the inventory of Haydn's collection, the composer's undoubted interest in prints issued by Macklin opens up the possibility that the composer acquired or subscribed to the Shakespeare prints, but that the series was not catalogued alongside the other prints that Haydn took back with him to Vienna. Item 609 in the inventory, which appears among a small number of items under a heading indicating a supplement to the engravings – as though they were only discovered by the compiler subsequent to the main inventory have been completed – simply indicates twenty-six separate engraved theatrical scenes, with no further information.[102] It seems clear that this item was a special collection of theatrical prints that the composer kept separately from his main portfolio of prints. Since the item appears almost at the end of the inventory, it is likely that the compiler of the inventory only came across the set late in his work and was reluctant at this late stage, seeing the end of his labour in sight, to provide identifying details. Perhaps he didn't understand what the series was about. He merely looked at the set to ascertain the nature of the prints and counted them. It has not been possible to discover any collection of theatrical prints that Haydn might have owned consisting of precisely twenty-six separate engravings that form a distinct entity. However, the number mentioned is sufficiently close to Bunbury's Shakespeare series to consider this identification plausible. Twenty Shakespeare prints were issued by Macklin between 1792 and 1796 and subsequently re-published as a set with a separate title-page. Two further prints which were probably intended as part of the series have been identified. Furthermore, Bunbury had previously designed three Shakespeare prints published before the Macklin series, which collectors of the Macklin series are likely to have acquired in order to make their set of 'Bunbury's Shakespeare' as complete as possible. (One of these designs has been mentioned already above.) Evidence that this may have happened in Haydn's case is the dedication of two of these earlier prints to Dora Jordan, one of Bunbury's favourite actresses. Haydn was also familiar with Mrs Jordan's reputation since he recorded details of her career in his journal. One of Bunbury's dedications reads: 'In admiration of those Talents which have given distinguish'd Eminence to the Character of Viola. / This scene from the Comedy of TWELFTH NIGHT is

101. *Cont.*
    different versions of the same subject. In the case of the last three prints, it can hardly be coincidental that Haydn selected the same subjects from other sources. The evidence suggests that Haydn is likely to have first become familiar with these latter three subjects in Macklin's gallery.

102. Under the heading 'NACHTRAG VON KUPFERSTICHEN / welche erst beim Schluß des Inventarii vorgefunden wurden. Sind nach No.54 [referring to the number of the last inventory item concerning a print from Haydn's portfolio] / 609. 26. Stück gestochene Theaterszenen.' Landon, *Haydn: Chronicle and Works*, V, 403.

dedicated by her Obedient Humble Servant / Henry Bunbury.' The impulse to make a dedication to a favourite actress by an admiring artist, which Bunbury here realized, forms a striking parallel with an uncharacteristic dedication by Haydn. Many years later, when Haydn was arranging Scottish songs for the Edinburgh publisher George Thomson, the composer recognized one of the songs sent to him as having been famously sung by Mrs Jordan. Haydn requested that his specially extended arrangement of this song be published separately from all the others he was working on and (in Haydn's own words) 'dedicated *in my name* to the celebrated Mistriss Jordan, as a tiny, tiny token of my esteem for her; for although I have not the honour of her acquaintance, I have the most profound respect for her great virtue and reputation'.[103] Since the form of this dedication is unique in Haydn's output, it seems plausible that its inspiration stemmed from the Bunbury print dedicated to the actress, which it is here suggested he took back with him to Vienna along with many others by Bunbury. Given that Haydn enjoyed the special patronage of the Duchess of York, the dedicatee of Macklin's Shakespeare prints, and his interest in Bunbury is beyond question, the hypothesis that the composer took out a subscription to *Bunbury's Shakespeare*, a highly appropriate undertaking for a man who was known in English as 'the musical Shakespeare' and who returned to Austria from London with a modern edition of all Shakespeare's works, is well founded.[104]

Haydn's reputation for wit and humour, identified in both his music and his own personal character, has been a feature of consideration of the composer since early in his career. Haydn's interest in Bunbury confirms and extends this analysis of the man and his music. The composer's admiration for Bunbury's work, however, provides new material to refine our understanding of this aspect of his character. Bunbury, as Haydn surely knew, had a reputation for making people laugh and laughing himself. Fanny Burney was one witness to his incessant laughter, though she found a negative aspect to this: Bunbury's 'general disposition to laugh at, censure or despise all around him'.[105] However, in terms of his pictorial work, Bunbury did this in such a way that, in contrast to the work of contemporary caricaturists, he gave no offence, a point acknowledged even by Fanny Burney, so that viewers

103. *Collected Correspondence and London Notebooks*, p. 198. For discussion of *The Bluebell of Scotland*, see: Tolley, "Exemplary patience', 121–25; Warwick Edwards, 'New Insights into the Chronology of Haydn's Folksong Arrangements: Reading between the Lines of George Thomson Correspondence', *Haydn-Studien*, 8 (2004), 325–40.
104. For Haydn and Shakespeare, see Elaine Sisman, 'Haydn, Shakespeare, and the Rules of Originality', in *Haydn and His World*, ed. by Elaine Sisman (Princeton, NJ: Princeton University Press, 1997), pp. 3–56. For Haydn's ownership of the complete works of Shakespeare, see Maria Hörwarthner, 'Joseph Haydn's Library: An Attempt at a Literary-Historical Reconstruction', in *Haydn and His World*, ed. by Sisman, pp. 395–462 (p. 399).
105. *Diary and Letters of Madame d'Arblay*, III (1905), 323.

from all social backgrounds could look at his work without risk of affront.

Haydn also liked to laugh. The London-based composer Clementi, who claimed to have met Haydn at Eszterháza in the early 1780s, said that whenever Haydn 'hears any of his own Pieces performed that are capricious *he laughs like a fool.*'[106] Any number of Haydn's compositions were described as 'capricious' in the eighteenth century; so – assuming Clementi's recollection to be accurate – Haydn presumably did a lot of laughing.

If Haydn laughed listening to his compositions, it seems reasonable to imagine that he expected others to laugh as well, at least at appropriate places. Anyone familiar with Sir Simon Rattle's 2007 recording of the finale of Symphony no. 90 with the Berlin Philharmonic Orchestra will know that the 'joke' at the heart of this movement has the power to provoke spontaneous and unbridled laughter from a large audience even in our own times.[107] Doubtless many other witticisms we recognize in Haydn's music did indeed provoke genuine laughter on first hearing in the eighteenth century. They just seemed funny.

The problem with laughter, however, is that it doesn't necessarily travel well, and what some people laugh at, and the way they laugh, may appear to others uncouth, inappropriate or beneath them. When at the end of his composing career Haydn introduced a chorus into the number in *Winter* in *The Seasons* where Hanne tells a light-hearted story, his setting of the country people's 'ho ho's' and their 'ha ha's' clearly characterizes their laughter as that of the coarse, peasant variety, perhaps something like that of the younger Haydn who apparently laughed 'like a fool' at his own compositions. Cultured audiences at first performances of *The Seasons* are likely to have been amused by this in large part because they would not have identified themselves with such behaviour.

Haydn, however, had enjoyed this kind of laughter from early in his career. One critic writing in 1777, noting that 'To arouse laughter, in whatever way, was [Haydn's] aim', made this comment not approvingly, but to reproach the composer for his supposed reliance on music associated with the low comedies traditionally performed in Vienna.[108] Five years later, in 1782, a more sympathetic critic took

106. Clementi reported this to Dr Burney in the mid-1780s: *The Letters of Dr Charles Burney*, ed. by Alvaro Ribeiro, 4 vols (Oxford: Clarendon Press, 1991–), I (1991), 400, n. 72.

107. Simon Rattle, Berliner Philharmoniker, *Haydn, Symphonies 88–92, Sinfonia Concertante*, EMI, 2007, disc 1, track 12. This performance includes the live audience reaction (including considerable laughter) at Haydn's 'joke', which with repeats occurs twice. There can be little doubt that Haydn expected similar responses from the symphony's original audiences.

108. Karl Ludwig Junker, *Zwanzig Componisten: eine Skizze* (1776). For full discussion of Junker's assessment of Haydn, see Gretchen A. Wheelock, *Haydn's Ingenious Jesting with Art: Contexts of Musical Wit and Humor* (New York: Schirmer, 1992). My translation of the quotation from Junker is Wheelock's.

the view that Haydn had come through a period in his career when his goal was provoking laughter in his audience and had begun a new phase in which his objective was rather to raise a smile on the lips of his listeners, something presented as more subtle and elevated, therefore rendering Haydn's music more generally desirable.[109]

Laughing like a fool was not at all what was expected in polite society, particularly in late eighteenth-century England, where conventions for how to react to amusing things demanded a much more refined response. Those concerned with codes of civility could point to the likes of Plato, Aristotle, Cicero and Erasmus to defend the view that laughter needed controlling.[110] This English sensibility is summed up, for instance, in advice given by Lord Chesterfield published in 1774:[111]

> Frequent and loud laughter is the characteristic of folly and ill manners: it is the manner in which the mob express their silly joy at silly things; and they call it being merry. In my mind there is nothing so illiberal, and so ill-bred, as audible laughter. True wit, or sense, never made anybody laugh; they are above it: they please the mind, and give a cheerfulness to the countenance. But it is low buffoonery, or silly accidents, that always excite laughter; and that is what people of sense and breeding should show themselves above.

Fanny Burney reveals a prejudice precisely along these lines when she baulked at Bunbury's constant habit of laughing aloud at himself, though she was prepared to take pleasure in his prints and even to encourage the king and queen to sample them without fear of offence.[112]

Given the social pitfalls of laughter in eighteenth-century England, it seems likely that a visiting composer from Austria in 1791, with a reputation for musical wit, would have needed help gauging how to pitch his humour and what kind of reactions to expect. What Haydn may not have been able to grasp fully in his limited understanding of the English language on first arriving in London, he might may well have felt he could comprehend through the medium of Bunbury's pictures, those that he acquired for his collection. What is undoubtedly the case is that after finally returning to Austria Haydn's particular brand of humour came to be identified as having a distinct 'English' aspect to it. For example, one commentator writing in 1801, dealing with the causes of Haydn's greatness, says that one part of it lies 'in that which the English call humour and for which the German word *Laune* [which

109. Wheelock, *Haydn's Ingenious Jesting with Art*, pp. 48–50.
110. Vic Gatrell, *City of Laughter: Sex and Satire in Eighteenth-Century London* (London: Atlantic, 2006), pp. 157–77.
111. Letter of 9 March 1748 to his son: see *Lord Chesterfield's Letters*, ed. by D. Roberts (Oxford: Oxford University Press, 1992), pp. 70–74 (p. 72) and Gatrell, *City of Laughter*, p. 164.
112. *Diary and Letters of Madame d'Arblay*, III (1905), 323.

also means 'humour'] will not do'.[113] Others made similar observations.[114]

What may be deduced from this is that Haydn's experience of English culture and society taught him not only something about self-deprecation whilst remaining witty, but also how, by maintaining more of a straight face rather than laughing aloud, the humour is actually intensified. A clear instance of this is the story of how Haydn, anonymously, delivered to his friend the pianist Therese Jansen (Mrs Bartolozzi), a composition for her to perform with a talented amateur violinist, whose technique was flawed when playing in higher registers. 'Jacob's Dream', the name Haydn wrote on the autograph of this composition, was also the title of one of the pictures in Macklin's Gallery, which perhaps provided inspiration:[115]

> What Haydn had foreseen duly came to pass. The dilettante remained stuck on the highest registers, where most of his passages lay. Soon Miss J[ansen] suspected that the unknown composer intended to depict the ladder to heaven that Jacob saw in his dream and then noticed how the dilettante now ponderously, uncertainly, stumbling, now reeling, skipping, climbed up and down this ladder. The thing seemed so funny to her that she could not hide her laughter, while the dilettante abused the unknown composer […] Only after five or six months did it come out that the sonata's author was Haydn.

Here the scene itself and the laughter it provoked are clearly worthy of Bunbury's most comic creations. Haydn envisages what is going to happen and composes accordingly. But in controlling the situation he is careful not to give the game away himself. Haydn had always written instrumental music that was perceived as 'capricious', to use an eighteenth-century term. But knowledge of Bunbury, it may be suggested, helped him to *see* the consequences of his capriciousness.

113. This appeared in an article by Triest concerning the development of music in eighteenth-century Germany published in the *Allgemeine musikalische Zeitung*, III (11 March 1801), pp. 405–10. The passage in question was quoted by Haydn's biographer Dies: *Biographische Nachrichten von Joseph Haydn*, ed. by Seeger, p. 202.

114. Haydn's friend and biographer Griesinger says something very similar: 'A harmless roguery, or what the British call *humour*, was one of Haydn's outstanding characteristics.': Georg August Griesinger, *Biographische Notizen über Joseph Haydn* (Leipzig: Breitkopf & Härtel, 1810), p. 107; translation from *Haydn: Two Contemporary Portraits*, trans. and ed. by Gotwals, p. 57.

115. Dies: *Biographische Nachrichten von Joseph Haydn*, ed. by Seeger, pp. 154–55; translation from *Haydn: Two Contemporary Portraits*, trans. and ed. by Gotwals, p. 171.

Thomas Hardy's Portrait
of Joseph Haydn

ALAN DAVISON

Welcome, great Master! to our favour'd Isle,
Already partial to thy name and style;
Long may thy fountain of invention run
In streams as rapid as it first begun;
While skill for each fantastic whim provides,
And certain science ev'ry current guides!
Charles Burney, Verses on the Arrival of Haydn in England

IT COMES AS NO SURPRISE that Haydn's first trip to England in 1791
heightened the literary efforts of both his supporters and his detractors. Charles
Burney celebrated with his effusive *Verses on the Arrival of Haydn in England*[1], while
in the same year William Jackson published his diatribe against modern music and

This chapter is based on a longer article published in *Eighteenth-Century Music,* 6 (2009): 209–
27. I would like to thank the two anonymous reviewers for the journal for offering useful criticisms
and suggestions for the article form of this material. Thanks also to the editor, W. Dean Sutcliffe,
and Keith Chapin, for their very helpful comments and for permission to republish this shortened
version. Several staff at the Royal College of Music, London, assisted me considerably with this
research, especially Paul Banks, Paul Collen, Jenny Nex and Lance Whitehead. I would also
like to thank Janet Snowman (Royal Academy of Music), staff at the Heinz Archive and Library

Fig. 1. Thomas Hardy, *Joseph Haydn*. Oil on canvas (1791).

the unnamed Haydn in his *Observations on the Present State of Music in London*.[2] These are just two examples of an ongoing debate conducted since the previous decade that encompassed a wide range of issues, including musical taste, modern versus ancient music, the nature of the symphony, the responsibility of the listener and indeed the nature of Haydn's genius. While contemporary support for Haydn in

Cont.
(National Portrait Gallery), Emma Floyd (Paul Mellon Centre for Studies in British Art), Sheila O'Connell (Department of Prints and Drawings at the British Museum), Alex Kidson (Liverpool Museum) and Elizabeth Barker (Mead Art Museum, Amherst College). My wife Natalie Nugent provided invaluable support and advice during my research on Hardy, while helpful feedback on a draft of this research was given by Erin Johnson-Hill.

1. Extract from *Verses on the Arrival of Haydn in England* (London: printed for Payne, 1791). The *Verses* are reproduced in full in Landon, *Haydn: Chronicle and Works*, III, 32–35. The poem's greatest critical acclaim appears to have come from Burney himself when he reviewed it in the *Monthly Review* of June 1791, when its authorship was still unknown to the public.

2. William Jackson, *Observations on the Present State of Music in London* (London: printed for Harrison, 1791).

Fig. 2. Thomas Hardy, *Joseph Haydn*. Stipple engraving (1792).

the form of published documents such as Burney's *Verses* is immediately recognizable to historians and musicologists, there is another piece of Haydn propaganda from the time that is less well understood: Thomas Hardy's oil portrait and subsequent engraving of the composer of 1791–92 (see Figs 1 and 2 respectively).

This oil portrait is familiar today as one of the most frequently reproduced images of the composer. The engraved version has been widely copied since it was first published in February 1792 by the music publisher John Bland. Bland almost certainly commissioned the oil portrait for use as the basis for the print. A detailed discussion of the visual traditions that formed the context for the portrait has been presented elsewhere,[3] as has a study of Haydn's concern for his image and reception more generally.[4] This essay will instead concentrate on the significance of Hardy's portrait

3. Alan Davison, 'Thomas Hardy's Portrait of Joseph Haydn: A Study in the Conventions of Late Eighteenth-Century British Portraiture', *Music in Art*, 33/1–2 (2008), 101–12. This was republished with some revisions in the *Journal of the Haydn Society of Great Britain*, 27 (2008), 2–15. The current chapter builds upon this research.

4. Thomas Tolley, *Painting the Cannon's Roar: Music, the Visual Arts and the Rise of an Attentive Public in the Age of Haydn, c. 1750–c. 1810* (Aldershot: Ashgate, 2001).

in relation to Haydn's reception in England at the time. The portrait is at first glance rather matter-of-fact, and hardly seems to evoke a sense of genius befitting the 'Shakespeare of music'. While it is certainly the case that the portrait conforms to a rather typical Georgian template, there are several clues indicating that Haydn was being presented here as much more than a generic successful businessman. Indeed, the portrait actually presents the composer as a creative genius, something he was acknowledged to be in his own lifetime. That changed dramatically, however, after his death.[5]

That a portrait is a form of propaganda is such a commonplace that it barely requires emphasis. What is more interesting for the historian or biographer is to what extent any given portrait responds to or reflects specific circumstances, and how it may in turn then provide an insight into those circumstances. The immediate context of Hardy's portrait of Haydn was the composer's visit to England and the interests of the two men closely associated with bringing him there: the impresario Johann Peter Salomon and the music publisher John Bland. For Burney's good friend Salomon there was the pressing concern of the publicity campaign being waged over Haydn, notably in connection with the competing concert series and the advocates of Ignaz Pleyel.[6] Bland was selling Haydn's music in competition with other publishers, and he appears to have commissioned oil portraits of several leading musicians of the day from Hardy, although the details surrounding this are unknown. Bland also published the engravings that were based upon them, proudly proclaiming in the captions that he possessed the original pictures. Bland had formed close ties with Salomon during the late 1780s and was, at his peak, the rival of the two other leading music retailers in London at the time: William Forster and Longman & Broderip.[7] Bland visited Haydn in November 1789 at Eszterháza to press for publishing rights, and probably also to encourage the composer to visit London. Haydn evidently thought highly of Bland, referring to his 'valued friendship' in a

---

5.   The reasons for the sharp decline in Haydn's reputation during the nineteenth century have been the focus of several studies, including Leon Botstein's 'The Consequence of Presumed Innocence: The Nineteenth-Century Reception of Joseph Haydn', in *Haydn Studies*, ed. by W. Dean Sutcliffe (Cambridge: Cambridge University Press, 1998), pp. 1–34; James Garratt, 'Haydn and Posterity: The Long Nineteenth Century', in *The Cambridge Companion to Haydn*, ed. by Caryl Clark (Cambridge: Cambridge University Press, 2005), pp. 226–38; and Howard Irving, 'Haydn and the Politics of the Picturesque', *Studies in Eighteenth-Century Culture*, 36 (2007), 213–34, where he outlines the rapid change in critical views on Haydn over the decades 1780 to 1820.

6.   Although Salomon's career was long thought to reach its zenith with Haydn's visits, Ian Woodfield argues that the reality was quite different. See his *Salomon and the Burneys: Private Patronage and a Public Career*, RMA Monographs, 12 (Aldershot: Ashgate, 2003).

7.   See Ian Woodfield, 'John Bland: London Retailer of the Music of Haydn and Mozart', *Music & Letters*, 81 (2000), 210–44, for an overview of Bland's activities as well as an insight into the intense commercial rivalry between the main music publishers at the time.

letter of 12 May 1790, and even stayed at the publisher's house on his very first night in London. In this same letter, Haydn wrote 'Concerning the portraits you ask for, you must be patient until I arrive in Vienna. I shall then be able to satisfy you.'[8] Bland was clearly seeking a portrait or portraits of Haydn, no doubt to support the marketing of Haydn's music, and, of course, he would eventually acquire one in the form of Hardy's oil painting.

As Thomas Tolley has shown, Bland was keen to stress his personal connection with the composer even prior to Haydn's first stay in London, and 'Bland's commission for the Hardy portrait, of course, served to confirm this connection at the expense of rivals'.[9] Moreover, Bland's role in Salomon's efforts to bring Haydn to England had been made public almost as soon as the composer arrived, via the announcement in the *Morning Chronicle* of 3 January that 'Yesterday arrived at Mr. BLAND's in Holborn, the celebrated Mr. HAYDN, the composer from Vienna, accompanied by Mr. SALOMON: and we understand that the public is indebted to Mr. BLAND as being the chief instrument of Mr. HAYDN'S coming to England.'[10]

Thomas Hardy, the man who actually executed the portrait, is something of an enigma, with a dearth of contemporary references to his name.[11] He painted a remarkable selection of musical sitters, including Haydn, Muzio Clementi, Wilhelm Cramer, Salomon, Pleyel, Samuel Arnold, Edward Miller and William Shield.[12] Many of Hardy's portraits are lost, or of unknown whereabouts. Fortunately, his

8.   The letter is translated in several sources, including Woodfield, 'John Bland', 227.

9.   Tolley, *Painting the Cannon's Roar*, p. 169.

10. Quoted in Landon, *Haydn: Chronicle and Works*, III, 31. Here Bland or one of his supporters is trying to cash in on the visit, but it would be Salomon that would end up with the most prestige, perhaps unfairly, as it turns out. See Woodfield, *Salomon and the Burneys*, chapter 9.

11. There is scant reference to Hardy in contemporary sources, including newspapers and journals. Moreover, he barely features in the memoirs or diaries of some people who might have been expected to mention him: Joseph Farington makes only passing reference to him (but does provide crucial information) in his monumental *Diaries*, Fanny Burney none at all, and so on. He is absent from several major histories, biographies or autobiographies, such as John Thomas Smith's *Nollekens and His Times* (London: Colburn, 1829), Edward Edwards's *Anecdotes of Painters who have Resided or Been Born in England* (London: Leigh and Sotheby, 1808) and so forth. The diaries of Mrs Papendiek end just at the time when Haydn arrives in England, and so no reference to Hardy is made, even if she had knowledge of him.

12. John Chaloner Smith's monumental *British Mezzotinto Portraits*, 4 vols (London: Sotheran, 1878–84), II, 662, lists a portrait by Hardy of a 'young man' to which 'the name of Dussek, the musician has been given […] but the authority is incomplete'. The print is held in the British Museum (ref. 1902.1011.247). It does not resemble Dussek at all, and shows a rather thin-faced aristocratic young man. Bland did in fact issue a print of Dussek, and while it is similar to Hardy's other portraits in general appearance, there is no name attached to it and on stylistic grounds it does not appear to be by Hardy.

portraits of musicians were engraved, and numerous copies are extant today. The original portraits of Haydn, Salomon and Shield are at the Royal College of Music, while that of Cramer can be found at the National Portrait Gallery in London.

What little is known of Hardy can be quickly outlined. He was one of three sons of a Derbyshire miner, William Hardy, and his wife, Mary.[13] Thomas was born in 1757 and died 'after a long illness' on 14 September 1804, according to an obituary in *The Gentleman's Magazine*.[14] He went to the Royal Academy schools in 1778, and exhibited over thirty paintings at the Academy exhibitions over the next two decades, nearly all portraits. Hardy worked not only as an oil painter and portraitist, but also as an engraver, producing prints both of his own originals and those of other, more notable painters such as Joshua Reynolds and William Beechey. He worked mainly in the two particularly common forms of engraving at the time: mezzotint and stipple. Why Bland chose Hardy is unknown, but it is worth noting that in the early 1790s the artist lived directly opposite the piano maker James Houston, while the latter was supplying Bland with pianos.[15]

While Hardy's connection to Bland provides the immediate and commercial motivation for his portrait of Haydn, the wider aesthetic and critical context must be considered in relation to the reception of the composer up to and during 1791. Well before Haydn's arrival, critics and supporters had been debating his music and his status as a genius, either directly or indirectly. Elaine Sisman and Thomas Bauman have both highlighted the connection between critical responses to Haydn and contemporary accounts of genius.[16] Sisman associates the frequent comparisons of Haydn with Shakespeare to the latter's status as a genius of originality, while

13. Hardy's father wrote *The Miner's Guide: or, Compleat Miner* (Sheffield: printed by Francis Lister, 1748), and in a copy held at the Derby Local Studies Library (accession number 1452) there are notes on the Hardy family by the nineteenth-century antiquarian William Bateman. Bateman mentions two brothers, William (a marble mason) and John (an engraver). Many thanks to Roger Flindall for providing a facsimile of Bateman's annotations. Both Thomas and John studied at the Royal Academy schools, although records for the latter at the Academy confusingly refer to a 'James' in the school register and a 'John' in the Council minutes. My thanks to Andrew Potter from the Royal Academy Library for this detail.

14. *The Gentleman's Magazine*, 74 (July–December 1804), 981.

15. J. Doane's *Musical Directory* (London: Westley, 1794), p. 34, gives Houston's address as 54 Great Marlborough Street, across the road from Hardy who lived at number 4. Hardy's addresses during the 1780s and 1790s are provided by the Royal Academy exhibition catalogues and by the various self-published prints. Richard Horward's map of London from the 1790s, 'Plan of the Cities of London and Westminster, the Borough of Southwark and Parts Adjoining', was consulted to pinpoint Hardy's location in relation to Houston.

16. Elaine Sisman, 'Haydn, Shakespeare, and the Rules of Originality', in *Haydn and His World*, ed. by Sisman (Princeton: Princeton University Press, 1997), pp. 3–56, and Thomas Bauman, 'Becoming Original: Haydn and the Cult of Genius', *The Musical Quarterly*, 87 (2005), 333–57.

Bauman argues that Haydn could be identified as a specific form of eighteenth-century genius, the 'learned' genius.[17]

While contemporary debates over the nature of genius may have been a pressing matter among intellectuals, however, notions of genius and originality as applied to Haydn often involved specific criticisms rather than philosophical musings. A survey of selected musical writings from the decade prior to Haydn's first visit will give an indication of what themes emerged in public debate, and show how some influential critics applied terms such as 'genius' and 'invention' in the case of Haydn.

The efforts of Haydn's advocates can be set against the backdrop of the wider debate over the merits of modern versus ancient music. Here the stage for the debate was, if not exactly set, then at least turgidly rehearsed by the music scholar and lawyer Sir John Hawkins, Burney's main antagonist in opinions on music.[18] In his five-volume *General History of the Science and Practice of Music* (1776), Hawkins railed against recent developments in music, and concluded his *History* with an attack on modern music and the wider society that encourages it:[19]

> The prevalence of a corrupt taste in music seems to be but the necessary result of that state of civil policy which enables, and that disposition which urges men to assume the character of judges of what they do not understand.

Decline in musical taste was thus a symptom of wider social decay, and the implication is clearly that it was the responsibility of the expert to guide the music lover towards what they should be listening to.

The earliest English biography of Haydn appeared in the following decade, in the anonymous 'Account of Joseph Haydn, a Celebrated Composer of Music', published in the *European Magazine, and London Review* in October 1784. If not actually written by Burney, it certainly conforms with some of his opinions. Here Haydn

---

17. A useful overview of theories of genius and creativity can be found in James Engell's *The Creative Imagination: Enlightenment to Romanticism* (Cambridge, MA: Harvard University Press, 1981). Kant's important writings on genius will not be considered in relation to Hardy's portrait. While enormously influential in Germany and more widely across nineteenth-century Europe, his impact upon English intellectuals was insignificant at the time, with only infrequent mention of him or his works in literature by the early 1790s. See Giuseppe Micheli, 'The Early Reception of Kant's Thought in England 1785–1805', in *Kant and His Influence*, ed. by George MacDonald Ross and Tony McWalter (London: Continuum, 2005), pp. 202–314.

18. Roger Lonsdale's *Dr. Charles Burney: A Literary Biography* (Oxford: Clarendon, 1965) is indispensable for biographical material on Burney, and the rivalry between the two men. Burney seems, unusually for him, to have been obsessive is his resentment of Hawkins. A defence of Hawkins can be found in Robert Stevenson's '"The Rivals" — Hawkins, Burney, and Boswell', *The Musical Quarterly*, 36 (1950), 67–82.

19. *A General History of the Science and Practice of Music*, 5 vols (London, 1776; reprinted New York: Dover, 1963), II, 919.

is praised for creating an '*original, masterly*, and *beautiful*' new species of music.[20] The 'Account' emphasizes Haydn's genius and tries to explain away the 'wildness' evident in some of his music, apparently in response to attacks from North German music critics. It is full of inaccuracies, but as Howard Irving notes, these are 'clearly motivated by an attempt to account for Haydn's "soaring genius," his early music's alleged lack of "regularity and consistency," and the "wildness of nature and luxuriance of fancy" that needed to be tamed through proper education'.[21] These sentiments can be aligned with the strong emphasis on the place of learning in the development of genius found in several philosophical texts in the eighteenth century.[22]

In the same year as the 'Account', William Jones published his *Treatise on the Art of Music*. A practical guide to music composition, the *Treatise* shows above all else the conservatism of English music theory at the time. In the chapter 'On the Analysis of Air, and the Conduct of Subject', where he outlines a very restricted approach to the treatment of melodic dissonance, Jones refers to Haydn in the following way:[23]

> As for *Haydn* and *Boccherini*, who merit a first place among the Moderns for *invention*, they are sometimes so desultory and unaccountable in their way of treating a Subject, that they may be reckoned among the wild warblers of the wood: And they seem to differ from some pieces of *Handel*, as the Talk and the Laughter of the Tea-table (where, perhaps, neither Wit nor Invention are wanting) differs from the Oratory of the bar and the Pulpit.

Neither for the first nor the last time, Handel is invoked as the touchstone of learnedness, and the more modern composers receive backhanded compliments for their invention while being derided for their apparently uncouth musical creations.

Jones was not alone, for Charles Dibdin's *Musical Tour* of 1788 follows up on the theme of undisciplined invention. The *Tour* is a typical eighteenth-century potpourri of criticism and musings in the form of letters. In letter XLIV he addresses melody and rules of composition, and Haydn is inevitably discussed. The main thrust of the

---

20. A. Peter Brown, 'The Earliest English Biography of Haydn', *The Musical Quarterly*, 59 (1973), 343. Italics original.

21. Irving, 'Haydn and the Politics of the Picturesque', 222.

22. See, for example, William Sharpe, *A Dissertation Upon Genius; or, An Attempt to shew, that the Several Instances of Distinction, and Degrees of Superiority in the Human Genius are not, Fundamentally, the Result of Nature, but the Effect of Acquisition* (London: printed for Bathurst, 1755), William Duff, *Essay on Original Genius* (London: printed for Edward and Charles Dilly, 1767), and Alexander Gerard, *Essay on Genius* (London: printed for Strahan, Cadell and Creech, 1774).

23. William Jones, *A Treatise on the Art of Music; In which the Elements of Harmony and Air are Practically Considered* (Colchester: printed for the author by Keymer, 1784), pp. 49–50.

letter is that 'simple unadorned melody [should] be accompanied only by such mod-ulations as arise from the general and perfect nature of the subject'.[24] Alas, some composers, even 'a man of such admirable genius' as Haydn, overdo things. Haydn is like a 'rope-dancer, who, though you cannot too much admire how prettily he frisks and jumps about, keeps you in a constant state of terror and anxiety for fear he should break his neck'.[25] Do Haydn's compositions, Dibdin asks, 'consist of any thing more than the strong effusions of genius turned into frenzy, and labouring as ineffectively to be heard as a flute in a belfry, or equity in a court of justice?'[26] As with Jones, it is not Haydn's originality or inventiveness in itself that is being ques-tioned, or even that he may be a genius – philosophical discussions over the nature of genius are not the concern here – but rather the intelligibility and taste of his music.

Staunch defence of Haydn was again at hand only a year later. Apart from his *Verses*, Burney's enthusiasm for Haydn is evident in the fourth volume (1789) of his monumental *General History of Music*. In chapter ten, 'Of the Progress of Music in GERMANY, during the present Century', he finally comes to discuss Haydn and makes his feelings readily apparent when writing of 'the admirable and matchless HAYDN!'[27] He defends his hero against claims that he composed in apparent igno-rance of the rules of composition, 'a censure which the admirable Haydn has long since silenced: for he is now as much respected by professors for his science as in-vention'.[28] Burney gives the music lover and performer a new weight of responsi-bility in dealing with Haydn's music: 'his compositions are in general so new to the player and hearer, that they are equally unable, at first, to keep pace with his inspi-ration'.[29] And, though his works may at first seem odd, 'by frequent repetition' both 'performer and hearer are at their ease'.[30]

Burney also emphasized the importance of repeated hearings in his famous 'Essay on Musical Criticism' contained in the *History*. Here, the point is made in relation to modern German music generally, and it is worth quoting at length:[31]

24. Charles Dibdin, *The Musical Tour of Mr. Dibdin; In which—Previous to his Embarkation for India—He Finished his General Career as A Public Character* (Sheffield: the author, 1788), p. 181.

25. Dibdin, *The Musical Tour*, p. 182.

26. Dibdin, *The Musical Tour*, p. 182.

27. Charles Burney, *A General History of Music, from the Earliest Ages to the Present Period*, 4 vols (London: author, 1776–89), with critical and historical notes by Frank Mercer (New York: Constable, 1957), II, 958.

28. Burney, *General History*, II, 959.

29. Burney, *General History*, II, 959.

30. Burney, *General History*, II, 960.

31. Burney, *General History*, II, 11.

[Music] is only understood and felt by such as can quit the plains of simplicity, penetrate the mazes of art and contrivance, climb mountains, dive into dells, or cross the seas in search of extraneous and exotic beauties with which the monotonous melody of popular Music has not yet embellished. What judgment and good taste admire at first hearing, makes no impression on the public in general, but by dint of repetition and habitude. […] The extraneous, and seemingly forced and affected modulation of the German composers of the present age, is only too much for us, because we have heard too little.

This directly challenges the views of Dibdin, and puts the onus on the concert-goer or music lover to make an effort rather than sit back and expect to be entertained.

The debate was far from over, however, and following on from Hawkins's efforts to protect the concert-going public from themselves was William Jackson's *Observations on the Present State of Music in London*, published as a pamphlet in October 1791. Unlike Hawkins, Jackson was writing after Haydn's music had become enormously successful in England during the 1780s, and so his criticisms are obviously a rearguard action. Jackson was an author, aspiring painter and composer, who seriously fell out with Burney around 1789 after he published a critical review of the latter's *History*.[32] Jackson's pamphlet is a biting attack on the moderns and a thinly disguised swipe at Haydn. Jackson outlined what he saw as the problematic qualities of various genres, but reserved particular criticism for the symphony. While first generously acknowledging the efforts of Richter and Abel, he soon changed his tone with more recent composers, who 'to be grand and original, have poured in such floods of nonsense, under the sublime idea of *being inspired*, that the present SYMPHONY bears the same relation to good Music, as the ravings of a Bedlamite do to sober sense'.[33] Crucially, Jackson is not only criticizing what he finds excessive in the music, but also mocking what, to his mind, was the contrived posturing of composers as inspired and original. Thus 'genius' in this form leads to a degradation of music.

Writing after Haydn's departure, John Marsh, the English composer, writer and friend of Burney, attempted to bring a conciliatory tone to the debate. Marsh wrote an essay that appeared in the *Monthly Magazine* in 1796, 'A Comparison between

32. See Richard McGrady's 'The Elegies of William Jackson and Thomas Linley the Elder', *Music & Letters*, 77 (1996), 209–27, for more on the relationship between the two men. For a discussion of Burney's other literary run-ins see Roger Lonsdale's 'Dr. Burney and the *Monthly Review*', *The Review of English Studies*, New Series, 14/56 (1963), 346–58, and 15/5 (1964), 27–37.

33. Jackson, *Observations*, p. 16. Jackson's focus on melody is significant, for in some later writings he explicitly links 'original melody' to genius. Writing shortly after Haydn's second visit, Jackson was keen to distinguish between mere talent and genius, and concluded that the defining characteristic of genius 'is *invention, a creation of something not before existing*; to which talents make no pretence' (Jackson, *The Four Ages; Together with Essays on Various Subjects* (London: printed for Cadell and Davies, 1798), p. 195). Italics original.

the Ancient and Modern Styles of Music, In which the Merits and Demerits of Each are Respectively Pointed Out'.[34] Marsh's essay provides the reader with an ostensibly even-handed guide to the virtues and limitations of the two styles. Marsh acknowledges that the consequence of inventiveness such as Haydn's could become hard to digest in the fleeting moment, and that 'it is impossible for any ear to receive and clearly distinguish the effect of many parts together, unless assisted by the eye in looking over the score, at least not till after several hearings'.[35] Here Marsh reinforces the notion that general pleasure might be forsaken, and, as with Burney, that repeated hearings are needed.

In summary, it would appear that the symphony epitomized all those things that were offensive to reactionaries, while for the 'moderns' it was held up as the ideal conglomeration of new trends. Haydn, being at the vanguard of modern – Viennese symphonic – music, was a pivotal figure for both his supporters and detractors, held up as the 'spiritual leader of the musical "moderns"'.[36] The arguments can be distilled down to a few recurring topics: genius, originality, rules, symphony and Haydn.

By the time Hardy's portrait of Haydn was exhibited at the Royal Academy in 1792, music lovers would have had ample time to digest the issues raised in the skirmishes of critics such as Burney and Jackson. Bland may well have thought that any publicity was good publicity, but he was obviously not content with just selling Haydn's music. At some stage he must have arranged for Haydn to sit for Hardy, and he finally obtained the painting of the Master he had desired since at least 1790. The resulting portrait was one of three the artist exhibited at the Royal Academy that year, the other two being of Salomon and the well known London actor Robert Baddely. The Salomon portrait must in some sense have been paired with the Haydn, as Salomon had taken credit for bringing Haydn over. They were not hung together, however, as their catalogue numbers indicate they were in different rooms. Paintings by non-Academicians had to go through a selection process in order to be hung, and so to have three portraits hung for that year was no mean achievement, and was a fine opportunity to display one's work to thousands of people and potential clients.[37]

34. C. L. Cudworth, 'An Essay by John Marsh', *Music & Letters*, 36 (1955), 155–64. Marsh had strong links to Bland, who published some of his songs and chamber music. Marsh's *Journal* refers to Bland as 'a great publisher of songs'; *The John Marsh Journals: The Life and Times of a Gentleman Composer (1752–1827)*, ed. by Brian Robins (Stuyvesant, NY: Pendragon, 1998), p. 454.
35. Cudworth, 'An Essay by John Marsh', 163.
36. Irving, 'Haydn and the Politics of the Picturesque', 231.
37. The average number of public visitors was in the order of 50,000 annually during the late 1780s and early 1790s. For a detailed study of the Royal Academy exhibitions during the relevant period see the collection of essays in *Art on the Line: The Royal Academy Exhibitions at Somerset House 1780–1836*, ed. by David Solkin (New Haven: Yale University Press, 2001). Especially informative is Marcia Pointon's 'Portrait! Portrait!! Portrait!!!', pp. 93–109.

Fig. 3. Facius (G. S. or J. G.) after Thomas Hardy, *Johann Peter Salomon.*
Stipple and line engraving (1792).

The precise date of the oil portrait is uncertain, but considering the fact that the engraving based upon it (see Fig. 3) was published in February 1792, and the Royal Academy exhibition opened in late April, some time late in 1791 or very early in 1792 would appear to be the likely range.[38] The portrait's fate after Bland is unknown, but it came into the possession of Alfred Hill late in the nineteenth century. It was exhibited at the Worshipful Company of Musicians' music loan exhibition held at Fishmonger's Hall in June–July 1904, and was reproduced in the illustrated

---

38. If the portrait was completed early in 1791, then it would not have made sense for Bland to wait so long before trying to cash in on the enthusiasm for Haydn's visit.

catalogue that followed in 1909. Hill gifted the portrait to the Royal College of Music in 1933, where it remains.

The roughly 64 by 76 cm dimensions of Hardy's portrait of Haydn are found repeatedly in late eighteenth-century England, as this was the smallest and cheapest of the commonly used standard sizes in portraiture.[39] Known as the 'head', the format actually shows the sitter from the waist up, and is typically rather minimal and unassuming. As with Hardy's other portraits of this format, Haydn engages the viewer with his eyes, and a very slight smile. The body is turned three-quarters but the head much less so, allowing for a near full-face view. Lighting comes from high to the left of the viewer, revealing all of the face, which thus lacks strong shadow. The right shoulder and coat collar are highlighted with diffuse lighting, creating the rather pastel-like effect found in Hardy's other portraits. The forehead is high and brilliantly lit, although a clear sense of Haydn's swarthy complexion is indicated by the ruddy cheeks. The result is a sharp contrast between the almost white purity of the forehead and the rather less noble skin tones that Haydn actually possessed. Haydn's very distinctive physiognomy is easily recognizable, especially with his prominent nose and rather protruding lower lip. He wears a dark coat with large buttons and a frilly silk necktie and cuffs. The tie and cuffs are effectively painted with lively and economical brush strokes, a typical feature of Hardy's portraits.

Other than Haydn himself, there are several other noteworthy features in the portrait. The armchair is covered with plush fabric, and a row of studs outlines the side of the right arm. Haydn holds a bound score with a marbled cover, red rectangular section on the spine, and possibly a gold crest. Although no title or text is present, Hardy has gone to some trouble to paint something absent from any of his other portraits of musicians, where only unbound sheet music or the score by itself is shown. In addition to the detailing on the score cover, Haydn also marks the work by prominently holding it up, marking a page with his second finger. This gesture is that of a man of letters pondering a venerable text, although in this case the implication is that it is Haydn's own work being contemplated. To the right of the score is a portion of a keyboard, visually separated from the composer through its positioning. It is clearly an English keyboard, although the nameboard is blank. Behind all of this is the clichéd red drape, although the familiar pilaster is absent.

The sheer succinctness of the 'head' portrait, even if driven by economic factors, led to a visual style of utmost brevity. Accoutrements, if any, take on a prominence and a strikingly direct relationship to the main subject of the painting, the sitter. Likewise, gesture and posture, and any deviation from an often unrelenting standard, gain a significance lacking in freer genres. While a larger-scale portrait might have

39. The other two sizes were the half-length portrait (127 cm by 102 cm) and the full-length portrait (239 cm by 147 cm).

enabled an artist to set up complex or narrative relationships between objects and the sitter, the head portrait necessarily had a directness that could be considered from the outset to be symbolic, and much more than a realistic representation of space.

It is easy for modern eyes to interpret the accoutrements shown in a portrait such as Hardy's Haydn in a rather facile manner, as little more than obvious and conventionalized signs of vocation.[40] Doubtless they are clues to the vocation and interests of the sitter, such as in paintings where an architect holds drawing plans or a judge holds tomes of law, and so forth. But what can be missed is the way in which these objects interrelate with the sitter, in a symbolic rather than literal space.[41] This almost 'abstracted' space takes on particular significance when multiple objects are shown, and the positioning of the objects, in relation both to each other and to the sitter, are emphasized due to the succinctness of the image.

By far the most prominent object in addition to the composer himself is the bound volume that one can only infer is of his music. Technically speaking, the score is quarter bound, in brown leather with the boards covered in marbled paper.[42] Being at the lower end of the leather-bound options may be significant, at least for the observant connoisseur of the day, as Paul Banks elaborates:[43]

> What the presence of a bound score tells us is, of course, a matter of interpretation, but it may be sending a subtlely modulated signal about the cultural status of Haydn's music – and one that implies the emergence of a notion of canon. That the score, whether printed or manuscript, is portrayed as meriting and receiving the protection and preservation of a binding, suggests the latter functions as a surrogate for the canon. Yet the binding itself is notable for its implied social context: not an ostentatious, top-of-the-range full binding, but an elegant, modest celebration of the contents implying, perhaps, a relatively broad social appeal of the music.

The score is not only emphasized in the painting's composition, but also frames Haydn off from the instrument, prioritizing his relationship to the musical text. Hardy has thus managed to imply that Haydn's connection to the keyboard is only

40. Ludmilla Jordanova, in her work on portraits of scientists, recognizes four functions for accoutrements: visual interest, following established conventions, conveying symbolic information and acting as symbols. Ludmilla Jordanova, *Defining Features: Scientific and Medical Portraits, 1660–2000* (London: National Portrait Gallery, 2000), p. 80.

41. Kate Retford, in her study of Georgian Conversation Pieces, argues that viewers would have understood the interior environment of the group portrait as a fabricated space: 'From the Interior to Interiority: The Conversation Piece in Georgian England', *Journal of Design History*, 20/4 (1997), 291–301.

42. My particular thanks to Professor Banks for highlighting various aspects of the volume to me, and raising the possible significance of the binding.

43. Paul Banks, personal communication, 16 July 2008.

indirect; the score (intellectual, non-manual work) is the primary object, and the keyboard shows his leadership of and connection to actual performances. In relation to these points, Simon McVeigh has observed that in London in the 1790s, 'composers were undoubtedly regarded above executants: one commentator directly contrasted "mere mechanical performers", their lives shortened by dissipation and debauchery, with long-lived composers, the real artists'.[44]

Hardy's other portraits, as indeed is the case with most other portraits of musicians from this time, tend to show the manuscript held loosely in the hand (such as his Clementi), or perhaps rolled up (as in his Cramer), with Reynolds's famous portrait of Burney as, at the time, a recent model for the latter. Holding up a book or other text of some sort strengthens the inference of ownership and the sense that such a book is a historically significant object.[45] The implication is that Haydn is doing to his own music what his champions said was expected of listeners of the day: that his music required repeated listening and study. Perhaps Haydn here presents his music as a model, an exemplar by which the works of followers or imitators will be judged.[46]

In contrast to the dramatic effects seen in paintings of romantic composers, there is at first glance little hint of the 'fire' that Haydn's supporters spoke of in this portrait. But there are subtle cues that indicate something of the fire still burning in the ageing composer. The portrait uses lighting and colour to suggest the creative energy of the composer through the brilliant highlighting of the forehead and the unusual placement of the drape. The latter falls across behind Haydn's head just in line with the most brilliant emphasis on the forehead, an effect that draws more attention to the glowing front of the cranium.

Compositionally, the painting provides a visual corollary to Haydn's own 'fantastic whim' controlled by 'certain science'. The surprising 'misplaced' drape, a whimsy of Hardy's visual play, is integrated within the overall design via the strong diagonal lines emanating from Haydn's head. Haydn's rather formal upright posture and the score held close to the body implies a man who controls and fully 'owns' the results of his creative process. No hastily scribbled notes on manuscript paper here. All in all, and within its own parameters, it is a perfectly judged reflection of Haydn's – and his supporters' – preferred form of genius in the English context: inspired and full of fire, capable of novelty and invention, and yet controlled by taste and judgement.

44. Simon McVeagh, *Concert Life in London from Mozart to Haydn* (Cambridge: Cambridge University Press, 1993), 204–05.

45. Laurent Dabos's historic portrait of Thomas Paine (*c.* 1791) is a good example of a significant text held aloft. It is in the National Portrait Gallery, London (ref. NPG 6804, 74 cm by 59 cm, oil on canvas).

46. On Haydn's own attempt to establish a reputation for priority and genius see Sisman, 'Haydn, Shakespeare, and the Rules of Originality'.

Fig. 4. George Dance, *Joseph Haydn*. Pencil on paper (1794).

Other than these painterly and compositional effects, further comment on Haydn's physiognomy is in order. Although the style of the painting suggests a matter-of-fact depiction, a comparison with another portrait, the profile drawing by George Dance, suggests otherwise (see Fig. 4). Dance was an architect who drew hundreds of profiles of acquaintances and friends. They are often unrelentingly dull, but seem to offer good likenesses, being in the tradition of the physiognomic silhouette. Here we can see that Haydn's forehead was much lower than that shown in Hardy's portrait, even taking into account the differing view of the head. Also clearly evident in Dance's portrait is the protruding lower lip and open mouth. Haydn suffered from nasal polyps, and may well have been breathing through his mouth when sitting for this.[47]

47. Peter Neugebauer, 'The "Case" of Joseph Haydn: A Rhinological Patient During the Eighteenth Century', *The Laryngoscope*, 110 (2000), 1078–81.

Fig. 5. John Watts, after Joshua Reynolds, *Giuseppe Baretti*.
Mezzotint engraving published by John Boydell (1780).

Hardy may have obtained his inspiration for the novel composition of this painting from a very well known portrait of similarly modest proportions that serves as
a precedent to Hardy's Haydn, quite possibly as a direct inspiration: Reynolds's famous Streatham portrait of the Italian author Giuseppe Baretti dating from 1773
(see Fig. 5). Baretti had been arrested in 1769 after a street brawl that left a man
dead. At the subsequent trial, Reynolds spoke in defence of his friend, and later
painted a portrait that aimed to situate the author firmly in the tradition of the
bookish scholar. Duncan Robinson has argued that the portrait 'was designed not
to stir controversy but to silence it'.[48] In showing Baretti as a myopic literary man,

---

48. Duncan Robinson, 'Giuseppe Baretti as a "Man of Great Humanity"', in *British Art 1740–1820:
     Essays in Honour of Robert R. Wark*, ed. by Guilland Sutherland (California: Huntington Library,
     1992), pp. 81–94 (at p. 93).

Reynolds distanced the writer from the more pervasive characterization of a hot-headed Italian. In both the portrait of Haydn and Baretti, the positioning in the armchair – and indeed the chair itself – is similar, and more significantly the red drape in both cases intersects diagonally across behind the sitter's head. Hardy was almost certainly aware of the portrait, for his younger brother John had engraved it by at least 1793.[49]

The reception history of the portrait from the time of its inception through to its apparent popularity now is another study in itself, although it is tempting to speculate on its trajectory. If our current response to the portrait is to view it as straightforward or even unimaginative, perhaps its appeal lies in the assumed direct access afforded by Hardy to the composer. It would indeed be an ironic twist of history if what was originally a carefully manipulated representation of a genius is now seen to be an unmediated likeness. The interpretation of the painting today – as that of little more than a portrait of a self-made man – is valid as a measure of the great aesthetic shifts that have occurred since the late eighteenth century. Neither our notion of genius nor our expectations of what genius should look like can be made to sit with what Hardy created. Haydn's reputation for genius and Hardy's subtle manipulation of portrait conventions have not fared well in the face of changing tastes, yet, in its own day, the portrait was a fine defence against Haydn's detractors.

---

49. An engraved version by 'J. Hardy' is listed in Henry Bromley's *Catalogue of Engraved Portraits* (London: Payne, 1793), p. 383.

A Matter of Words:
Haydn, Holcroft and Anne Hunter

CAROLINE GRIGSON

IT IS WELL KNOWN that Haydn made two very productive visits to London in the early 1790s, both in terms of music written and performed and in terms of social success. Among the musical pieces that he composed during those visits were his two sets of six Original Canzonettas, produced in collaboration with the poet Anne Hunter. She wrote all the words for the first set and it is usually assumed that, as well as writing the words for one of the poems in the second set, 'The Wanderer', she chose the words of the remaining five. However, in the course of writing a biography of Anne,[1] it became clear that two others were involved in the production of the second set, namely the poet, playwright and actor Thomas Holcroft and, most probably, the man who published both sets, Domenico Corri. Holcroft had previously written the English words for some of the arrangements of Haydn's songs made by the composer William Shield, who published them in London in the 1780s. After Haydn's final departure from London, Anne continued to write texts for some of his compositions, but there is no indication that the two were in correspondence.

---

1.   Details of Anne Hunter's life are taken from *The Life and Poetry of Anne Hunter: Haydn's Tuneful Voice*, ed. by Caroline Grigson, introd. Isobel Armstrong (Liverpool: Liverpool University Press, 2009).

Anne Hunter

Anne Hunter (1742–1821) was the eldest of eight children of a Scot, Robert Home, surgeon to General Burgoyne's Regiment of Horse, and his wife, Mary Hutchinson, who may have been English. Although Anne was probably born in Ireland, most of her childhood was spent in York, Hull and Scotland. At the end of the Seven Years War in 1763, Robert Home brought his family to London where he, his wife and Anne remained for the rest of their lives.

In 1764 Anne Home's first published poem 'Adieu ye Streams' appeared anonymously in an anthology of poetry, written for the tune of the famous Scottish lament 'The Flowers of the Forest'.[2] She married the up-and-coming surgeon and anatomist John Hunter (1728–93) in 1771 and was always thereafter referred to as Mrs John Hunter. She was soon established as one of the most successful songwriters of her generation,[3] but her poems and songs were either published anonymously or attributed only to 'A Lady'. Sometimes she wrote both words and music, such as her *Nine Canzonetts for two voices; and Six Airs with an Accompanyment for the Piano-forte by a Lady*, which were published in about 1782.[4] Various broadsheets with both words and music composed by Anne appeared from time to time, but it was the words of her songs that were the most successful. For example, her 'Lamentation of Mary Queen of Scots' was reprinted in various forms no fewer than forty times before the end of the century, and 'The Death Song of the Cherokee Indians' and 'Adieu ye Streams' each about twenty times, always anonymously.

A few years before Haydn's first visit to London, Anne and John Hunter had moved to a grand house in Leicester Square. Hunter had by then achieved considerable social and financial success and was Surgeon Extraordinary to the king, and surgeon general to the army. There was a strange dichotomy between the activities in the Leicester Square house, where the family lived and where Hunter received his patients, and the building at the rear, in what is now Charing Cross Road, which housed his dissecting rooms, his anatomy school and his immense anatomical collection. It was there, in the dead of night, that the 'sack-em-up man' would deliver corpses stolen from graveyards for dissection.[5]

2.   *The Black Bird: A Choice Collection of the Most Celebrated Songs: Few of which are to be Found in any other Collection,* [ed. by] William Hunter (Edinburgh: printed by J. Bruce, sold by John Moir, 1764), 12.

3.   A. Peter Brown, 'Musical Settings of Anne Hunter's Poetry: From National Song to Canzonetta', *Journal of the American Musicological Society,* 47 (1994), 39–89.

4.   *Nine Canzonetts for Two Voices; and Six Airs with an Accompanyment for the Piano-forte by a LADY to which is added the Death Song of the Cherokee Indians* (London: Longman & Broderip, [n. d.]).

5.   For details of John Hunter's life, see Wendy Moore, *The Knife Man* (London: Bantam Press, 2005).

Anne Hunter and the six Original Canzonettas

Haydn arrived in London on 1 January 1791 at the invitation of the composer and impresario Johann Peter Salomon. Later in 1791 or in the first half of the following year Haydn composed his first set of six Original Canzonettas. Anne wrote the words of all but one of these canzonettas especially for him; the poem 'Pleasing pain' was evidently written earlier, since it has survived in a manuscript dated 1767 preserved in the archives of the Royal College of Surgeons.[6] How the collaboration came about is uncertain. For his Lieder texts several years previously Haydn had written to his publisher Artaria that as well as the cheerful texts that he already had, he wanted new, gentler ones, but 'the content of these can be melancholy, too: so that I have shadow and light'.[7] Those acquainted with Anne Hunter's published works would have known that she could provide vigour, melancholy, shadow and light, in contrast to the pastoral nature that characterized so many of the songs of the time.

Anne Hunter was a second-generation bluestocking. In 1786 or 1787 she began to hold weekly evening parties during the Season, devoted to conversation and music, at their house in Leicester Square. It is usually assumed that Haydn attended these as a guest, though if he did it seems rather odd that the great composer is not included in the surviving lists of those who attended. Nevertheless it is well known that Haydn did make at least two visits to the household on a very different matter: to consult John Hunter about the polyps in his nose. He described Hunter as 'the greatest and most famous surgeon in London'.[8] On the first occasion, Hunter inspected Haydn's nasal polyps and offered to remove them, but no operation took place. Then in June 1792, or just before, Haydn called again, the visit vividly described in his own words as translated by Landon:[9]

> Shortly before my departure Mr. H. asked me to come and see him about some urgent matters. I went there. After the first exchange of greetings a few brawny fellows entered the room, grabbed me, and wanted to force me into a chair. I yelled, kicked until I had freed myself, and made it clear to Mr. H., who already had his instruments ready for the operation, that I did not want to undergo the operation. He was very astonished at my obstinacy, and it seemed to me that he pitied me for not wanting to undergo the happy experience of enjoying his skill. I excused

6.   'Ode', 1767, in London, Royal College of Surgeons of England, The Hunter-Baillie Papers, 1704–1923, Anne Hunter, Poems, vol. 1, MS0014/13.

7.   *Collected Correspondence and London Notebooks*, p. 32; A. Peter Brown, 'Notes on Joseph Haydn's Lieder and Canzonettas', in *For the Love of Music, Festschrift in Honor of Theodore Front on his 90th Birthday*, ed. by Darwin F. Scott (Lucca: LIM Antiqua, 2002), 77–104.

8.   *Collected Correspondence and London Notebooks*, p. 253.

9.   Landon, *Haydn: Chronicle and Works*, III, 178–79.

myself saying that there was not time, due to my forthcoming departure, and took my leave of him.

It is possible that Anne, hearing that Haydn was in her husband's consulting room, invited the great man upstairs for tea, and that the relationship developed from there. Alternatively, perhaps their collaboration was initiated by someone else, such as the music historian Charles Burney who had done much to facilitate Haydn's visit to England, including the award of his doctorate at Oxford. Burney would have known her work too. Indeed a letter from Haydn to Burney, written during his second London visit, refers to a canzonetta in Burney's keeping which Landon has suggested may have been one of Anne's.[10] Another who might have effected an introduction was Salomon. He too might have been acquainted with Anne from this time since a few years later he used some of her poems in his own six English Canzonets.[11]

A third person who may have played a role in bringing about the collaboration between Anne and Haydn is Domenico Corri, since the Canzonettas were eventually published by the firm of Corri & Dussek. Corri was a composer and singing teacher as well as a publisher. Born in Rome, he arrived in Scotland in 1771 at the invitation of Charles Burney to conduct concerts at St Cecilia's Hall in Edinburgh. He moved into publishing in about 1779, setting up business in Edinburgh with his brother Natale and James Sutherland. The firm Corri & Sutherland survived until Sutherland's death in 1790 when Domenico moved to London, but Natale continued to publish music in Edinburgh as Corri & Co. Although he was not actively involved in publishing at the time of Haydn's first visit to London in 1791–92, Domenico Corri may already have recognized in Anne someone who might write words for Haydn's music with a view to future publication. As we have seen, Anne was an experienced song-writer, and although most of her work appeared anonymously, Corri was already familiar with some of it, having published her 'Queen Mary's Lamentation' in at least two collections. In one of these it appears as a duet, based on the solo version which in both is attributed to Tommaso Giordani.[12]

When Haydn left England in June 1792, the Canzonettas were still unpublished. In February 1794 Haydn returned to London, and on 28 May the first set of his six

10.   *Collected Correspondence and London Notebooks*, p. 145; Joyce Hemlow, *A Catalogue of the Burney Family Correspondence, 1749–1878* (New York: New York Public Library, 1971).

11.   Johann Peter Salomon, *Six English Canzonets: with an Accompaniment for the Piano Forte* (London: printed for the author, and sold by Birchall, [1805]).

12.   *A New and Complete Collection of the Most Favourite Scots Songs including a few English and Irish* (Edinburgh: Corri and Sutherland, [c. 1785]), pp. 26–27; *Select Collection of the Most Admired Songs, Duetts, &c*, 3 vols (London, Edinburgh: Corri, Dussek, [c. 1790]), III: *National Airs*, 71.

Original Canzonettas was finally published by Corri & Dussek and sold by them at their offices, 67 Dean Street in London and in Bridge Street in Edinburgh, as well as by Haydn himself at his London lodgings, 1 Bury Street. They were dedicated to Mrs John Hunter, but with no indication that she had composed the words. Anne was by then a widow, living in much reduced circumstances in a small villa in Blackheath. Her husband had died in October 1793, deeply in debt, having spent most of his considerable income on amassing his enormous anatomical collection. Anne was in deep mourning; convention dictated that she was allowed no visitors – apart from family members and close female friends – and that she must never 'go into company'.[13] It was essential that she adhere to the strict conventions of the time as she was financially dependent on a small two-year pension, the King's Bounty, which had been arranged for her by friends in high places – William Eden, Lord Auckland and Sir Archibald MacDonald.

The second set of six Original Canzonettas

It was during Haydn's second London visit that he composed his second set of six Original Canzonettas. As well as contributing the first poem ('The Wanderer'), Anne is credited with having assisted Haydn in the choice of the other five poems for this set. If this is true their collaboration must have taken place towards the end of Haydn's visit, as Anne was simply unavailable for at least a year following the death of her husband in October 1793, due to her observance of the mourning conventions described above. By April 1795 however, Haydn was able to visit Anne at her home in Blackheath. The visit was arranged by Haydn's friend and publisher Domenico Corri, whom Anne employed as a singing teacher for Isabella Elliot (the teenage daughter of a minor diplomat, Hugh Elliot), who was boarding with her. On 19 April 1795, Isabella wrote excitedly to her father:[14]

> A great event took place in our Chateau, likewise, the famous Doctor Haydn came down on Fryday the 17th, I think his music is charming, it is really quite delightful.

It may have been on this occasion that Anne helped the composer with the choice of texts for his second set of six Original Canzonettas. One can imagine their working together, Anne singing, Haydn trying out the accompaniment on her piano, listened to by an admiring Isabella.

Landon has pointed out that the second set appeared in two different editions,

13. Letter from Isabella Elliot to Hugh Elliot, 3 May 1795. Edinburgh, National Library of Scotland, MS 12961, fol. 164.
14. Letter from Isabella Elliot to Hugh Elliot, 19 April 1795. NLS, MS 12961, fol. 162.

both published by Corri & Dussek after Haydn's departure in 1795.[15] Both editions have the same title-page, presumably printed from the same plate, with a dedication to Lady Charlotte Bertie, one of the daughters of Haydn's friend Willoughby Bertie, 4th Earl of Abingdon, the musical impresario who had organized concerts in the Hanover Square Rooms in the early 1780s. Like Anne, Lady Charlotte lived in difficult circumstances – her mother had recently died and her father was imprisoned for libel from January to March 1795.

Five of the canzonettas have the same music and words in both editions, but the text of the sixth is quite different. The very racy words of 'Transport of Pleasure' in the first edition are replaced in the second by the much more sedate 'Content':

> **'Transport of Pleasure'**
> What though no high descent I claim,
> No line of Kings or race divine;
> Not all the mighty Sons of fame
> Can vaunt of joys surpassing mine.
> Possess'd of blooming Julia's charms
> My heart alive to love's alarms,
> Transported with pleasure,
> I'm blest beyond measure,
> And die with delight in her arms.
>
> What though no robe of Tyrian dye,
> No gold of Ophir I can boast,
> Nor fields, nor flocks, yet rich am I
> In wealth the gods might envy most.
> For mine are blooming Julia's charms,
> While Love my throbbing heart alarms,
> Transported with pleasure,
> I'm blest beyond measure
> I die with delight in her arms

15. Joseph Haydn, *Content: facsimile reproduction of four versions* (Cardiff: University College Cardiff Press, 1983).

'Content'

Ah me, how scanty is my store!
Yet, for myself, I'd ne'er repine,
Tho' of the flocks that whiten o'er
Yon plain, one lamb were only mine.
'Tis for my lovely maid alone,
This heart has e'er ambition known;
This heart, secure in its treasure,
Is bless'd beyond measure,
Nor envies the monarch his throne.
When in her sight from morn to eve,

The hours they pass unheeded by;
No dark distrust our bosoms grieve,
And care and doubt far distant fly.
'Tis for my lovely maid alone,
This heart, secure in its treasure,
Is bless'd beyond measure,
Nor envies the monarch his throne.

Comparison of the two poems reveals that 'Content' is based on 'Transport' – many of the words are repeated, but the tone of the new text is one of pastoral contentment, not sensual delight. The music for both versions is the same as Haydn's song 'Der verdienstvolle Sylvius' (Hob.XXVIa:36*bis*), probably composed in the 1780s and first published in Vienna in 1794. Haydn had a copy with him during his second visit and sang it himself at two soirées attended by members of the royal family.[16] For the two English versions, the song was transposed up a semitone, from A flat major to A major. 'Transport of Pleasure' was published in August 1795; 'Content' was published the following October.[17] The first stanza of 'Content' shares some of the pastoral imagery and a reference to monarchy with 'Der verdienstvolle Sylvius'. There is a similarly tenuous link between 'Der verdienstvolle Sylvius' and another text by Anne Hunter, inscribed 'Song (from the German). Landon's English translation of 'Der verdienstvolle Sylvius' is given below, followed by Hunter's 'Song (from the German)'.[18] It is possible that she offered this English text for inclusion in the second set before 'Transport of Pleasure' was decided upon.

16. *Haydn*, ed. by David Wyn Jones, Oxford Composer Companions (Oxford: Oxford University Press, 2002), p. 370.
17. For all four versions see Haydn, *Content: facsimile reproduction*.
18. Anne Hunter, 'Songs written for Music between the years 1762 and 1815–1818', RCSE MS0014/15, fol. 14v.

'Der verdienstvolle Sylvius' (English translation)
Of all mortals on earth,
I am the poorest:
Two lambs, they are my herd;
My field is a patch of clover.
But if one reckons merit,
Surely I must be King,
For I am the most infatuated,
Of all mortals on earth.

'Song (from the German)' (Anne Hunter)
Alas! I am so very poor,
   One little Lamb is all my flock,
The grass before my Cottage door
   Is all my Land; so small my stock!

Yet I am sure that heart of thine,
   That tender heart; is all my own:
And blush that I should e'er repine
   Tho' poor, neglected, and unknown.

The earliest advertisement for the second set appeared in the *Morning Chronicle* on 20 August 1795, five days after Haydn's departure. Under the heading 'New Music, published this day' was listed *Dr. Haydn's Second Set of English Canzonettas, the words by Shakespeare, Metastasio, Holcroft, etc etc, price 7s.6d.*

The important point to notice here is the inclusion of the name Holcroft. Thomas Holcroft (1745–1809) was a jobbing poet, playwright, actor and radical thinker. His name has never previously been associated with the Canzonettas.

No poets' names are mentioned, however, in the advertisement that appeared two months later, in both the *Sun* (14 October) and the *Courier and Evening Gazette* (27 October). This notice also appeared under the words 'New Music, published this day', so one can assume that the two advertisements refer to the two editions of the second set; the first including 'Transport of Pleasure', the second having instead the song 'Content'. Since Thomas Holcroft's name is associated only with the first advertisement, it is possible that he was the author of 'Transport of Pleasure'. As the first edition of the second set was published after Haydn's final departure from England, the substitution must also have been effected after then.

The identification of Holcroft as someone involved in the production of texts for Haydn's canzonettas leads one to the possibility that he acted, as Schroeder has suggested, as the composer's advisor on English poetry.[19] Perhaps on his return to London,

---

19. David P. Schroeder, *Haydn and the Enlightenment: The Late Symphonies and their Audience* (Oxford: Clarendon, 1990), pp. 118–19.

finding Anne Hunter unavailable to resume cooperation in the production of a second set of Canzonettas, Haydn turned to Holcroft instead, and Anne had nothing to do with it. The one poem of hers that is included, 'The Wanderer', might well have been given to Haydn during his first visit. Thus Holcroft may have written the unattributed texts for 'Sailor's song', 'Piercing eyes', 'Transport of Pleasure' and the version of 'She never told her Love' ('after Shakespeare'), as well as suggesting 'Sympathy', which though credited to Metastasio was actually written by John Hoole (1727–1803), and published in his translation of Metastasio's drama *Olympiad* in 1767.[20]

Landon suggested that the substitution of 'Transport of Pleasure' with 'Content' may have been because Lady Charlotte found the words too licentious,[21] but whether Holcroft was involved in the substitution is not known.

Thomas Holcroft, William Shield and Joseph Haydn

It is often stated that Holcroft was a close friend of Haydn's, though there is not much evidence for this. Haydn did have one of Holcroft's novels, however, *The Adventures of Hugh Trevor*, in his library,[22] and Holcroft's adulatory poem 'Haydn' was published several times, first in September 1794, early in Haydn's second visit:[23]

'To Haydn' (Thomas Holcroft)
Who is the mighty Master, that can trace
Th' eternal lineaments of Nature's face?
'Mid endless dissonance, what mortal ear
Could e'er her peal of perfect concord hear?
Answer, Oh HAYDN! Strike the magic chord!
And, as thou strik'st, reply, and proof afford.

Whene'er thy Genius, flashing native fire,
Bids the soul tremble with the trembling lyre,
The hunter's clatt'ring hoof, the peasant-shout,
The warrior-onset, or the battle's rout,
Din clamour, uproar, murder's midnight knell,
Hyæna-shrieks, the warhoop, scream and yell –
All sounds, however mingled, strange, uncouth,
Resolve to fitness, system, sense, and truth!
To others noise and jangling; but to thee
'Tis one grand solemn swell of endless harmony.

20. Brown, 'Notes on Haydn's Lieder and Canzonettas', pp. 77–104.
21. Haydn, *Content: facsimile reproduction*.
22. Maria Hörwarthner, 'Joseph Haydn's Library: Attempt at a Literary–Historical Reconstruction', trans. Kathrine Talbot, in *Haydn and His World*, ed. by Elaine Sisman (Princeton: Princeton University Press, 1997), p. 437.
23. *Whitehall Evening Post*, 11 September 1794.

When dark and unknown terrors intervene,
And men aghast survey the horrid scene;
Then, when rejoicing fiends flit, gleam, and scowl,
And bid the huge tormented tempest howl;
When fire-fraught thunders roll, when whirlwinds rise,
And earthquakes bellow to the frantic skies,
'Tis the distracted ear, in racking gloom,
Suspects the wreck of worlds, and gen'ral doom:
Then HAYDN stands; collecting Nature's tears,
And consonance sublime amid confusion hears.

Further, it is evident from the following letter that the composer sent two songs to Holcroft during his second visit and that they intended to meet:[24]

> Dear Sir!
>   I tack me the Liberty to Send you the Canon, and the 2 songs and if it is possible, I self will come to you to day, or to morrow. I was oblieged to tack a Medicine to day, perhaps I see you this Evening.
>   I am
>   Sir with greatest Respect
>   Your
>   Oblig Ser^v
>   Haydn

So which were the two songs? Landon suggested that one was 'Eine sehr gewöhnliche Geschichte' (Hob.XXVIa:4), as Holcroft had written an English version of it entitled 'An Old Story'. That had been published well before, however, in 1786, in an English version of the first twelve of Haydn's German Lieder (Hob.XXVIa:1–12).[25] It seems more likely therefore that one of the songs was 'Der verdienstvolle Sylvius' (Hob.XXVIa:36*bis*) which as we have seen was probably composed by 1794.

Holcroft's relationship with Haydn's songs had begun well before the composer's first visit to London. The English composer William Shield had published arrangements of many of Haydn's songs, some with the German texts and others translated into English by various people including Holcroft.[26] The other two songs in the twelve Ballads for which Holcroft wrote English words were 'The Forsaken Lady' ('Die Verlassene', Hob.XXVIa:5) and 'The Knitting Girl' ('Das strickende Mädchen',

---

24. Landon, *Haydn: Chronicle and Works*, III, 273.
25. Joseph Haydn, *Twelve Ballads Composed by the Celebrated Haydn, of Vienna, Adapted to the English Words with an Accompaniment for the Harpsichord or Piano Forte by Willm. Shield* (London: Longman & Broderip, [1786]).
26. Haydn, *Twelve Ballads [...] Adapted [...] by Willm. Shield*, [1786].

Hob.XXVIa:1). Holcroft's words are adaptations rather than translations. The German text of 'Das strickende Mädchen' was itself a translation of 'The Knotting Song' written by the seventeenth-century poet Sir Charles Sedley.[27]

Holcroft also published the English words of yet another song apparently by Haydn in some additions to the text of the comic opera *The Noble Peasant*. It is not so much an opera, as a play punctuated by songs, most of which were composed by William Shield.[28] However, in a subsequent publication of the words only, 'as performed at the Theatre Royal Haymarket in 1784', six additional song texts were added. Here the music for one of them, 'Adela', was attributed to Haydn:[29]

'Song. Adela. Haydn' (Thomas Holcroft)
He who loves his mistress truly
Ever anxious for her fame
Scorns to let a thought unruly
Taint his ardent, gen'rous flame:
Sooner far would hopeless perish,
Than indulge impure desires,
Tho' thro' life he'll constant cherish
Gentle hopes and holy fires,
If the Lover doth not so,
Virgins mark him for your foe;

Ever faithful, ever tender,
Ever watchful for the day,
When his valour may defend her,
Not his cunning may betray.
Selfish snares so much detesting,
If unequal love denies,
(Pity's tear alone requesting)
He a willing martyr dies.
If the Lover doth not so,
Virgins mark him for your foe.

Holcroft's verses here do not appear to be a translation of the words of any of Haydn's German songs. Like many of the other songs and poems that Holcroft wrote, they are sexually suggestive and similar in tone to 'Transport of Pleasure'. Without the music, however, this song remains a mystery.

It may be a coincidence that Holcroft, like Haydn, had some years previously

27. Hoboken, *Werkverzeichnis*, II, 240.
28. William Shield, *The Noble Peasant: A Comic-Opera set to music by William Shield* (London: printed for W. Napier, [1784]).
29. Thomas Holcroft, *Songs, Duets, Glees, Choruses, &c. in the Comic Opera of the Noble Peasant* (London: Robinson, 1784).

consulted John Hunter about an ailment, the nature of which is unknown, and for which Hunter had advised sea bathing.[30] Instead of departing for the seaside as he had planned in the summer of 1795, however, Holcroft remained in London as a warrant had been issued for his arrest and he wished to prepare his defence. On 6 October he was indicted for high treason and imprisoned in Newgate, but two months later he was brought to trial and honourably acquitted. After several years on the continent he returned to London and died in 1809.[31]

More songs by Anne Hunter

The Canzonettas were not the end of Anne Hunter's relationship with Haydn. It may have been on the occasion of his visit to her in Blackheath in 1795 that she gave him her most celebrated poem, 'O Tuneful Voice'. The poem is said to have been her farewell to the great composer. Haydn's setting was first published in a bilingual edition by Breitkopf & Härtel in 1806, but another setting, together with three other songs by Anne, had already been included in Johann Peter Salomon's six English Canzonets published in London in 1805.[32] Anne must have given the songs to Salomon, as the two other poems by her that Salomon included are known only from this volume.

Anne may also have given Haydn 'The Spirit's Song', which he thought was written by Shakespeare; the song was first published in German in Vienna by Mollo in about 1801, and then in a bilingual version by Kunst- und Industrie-Komptoir, also in Vienna, in 1803.[33] The words were included in a collection of her poetry published in 1802, in which she refers to it as a song 'already well known to the musical world',[34] which suggests that it was already circulating, perhaps in published form, to some acclaim. It does not follow, however, that the music of that earlier version was written by Haydn. Indeed, she might have composed the setting herself. It has been suggested that the poem might have originally been intended for inclusion in the second set of Canzonettas, but not used because its mood is similar to the one song therein written by her – 'The Wanderer'.[35]

30. Thomas Holcroft, *The Life of Thomas Holcroft*, 2 vols, ed. by Elbridge Colby (London: Constable, 1925), II, 39.

31. Gary Kelly, 'Thomas Holcroft (1745–1809)', *Oxford Dictionary of National Biography* (Oxford: Oxford University Press, 2004); www.oxforddnb.com/view/article/13487 accessed 11 March 2010.

32. Johann Peter Salomon, *Six English Canzonets: with an Accompaniment for the Piano Forte* (London: printed for the author, and sold by Birchall, [1805]).

33. Hoboken, *Werkverzeichnis*, II, 267.

34. Hunter, Mrs John, *Poems* (London: Payne, 1802), p. [v]; p. 106.

35. *Haydn*, ed. by Jones (2002), p. 371.

Anne wrote at least two more poems for Haydn, for which no settings can be traced. The first, 'A Soldier Song',[36] was written in 1792 during his first visit and so may have been intended for the first set of six Original Canzonettas:

'A Soldier Song, written for Dr Haydn, 1792' (Anne Hunter)
To war, to war, and glorious deeds,
Follow where martial honor leads!
Bellona in terrifick charms
Calls us aloud, to arms! to arms!

Nor love, nor wine the soldiers pleasure;
Nor hopes for age of ease & treasure,
Shall make us e'er the field forego -
Bosoms high with courage bounding
Neighing steeds, and trumpets sounding
On we rush to meet the foe.

It is particularly interesting because of its early date and martial tone: many of Haydn's heroic compositions were not written until later, beginning with those of his second London visit, including the unfinished ode the *Invocation of Neptune* which gloats over Britain's riches, and the lively and jingoistic 'Sailor's Song', the first of the second set of Canzonettas.[37]

A second poem, without a title, was apparently written for an existing song of Haydn's which has not been identified:[38]

'Song – Written for an Air of Dr Haydn's' (Anne Hunter)
Where the green ivy twining,
Binds round the burn's brow,
I heard a voice complaining
In numbers sad and low.

Alas! she's gone for ever,
Now low in earth she lies;
And I, forlorn, shall never
Behold those speaking eyes.

36. Aberdeen University, Special Libraries and Archives, MS 2206/22/11, 'Odes, ballads, songs, sonnets and other poems by Mrs Hunter of Leicester Square, London'.
37. Nicholas Mathew, 'Heroic Haydn, the Occasional Work and "Modern" Political Music', *Eighteenth-Century Music*, 4 (2007), 7–25.
38. Aberdeen University, SLA MS 2206/22/11, 'Odes, ballads, songs, sonnets' *etc*; RCSE MS0014/15, Anne Hunter, 'Songs written for Music between the years 1762 and 1815–1818', fol. 14v; Hunter, *Poems*, p. 106, 'Song'.

The pangs of grief beguiling,
She sooth'd our parting hour;
Amidst her tears soft smiling,
Like sunbeams thro' a shower.

But, ah! she's gone for ever,
Now low in earth she lies,
And I, forlorn, must never
Behold those speaking eyes.

After Haydn's departure, the restrictions of widowhood eased and Anne was employed for several years as a companion to various 'young ladies of fortune'. Some of her friends, including Isabella Elliot's uncle by marriage, Lord Auckland, and various colleagues of her husband, finally persuaded the government to purchase John Hunter's anatomical collection (much of which survives to this day in the Hunterian Museum in the Royal College of Surgeons in London) and she was able to set up on her own in a house in Mayfair where she continued to write poetry.

The Creation

Anne Hunter's 'collaboration' with Haydn did not cease when he left London for the last time in the summer of 1795, though it continued only in an indirect fashion.

The English libretto of Haydn's oratorio *The Creation* is famously awkward, a fact that was realized as soon as it received its first London performances in 1800. Anne set about writing her own alternative libretto, and her words, though more poetical, are also difficult to sing. The manuscript of her libretto survives in the Royal College of Surgeons[39] and this translation was first performed in London on 15 September 1993.[40] There is absolutely no record, however, that Haydn ever had sight of Anne's text; if a copy had been sent to him, it would surely have survived amongst his papers.

Haydn and George Thomson's Welsh and Scottish Airs

The Edinburgh impresario George Thomson collected a great many Scots, Welsh and Irish folk songs and commissioned various notable composers, including Haydn,

---

39. RCSE MS0014/17, Anne Hunter, 'The Creation'.
40. Aileen K. Adams, 'A New Libretto for "The Creation"', *Haydn Society of Great Britain Journal*, 14 (1994), 25–26; Hunter's words are included in 'The World Premier Performance of "The Creation" by Joseph Haydn to the words of Anne Hunter', Festival Hall Concert programme (London: The South Bank Centre, 1993).

Beethoven, Kozeluch and Pleyel to undertake settings of the melodies. He also persuaded various poets to rewrite the words, or even to write completely new ones to fit the music. It is clear from Thomson's surviving correspondence that whereas the composers were paid, the poets were not.[41] Anne Hunter was one of the people whom he approached for texts. Haydn wrote a new setting for her song 'Queen Mary's Lamentation' which is included in Thomson's *Select Collection of Original Scottish Airs*,[42] and she wrote the words for seventeen of the songs in his *Welsh Airs*,[43] seven of which have arrangements of music attributed to Haydn (though two of these were actually arranged by his pupil Sigismund Neukomm).[44] There is no evidence that Anne was in touch with Haydn over the settings of her words, since all communication with the composers and the poets was conducted by Thomson himself.[45]

Both Haydn and Holcroft died in 1809. Anne Hunter died in 1821 aged 79 or 80; she continued to write and publish songs and poetry until the end of her life.

41. London, British Library, Add. MSS 35263–35269.
42. *A Select Collection of Original Scottish Airs for the Voice, with […] Symphonies and Accompaniments for the Piano Forte, Violin and Violoncello by Pleyel, Kozeluch and Haydn; With Select […] Verses […] Adapted to the Airs, including over One Hundred New Songs by Burns* [ed. by George Thomson], 3 vols (London: Preston, 1801–02).
43. *A Select Collection of Original Welsh Airs Adapted for the Voice, United to Characteristic English Poetry […] with Symphonies and Accompaniments Composed Chiefly by Joseph Haydn. (vol. 3: Accompaniments […] Composed Partly by Haydn but Chiefly by Beethoven)* (London: Preston, 1809–17).
44. Marjorie Rycroft, 'Haydn's Welsh songs: George Thomson's Musical and Literary Sources', *Welsh Music History*, 7 (2007), 92–160.
45. London, British Library, Add. MSS 35263–35269.

Haydn's Music and
Clementi's Publishing Circle

DAVID ROWLAND

WHILE ON HIS FIRST major European tour, Clementi arrived in Vienna on 19 December 1781.[1] According to the account of Clementi's life in the *Quarterly Musical Magazine and Review*,[2] he made Haydn's acquaintance during this visit. Clementi's son, Charles, later reports that his father broadly confirms the accuracy of this account.[3] Charles Burney, too, confirms that the two men met some time in the early 1780s, commenting that 'Clementi, who saw him [Haydn] in Hungary at Prince Esterhausi's says he is a little, brown complexioned Man'.[4] It was around this time, then, that on 18 June 1783, Haydn wrote to Artaria thanking the publisher for sending him some of Clementi's recent piano sonatas, presumably his op. 7 or op. 9,[5] both of which had been published within the previous year by Artaria,

---

1. The date is given in a letter written by Clementi to his father five days later. See *Muzio Clementi: Opera Omnia*, ed. Roberto Illiano (Bologna: Ut Orpheus, 2000–), XIV: *The Correspondence of Muzio Clementi*, ed. by David Rowland (2010), pp. [5]-7.
2. *Quarterly Musical Magazine and Review*, II (1820), 311.
3. Letter dated 20 January 1824 from Charles (Karl) Clementi, to John Davis Sainsbury. See *Correspondence*, ed. Rowland, pp. 309–12.
4. From a manuscript of Burney's 'Materials Towards the History of German Music & Musicians' (Yale, Beinecke Library, Osborn shelves, C 100, p. 7), quoted in *The Letters of Dr Charles Burney*, ed. by Alvaro Ribeiro, 4 vols (Oxford: Clarendon Press, 1991–), I (1991), 400, n. 72.
5. For publication details see Alan Tyson, *Thematic Catalogue of the Works of Muzio Clementi* (Tutzing: Hans Schneider, 1967), pp. 43, 45.

Fig. 1. Thomas Hardy, *Muzio Clementi* (1794).

adding 'they are very beautiful; if the author is in Vienna, please present my compliments to him when opportunity offers'.[6] Clementi had in fact left Vienna some time previously, probably in May 1782.[7] It is just possible, however, that he made return visits in the course of the following three years, although details of his various European adventures at this time are hard to come by. From at least the end of 1785 onwards Clementi was in London, playing a major role in the concert life of the city. During the course of Haydn's visits to London in the 1790s, works by both composers were played at the Salomon concerts and the Opera Concert of 1795,

6.   *Collected Correspondence and London Notebooks*, p. 42.
7.   In a letter to his father dated 8 May 1782, Mozart revealed that 'I hear Clementi is leaving Vienna tomorrow'; see *The Letters of Mozart and his Family*, ed. by Emily Anderson, 3rd edn revised by Stanley Sadie and Fiona Smart (London: Macmillan Press, 1985), p. 805.

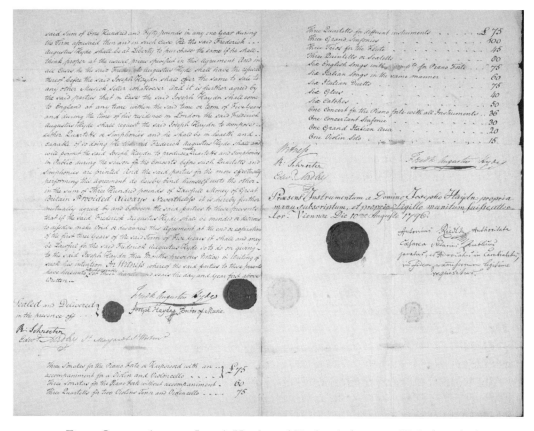

Fig. 2. Contract between Joseph Haydn and Frederick Augustus Hyde (1796), showing the prices agreed for works to be published, signed by Haydn and Hyde, and witnessed by Rebecca Schroeter. BL, MS Mus. 1713.

and although Clementi's reputation as a composer suffered by comparison with Haydn, the two men retained their friendship. Haydn interacted socially with Clementi[8] and when the former returned to Austria in 1795, he took with him Clementi's gift of a piece of coconut shell embellished with silver trimmings.[9]

Just before Haydn left London in the middle of August 1795, Clementi's career began to take a new direction. The end of May 1795 saw the bankruptcy of the music publisher and retailer Longman & Broderip,[10] one result of which was the appointment of Clementi and four others as assignees whose role was to look after

8.   See Landon, *Haydn: Chronicle and Works*, III, esp. pp. 27, 116.

9.   Landon, *Haydn: Chronicle and Works*, III, 320.

10. For details of this company's history see Jenny Nex, 'Longman & Broderip' in *The Music Trade in Georgian England*, ed. by Michael Kassler (Farnham: Ashgate, 2011), pp. 9–93.

the affairs of the company and the interests of the creditors.[11] They did this for a little over three years, during which time the company continued to trade under the same name despite the fact that new personnel were involved in its management and both James Longman and Francis Broderip spent periods of time in jail. On 1 November 1798, however, the firm was sold. Part of the business continued at the firm's premises in the Haymarket under Francis Broderip and a new partner, George Wilkinson. The other part of the business, which traded from the firm's Cheapside premises and which also used the company's Tottenham Court Road factory, was bought by Clementi and five other partners: Frederick Augustus Hyde, John Longman, Frederick William Collard, Josiah Banger and David Davis.

Clementi's personal relationship with Haydn ensured that the new company of Longman, Clementi & Co. had strong links with the composer, but that was not the only significant connection. Under Longman & Broderip, the firm had already published over a hundred editions of Haydn's music, many of which were subsequently re-issued under the imprint of the new company, as we shall see. Probably the most important connection between Haydn and the new company in its early days, however, was a contract that had been drawn up in 1796 between Haydn and Frederick Augustus Hyde, one of the new firm's partners from 1798.[12] The document itself is now held in the British Library (MS Mus. 1713: see Fig. 2); a full facsimile and transcription was published over a decade ago to accompany a chapter by Albi Rosenthal[13] and more recently a transcription has been published as an appendix to the correspondence of Clementi, his family and business partners.[14]

The contract is dated 30 July 1796 and was signed in London by Hyde and less than a fortnight later by Haydn in Vienna, on 10 August. In summary, it states that:

- The agreement was for a five-year period.
- Haydn would write new works at Hyde's request and deliver them to him according to the price list set out at the end of the contract (see below).
- The works written under the terms of the contract would become Hyde's exclusive property and could not be sold by Haydn to anyone else.
- Hyde would purchase music to the value of £150 per year for the five-year period.
- Payment would be due on the delivery of each work.

11. See Nex, 'Longman & Broderip', p. 78.

12. For details of these partners see David Rowland, 'Clementi's Music Business' in *The Music Trade*, ed. by Michael Kassler, pp. 125–34.

13. Albi Rosenthal, 'The contract between Joseph Haydn and Frederick Augustus Hyde (1796)' in *Studies in Music History Presented to H. C. Robbins Landon on his Seventieth Birthday*, ed. by Otto Biba and David Wyn Jones (London: Thames and Hudson, 1996), pp. 72–81.

14. See *Correspondence*, ed. Rowland, Appendix 5, pp. [403]–407.

- If Haydn wrote music to a greater value than £150 in a year, Hyde would have first refusal to purchase it at the rates listed in the contract.
- If Haydn visited England within the five-year period, any new symphonies or quartets that he wrote could be performed in public before they were published by Hyde.
- Hyde could cancel the contract after the first three years so long as he gave Haydn three months' notice.

The price list that forms the final part of the contract is as follows:

Three Sonatas for the Piano Forte or Harpsicord with an accompaniment for a Violin and Violoncello	£75
Three Sonatas for the Piano Forte without accompaniment	£60
Three Quartetts for two Violins Tenor and Violoncello	£75
Three Quartetts for different instruments	£75
Three Grand Sinfonies	£100
Three Trios for the Flute	£45
Three Quintetts or Sextetts	£80
Six English Songs with accomp[animen]ts. for Piano Forte	£75
Six Italian songs in the same manner	£60
Six Italian Duetts	£75
Six Glees	£40
Six Catches	£50
One Concert for the Piano forte with all Instruments	£36
One Concertant Sinfonie	£30
One Grand Italian Aria	£20
One Violin Solo	£15

The list cannot have constituted an order or commission, since the total price of works listed (£911) exceeded the total value of the music that Hyde had agreed to purchase (£750 at £150 per year). Rather, the purpose seems to have been to guarantee Haydn the amount he would receive if he sent Hyde the works listed for publication in London. It must therefore have been up to the composer to decide exactly what was sent to Hyde, which explains how two sets of three quartets came to be composed under the agreement despite only one set being listed.

The most striking element of the contract, however, is the nature of its exclusive provisions, including its international scope:

> From and after such new and Original Musick shall be so written for and delivered to the said Frederick Augustus Hyde the same shall become his absolute Property and no copy thereof shall be delivered or sold by him the said Joseph Haydn to any other Person or Persons under any pretence or upon any Account whatsoever.

According to these terms, works published by Hyde could not be published by anyone else anywhere in Europe. This arrangement would have put Hyde in a powerful position among London publishers and must have been one of the reasons why he was attractive as a partner to Clementi, Banger, Collard, Davis and Longman in 1798. But how usual was this sort of exclusivity in contracts of the period? The question is impossible to answer with any certainty, because too few contracts between publisher and composer survive. There are similarities, however, in the arrangements that Clementi's company had with other prominent composers of the time. Dussek, for example, is revealed by Clementi's letter to Artaria of 29 November 1799 to have taken out an exclusive contract for new publications with Longman, Clementi & Co.;[15] a letter from Dussek to Birchall dated 8 October 1806 stating that the contract was to expire on 4 November of the same year indicates that the term of this contract was seven years (although it was not explicitly international in scope).[16] Further, a letter from Clementi & Co. to Pleyel dated 9 December 1801[17] reveals that the firm also had an understanding (i.e. a contract in all but name) with Viotti that no other publisher would have his works, an arrangement which turned out to be more or less true, at least as far as London was concerned.[18] The same letter also refers to a current agreement with Haydn, even though the five-year contract with Hyde would by that time no longer have been in force. No evidence of any continuing contract with Haydn exists, however, so perhaps the intention was to impress Pleyel by stretching the truth a little; or perhaps the letter writer was unaware, or had simply forgotten, that the contract had expired.

Clementi's correspondence shows that he tried to negotiate an exclusive contract with Beethoven, but only for the British dominions. On 4 August 1804, Clementi wrote to his business partner Collard from Berlin about a deal he had struck with the publisher Gottfried Christoph Härtel:[19]

> He has promised me to engage Beethoven to send him <u>all</u> his new MSS, & we shall have them for the <u>British Dominions</u> for <u>half</u> <u>the</u> <u>price</u> <u>he</u> <u>gives</u> <u>him</u>. He is to have all that Haydn means to publish […] Writing to <u>him</u> or <u>Beethoven</u> is now

---

15. See *Correspondence*, ed. Rowland, pp. 37–38.
16. London, British Library, Additional MS 33965, fol. 200. For Dussek's business dealings see David Rowland, 'Dussek in London's Commercial World', in *Jan Ladislav Dussek (1760-1812): A Bohemian Composer "en voyage" through Europe*, ed. by Roberto Illiano and Rohan Stewart-MacDonald (Bologna: Ut Orpheus, 2012), pp. 87–111.
17. See *Correspondence*, ed. Rowland, pp. 79–80.
18. For further details of the firm's relationship with Viotti see David Rowland, 'Viotti and Clementi: Friendship, Publishing, the Philharmonic Society and the Royal Academy of Music' in *Giovanni Battista Viotti: A Composer Between the Two Revolutions*, ed. by Massimiliano Sala (Bologna: Ut Orpheus Edizioni, 2006), pp. 377–94.
19. The full text of the letter is in *Correspondence*, ed. Rowland, pp. 120–22.

become superfluous to say no more, since my conference w[ith]. Härtel, for now with <u>less</u> trouble & <u>much less</u> expense we shall get all we want.

Clementi's optimism was misplaced. Although he did eventually secure a contract with Beethoven three years later, it was not the exclusive deal that he had hoped for and he had to settle instead for a contract for six specific works. This more specific kind of contract had much in common with two more or less contemporary contracts that Viotti negotiated with French publishers, dating from 1796 and 1802, both of which refer to a small group of named works.[20]

Whatever Hyde may have hoped, no contract with Haydn could ever have turned out to have been internationally exclusive in practice, largely because such an arrangement would have been unenforceable. Before the development of international copyright and the protection it afforded, the most that any composer or publisher could hope for by way of cooperation and respecting of business rights across national boundaries was almost simultaneous publication in a number of countries by a small network of publishers. This was the best that could be done to prevent the worst abuses of pirate publishers. Sometimes composers attempted to make the arrangements for simultaneous publication themselves, but the negotiations between Beethoven, Breitkopf & Härtel and Clementi & Co. show how publishers preferred a situation in which one of their number acted as the lead, purchasing rights from the composer which were then sold to international partners. These sorts of arrangements worked with varying degrees of success, with negotiations and timely publication increasingly difficult when countries were at war, and composers never being entirely faithful to the terms imposed on them, whatever they might be. Given this context, it is not suprising, then, that Haydn did not follow the terms of his contract with Hyde to the letter. Even so, the degree of loyalty that it commanded from Haydn seems to have been of benefit to Hyde. The composer was certainly careful on occasion not to breach the contract by publishing works in Vienna ahead of their appearance in London, even though he made his own arrangements with Artaria and others for the publication of several works that should have fallen within its terms. Meanwhile, Longman, Clementi & Co. seem to have been confident that the contract's terms meant that they could sell Haydn's works to publishers on the continent, as will become apparent.

Why did Haydn entrust such an important contract to Hyde, rather than to other London publishers? The reason almost certainly has to do with the development of Hyde's career in the 1790s, as well as the plight of the publishers with whom Haydn had dealings in the early and mid-1790s. According to the evidence presented in a legal dispute between the publisher Forster and Longman, Hyde started work at

20. François Lesure, 'Deux contrats d'édition de Viotti (1796–1802)' in *Festschrift Albi Rosenthal*, ed. by Rudolf Elvers (Tutzing: Hans Schneider, 1984), pp. 221–26.

Longman & Broderip in 1786, becoming a shopman in the firm by 1791.[21] Evidence that he then worked with the publisher Joseph Buckinger[22] is found in two Stationers' Hall entries in which Hyde appears as a signatory to the registration of two songs published by Buckinger. The first, *The Tint on the Cheek of my Love* (words by Carey, music by Carter), was registered by Hyde on 14 December 1793 and the second, *The Gentle Shepherdess* (words by Cunningham, music by Welsh), was registered by Hyde on 21 March 1794. Sometime in the course of the following twelve months Hyde formed a partnership with John Lewis Vautier Sollicoffre and James Henry Houston, known as Lewis, Houston & Hyde. Their first entry at Stationers' Hall was made on 18 March 1795 and adverts in the press describe them as successors to John Bland, Haydn's publisher. Their final Stationers' Hall entry was made on 10 October 1795, and on 1 December of the same year the partnership was dissolved.[23] Shortly afterwards Hyde seems once more to have been working for Longman & Broderip (who had by now become bankrupt, but who continued to trade), because on 9 May 1796 he registered at Stationers' Hall a collection of Canzonets and an Elegy by Shield which had been published for the author by that firm. A further connection between Hyde and Longman & Broderip is found in the publication of Hyde's own compilation of *A Miscellaneous Collection of Songs, Ballads, Canzonets, Duets, Trios, Glees, & Elegies; in Two Vols., Properly Adapted for the Voice and Piano-Forte*. The work was printed for Hyde, F. W. Collard and Davis (two of Hyde's and Clementi's partners from 1798) by Longman & Broderip. Finally Hyde registered Suett's *Sylvia Again is True and Kind*, published by Longman & Broderip, at Stationers' Hall on 1 August 1798, just three months before Hyde became a partner in the firm's successor, Longman, Clementi & Co. All of this evidence shows that Hyde had gathered several years' experience of the London music publishing trade and was becoming an increasingly senior figure within it. He had been a partner in the successor firm to Haydn's publisher Bland and was evidently an influential figure within another firm strongly associated with the composer, Longman & Broderip. Bland was finished and in the absence of other major rivals with whom Haydn was prepared to do business, as well as the uncertainty surrounding Longman & Broderip following their bankruptcy, Hyde must have seemed a relatively safe option with whom to collaborate, especially given his good contacts in the music trade and the high prices he was prepared to offer.

What negotiations did Hyde have with Haydn prior to signing the contract? The only evidence we have is the contract document itself. The information it contains

---

21. Nex, 'Longman & Broderip', p. 55.
22. For information on Buckinger see Charles Humphries and William C. Smith, *Music Publishing in the British Isles*, 2nd edn (Oxford: Blackwell, 1970).
23. *London Gazette*, 1795, p. 1350.

suggests that any discussions beforehand would have been mainly in general terms about what forms of works might be envisaged, rather than about specific works. Such discussions would have had to take place before Haydn left England in the middle of August 1795 (i.e. nearly a year before the contract was agreed), but may have been continued through correspondence. If Haydn held discussions with Hyde in the months before leaving the country, the latter would have been acting as one of the partners of the firm Lewis, Houston & Hyde that had taken over the business of Bland. If the discussion took place after his departure and by correspondence, Hyde would either have been acting for Lewis, Houston & Hyde, or perhaps in connection with the bankrupt firm Longman & Broderip.

Hyde must have been disappointed by the amount of music that was published as a result of the contract. The only works that can be identified with it that were published for almost three years after it was signed are the Piano Trios Hob.XV:27–29, dedicated to Therese Bartolozzi – the first category on the contract's price list. Longman & Broderip advertised them as shortly to be published in *E. Johnson's British Gazette and Sunday Monitor* on 19 March 1797 and in *The Oracle and Public Advertiser* on 21 March 1797. If the publication schedule for these trios was similar to that for the first three quartets of op. 76, then this would have been the time at which the company received the manuscript from Haydn, or perhaps from Therese Bartolozzi, who had by this time left London. The works were listed among the new music advertised by Longman & Broderip in *The Oracle & Public Advertiser* on 20 April and they were registered at Stationers' Hall on 27 April.[24] Continental editions by André and Artaria followed later that year; whether or not Hyde had any involvement with these editions is not known.

The next works to be published as a result of the contract with Hyde were the Quartets op. 76. Haydn reported in a letter of 15 August 1799 to Artaria that 'I sent the first 3 Quartets as early as 27th March.'[25] If one assumes once again that the publisher would place advance notices of publication in the press as soon as the manuscript arrived from the composer, then that must have taken place around 19 April, when *The Times* advertised the works as shortly to be published by Longman, Clementi & Co. The quartets were then engraved, entered at Stationers' Hall on 13 June, advertised on the same day in *The Oracle and Daily Advertiser* and on 15 June in the *The Morning Chronicle*, with further advertisements over the next two months. As with the trios, the speed with which these works were engraved, and the publicity that they received in the press, illustrate the importance that Longman, Clementi & Co. attached to them. The firm also took the opportunity to capitalize on their

24. Hoboken, *Werkverzeichnis*, I, 711.
25. *Collected Correspondence and London Notebooks*, p. 163.

investment by signing a contract with Pleyel on 2 August 1799[26] permitting publication in Paris engraved from the same source as the London edition.[27] The new French edition was advertised in the *Journal typographique et bibliographique* on 6 November of the same year.[28] Meanwhile, Artaria had also published the quartets, advertising them in the *Wiener Zeitung* on 17 July[29]; again, we know nothing of any involvement of Hyde.

Haydn evidently considered that the second set of three Quartets op. 76 came within the terms of the contract with Hyde. With these pieces, however, the course of publication did not run so smoothly. In his letter of 15 August 1799 to Artaria, Haydn mentioned that he had dispatched the quartets to London on 15 June 1799, but had received no acknowledgement of their arrival. Anxious to protect his fee of £75 Haydn expresses concern that[30]

> If the publication in Vienna should be earlier than that in London (which I hope will not be the case), and if the gentlemen were to discover that you at once received the same 3 Quartets from me, I should lose £75 Sterling, which would be a serious matter. You must therefore take immediate action, *sub rosa*, to ascertain positively whether the first 3 are out, and likewise approximately when the last 3 will appear, so that I won't have a double fine imposed on me.

By the time the letter was written the first set had been published in London, so Haydn had no reason to worry about those works; but he did have cause for concern about the second set, which were almost certainly still *en route*. If the newspaper announcements of the imminent publication in London of the second set of op. 76 were prompted by the arrival there of the manuscript from Vienna (as is the inference with the first set), the works cannot have arrived in London until the beginning of 1800: *The Times* announced their forthcoming publication on 7 January. No further announcements were made until 7, 8 and 11 April, when their publication was advertised in *The Oracle and Daily Advertiser*, *The Morning Post* and *The Morning Chronicle*; no entry can be traced at Stationers' Hall. Meanwhile, Artaria had already announced the quartets in the *Wiener Zeitung* on 7 December 1799, so that Haydn's concerns that he may not be paid by the London firm were amply justified. In the event there is no evidence that payment was withheld.

Prior to the eventual publication of the second set of op. 76 by Longman,

26. Max Unger, *Muzio Clementis Leben* (Langensalza: Herman Beyer & Söhne, 1914), p. 102.
27. Joseph Haydn, *Werke* (Munich: Henle), XII/6: *Streichquartette: Opus 76, Op. 77 und Op. 103*, ed. by Horst Walter (2003), pp. xiii, 182, 184.
28. Rita Benton and Jeanne Halley, *Pleyel as Music Publisher: A Documentary Sourcebook of Early 19th-Century Music* (Stuyvesant, NY: Pendragon, 1990), p. 106.
29. Haydn, *Werke*, XII/6: *Streichquartette: Opus 76, Op. 77 und Op. 103*, ed. by Walter, p. 180.
30. *Collected Correspondence and London Notebooks*, p. 163.

Clementi & Co., one further item relating to the contract's price list had been published by the firm in London: the Sonata Hob.XVI:52, dedicated to Therese Bartolozzi. The circumstances of the publication of this sonata have been described in detail elsewhere.[31] In short, the London publication of this work seems to have been prompted by Therese Bartolozzi's discovery that Artaria had already published the Sonata in Vienna in December 1798. It appears therefore that Longman, Clementi & Co. received a copy of the sonata either from Vienna, or from a contact of Therese Bartolozzi's in London. The firm had it engraved and it was advertised as forthcoming in *The Oracle and Daily Advertiser* on 24 October 1799 and *The Times* on 29 October. The actual publication was announced two months later in *The Oracle and Daily Advertiser* and *The Morning Chronicle* on 27 December, though apparently no entry at Stationers' Hall was made.

The three accompanied sonatas, the six quartets and the solo piano sonata are the only works that can definitely be associated with Hyde's contract. According to the price list, this might have amounted to some £245 worth of music, a long way short of the £150 per year over five years that the contract anticipated. It is possible, however, that one further work, the *Battle of the Nile*, was published within the five-year period, but the lack of definitive publication details make it impossible to assign a certain publication date. No press announcements have come to light and no entry can be found for the work at Stationers' Hall. It was published by Clementi, Banger, Hyde, Collard & Davis, so that it cannot have appeared before March 1801 (when John Longman left the partnership).[32] However, the firm is described on the title-page as 'Late Longman & Broderip', the firm's title up to 1798, so it seems likely that the work was published while the name Longman was still a recent memory in connection with the firm, which may bring the work within the timeframe of the Hyde contract.

One of the reasons why so little of Haydn's music was published as a result of Hyde's contract is revealed in a letter written by Griesinger to Härtel on 12 June 1799:[33]

> His [Haydn's] publisher in England is a Mr. Bay, a rather unimportant man as Haydn said, but associated with Clementi and Broderip. His agreement is for five years, of which three are now finished, and Bay has agreed to take everything he composes, and the price for every psalm, sonata, etc. has been established beforehand. But because of the great amount of work on his [Haydn's] shoulders, he has only delivered some quartets in these three years, and these were sent to England

31. See W. Oliver Strunk, 'Notes on a Haydn Autograph', *The Musical Quarterly*, 20 (1934), 192–205, much of which is summarized in Landon, *Haydn: Chronicle and Works*, III, 440 ff.

32. For a summary of the partnership changes of the firm see 'Chronology of the Business begun by James Longman', *The Music Trade*, ed. by Kassler, pp. 3–7 (p. 5).

33. Landon, *Haydn: Chronicle and Works*, IV, 469.

quite recently. Bay is pushing him especially hard for piano sonatas, but up to now he hasn't been able to fulfil his wish.

The letter identifies a Mr Bay as Haydn's English publisher, yet the details of the account make it clear that it must refer to Hyde's contract for the following reasons. The timescale referred to in the letter corresponds with the provisions of the contract; it was for a five-year period, three years of which had almost passed. The letter also refers to the all-encompassing nature of the contract – it was for 'everything he [Haydn] composes' – and the reference to the quartets that had recently been sent to London corresponds with what is known about op. 76. So who was Bay? So far, no evidence has been discovered in contemporary sources that sheds any light on his identity. However, the fact that he was associated with Clementi and Broderip, according to the letter, suggests that he was probably a member of Longman & Broderip, subsequently Longman, Clementi & Co., perhaps a clerk; later correspondence of Clementi & Co. was sometimes entrusted to members of the firm, so perhaps Bay had been given the responsibility of following up the business relating to Hyde's contract on his behalf. Whatever the details of Bay's role, the letter is clear about why Haydn had sent so little to London: he simply had too much work to do.

One project on which Haydn was certainly spending a lot of time during these years was the composition of *The Creation*. As Griesinger reminds us, the exclusive nature of the Hyde contract meant that it could extend to works not explicitly listed and priced there; in the event, Longman, Clementi & Co. acted not as publisher, but as distributor of the work in London, which was published for the composer in score by Artaria in Vienna on 28 February 1800. Although the distribution was ultimately carried out successfully, a series of letters from 1800 involving Charles Burney, Clementi and Haydn himself reveal that the process caused considerable anxiety to the parties concerned.

According to a letter from Burney to Longman, Clementi & Co. dated 11 January 1800[34] Haydn had written to Burney on 18 July 1799 asking for help with procuring subscribers for the publication of *The Creation*. The January letter reveals that Burney had responded positively to Haydn's request. He had, however, asked that publication be delayed until the following spring, because he and many potential subscribers were about to leave London for the country, making it difficult to secure as many as he hoped. Nevertheless, he began collecting a list of subscribers and sent names to Haydn,[35] but received no response. He had therefore sent a further list to Haydn on 8 January 1800, but he must then have heard something about the

---

34. See *Correspondence*, ed. Rowland, pp. 46–48.

35. Via a letter that Salomon had written, according to Burney's letter to Clementi of 26 May 1800 – see below.

progress of publication in Vienna, because when he wrote to Longman, Clementi & Co. on 11 January he was concerned that the edition would be published without the names that he had supplied. He also expressed concern that the terms of subscription had apparently changed since he first wrote to Haydn on the subject.

A month after the publication of the full score in Vienna, on 27 March 1800 an advertisement in *The Morning Chronicle* stated that Longman, Clementi & Co. had purchased 'the entire COPY RIGHT of Haydn's Grand Oratorio' and that 'it will be very shortly published, for Voices and Piano Forte, arranged by Mr. Clementi' in advance of public performances under the direction of Salomon, according to 'the style pointed out to him' by the composer. Whether Longman, Clementi & Co. considered the arrangement to be within the first-refusal provisions of Hyde's contract is not known: Hyde was still a partner in the firm and the contract had yet to expire. In any event the firm had identified an excellent opportunity to make money by selling copies of the vocal score. Meanwhile, around this time or a little afterwards, the London copies of *The Creation* were dispatched from Vienna. Haydn later wrote to Artaria on 22 August 1800 saying that the copies had been sent 'more than 3 months ago',[36] probably meaning April, or early May. In the same letter Haydn also reported to Artaria that he had received a letter from Clementi dated 16 July in which the latter had indicated that the printed copies had not arrived. The delay in the dispatch may initially have been of some comfort to Burney, who was still anxious about including subscribers' names when he wrote to Clementi on 26 May,[37] but by the time the printed copies arrived towards the end of July Burney's anxiety was of a different sort. According to another letter of Burney's to Longman, Clementi & Co. on 25 July[38] the scores of *The Creation* had arrived from Vienna, and Burney had been informed on the previous day that they were ready for collection, subject to clarifying how many copies Burney required. On 25 July the firm announced in the press the arrival of the work from Vienna and Burney was anxious to distribute the copies to subscribers before they left London for the country, so he sent his servant to Longman, Clementi & Co. sometime on 24 or 25 July, only to be told that the books could not be sent until somebody whose name the servant cannot remember came to town.

The copies were presumably dispatched to subscribers shortly after this, and Burney must eventually have been satisfied, because there seems to have been no further correspondence between him and the firm on the subject. Meanwhile, it was Haydn's turn to be anxious. In his letter of 22 August[39] to Artaria, he expressed concern that

36. *Collected Correspondence and London Notebooks*, p. 174.
37. See *Correspondence*, ed. Rowland, p. 55–56.
38. *Correspondence*, ed. Rowland, pp. 63–64.
39. *Collected Correspondence and London Notebooks*, p. 174.

he was 'in danger of losing two thousand Gulden, because Herr Clementi has already published the work himself'. Haydn must have known of Clementi's intention to publish the work, as advertised in the press on 27 March (see above), but he cannot have been aware that publication as a vocal score had been delayed. In fact, it was not until the early days of the following year that Longman, Clementi & Co. published it; the first notice of their publication appeared in *The Morning Post* on 5 January 1801. Haydn did not lose his payment, because in the final piece of surviving correspondence between the relevant parties, Haydn's letter to Hyde and Clementi of 28 April 1801,[40] the composer acknowledges receipt of 100 guineas and reminds the two partners that he was owed further remuneration on account of the 212 copies that Artaria had sent to London.

Once Hyde's contract with Haydn had expired, the firm needed to establish a new relationship with the composer. A convenient arrangement would have been a collaboration with Artaria, since it is evident that Clementi's firm already had a business association with the Viennese publishers. On 21 December 1798 Clementi had written to Artaria in order to establish a mutually beneficial business relationship:[41]

Being an associate of Longman, Hyde, and others, it would give me great pleasure to enter into correspondence with you, to the mutual advantage of both parties. But first of all, might we ask you to send us your catalogue, and we will send you ours as soon as it is ready. We have a range of excellent new works, and I hope that if we do enter into trading business with each other, both of us will find it mutually beneficial.

Clementi's letter of 24 June 1799 reveals that Artaria had not yet responded to the request to send a catalogue:[42]

On the occasion of the departure of my illustrious Pupil Giovanni Battista Cramer who is leaving tomorrow for Germany I am sending you our Catalogue, and would ask you to send us yours at the earliest opportunity. In this way, we'll make a favourable exchange.

Five months later, on 29 November 1799, Clementi wrote again:[43]

Now that you know what we have, we would like to receive your orders and for whatever you take from our catalogue we ask you to send us the equivalent from your catalogue. You could send us two copies of every popular publication that

40. See *Correspondence*, ed. Rowland, pp. 73–74 and *Collected Correspondence and London Notebooks*, p. 179.
41. *Correspondence*, ed. Rowland, pp. 31–32.
42. *Correspondence*, ed. Rowland, pp. 34–35.
43. *Correspondence*, ed. Rowland, pp. 37–38.

you have printed in the past twelve months, and especially vocal music, military music, Sonatas for pianoforte and Haydn's new Symphonies for full orchestra.

A much later letter from Frederick William Collard (Clementi's business partner), written on 7 May 1817[44] in order to re-establish the relationship between the two firms following the disruption of the Napoleonic wars and the establishment of peace in Europe, reveals the details of the arrangement that had earlier existed between the two firms; Collard asks if Artaria would be willing 'to make an exchange with us as formerly viz. page for page'. It is also clear from later correspondence that Clementi had much more than a business relationship with his Viennese counterparts. Clementi stayed with Artaria when he later visited Vienna and he also asked Artaria to act as an intermediary with the piano-making firm Streicher in order to secure some leather for piano hammer coverings.[45]

At some time, either during the term of the Haydn–Hyde contract, or after it expired in the summer of 1801, Clementi, or one of his representatives, must have begun negotiating with Haydn and/or Artaria over the publication of the F minor Piano Variations (Hob.XVII:6) which Clementi & Co. published as op. 89, and the Quartets op. 77 (Hob.III:81, 82). The Variations had been published by Artaria in 1799, while the contract was still in force, but were not published in London until 1802, where they were advertised in *The Times* on 27 April. Evidently the London edition was copied from Artaria's.[46] If the works were considered to come within the remit of the contract with Hyde, it appears that either Hyde (and therefore Clementi & Co.) had agreed in this instance that publication could proceed in Vienna ahead of London, or that the composer had the pieces published in Vienna without the permission of the London publisher.

The op. 77 Quartets were also copied in London from Artaria's edition.[47] Although the publication dates are less certain, the Vienna edition appeared over a year after the Haydn–Hyde contract had expired. Artaria had published them in Vienna in November 1802 and Clementi & Co. must have been expecting receipt of them in London at the same time, because on 26 October Clementi & Co. reported to Pleyel that they had 'not as yet received the copy of Haydn's 2 Quartetts'.[48] Information on the works' London publication is sparse – they were not entered at Stationers' Hall and neither do they seem to have been advertised in the press.

Following the publication of the F minor Piano Variations and the op. 77

---

44. *Correspondence*, ed. Rowland, p. 246.

45. See Clementi's letter to Artaria on 6 August 1827; *Correspondence*, ed. Rowland, pp. 345–46.

46. Joseph Haydn, *Werke* (Munich: Henle), XIX/XX: *Klavierstücke und Werke für Klavier zu vier Händen*, ed. by Sonja Gerlach (2006), p. 159.

47. Haydn, *Werke*, XII/6: *Streichquartette: Opus 76, Op. 77 und Op. 103*, ed. by Walter, p. 205.

48. See *Correspondence*, ed. Rowland, p. 99.

Quartets, Clementi & Co. published no new music by Haydn for several years. This inactivity may have had something to do with Clementi's absence from London. He departed for the continent in the summer of 1802 and spent the following eight years travelling in increasingly difficult circumstances in France, Russia, Germany, Austria and Italy. Much of his activity during those years was spent enhancing his company's business prospects. During a visit to Berlin in 1804, Clementi had extensive discussions with Härtel about the publication of Beethoven's and Haydn's music. As we have seen, Clementi had to settle for a contract for only six of Beethoven's works. Similarly with Haydn's music, in 1804 Clementi believed that he could secure the rights for everything the composer wrote, in collaboration with Härtel. On 4 August 1804, Clementi wrote to his business partner Frederick William Collard:[49]

> He [Härtel] is to have all that Haydn means to publish, & has likewise promised to send you whatever he gets <u>from</u> his pen. He has shown me the 2 songs which the good Doctor gave me a sight of, with the promise in his usual polite way – I mean the Doctor's – that I should be the <u>sole</u> possessor […] Härtel expects very soon to get from Haydn his Sonata dedicated to M<u>me</u> Moreau which he'll send you! Now for a secret! but mind it is to be kept <u>inviolable</u>; – the said editor is to have all Haydn's <u>famous canons</u>; & what is more he hopes to possess them even <u>before</u> the death of that otherwise <u>immortal</u> <u>author.</u>

Not a great deal arose from Clementi's dealings with Härtel over the publication of Haydn's music. The two songs referred to here are identified later in Clementi's letter as 'O Tuneful Voice' (Hob.XXVIa:42) and 'What Art Expresses' (Hob.XXVIb:3). Only the first of these, 'O Tuneful Voice', was published by both Breitkopf & Härtel and Clementi & Co. in parallel first editions, probably in 1806.[50] The other song, 'What Art Expresses', was published by Breitkopf & Härtel in 1806,[51] but there is no record that Clementi & Co. ever published it, perhaps because the Breitkopf & Härtel publication gave the text in two languages, German and English: only 'O Tuneful Voice' is included in the company's 1823 catalogue.[52]

49. *Correspondence*, ed. Rowland, pp. 120–21.

50. It was advertised in *Allgemeine musikalische Zeitung* on 19 February 1806; the London edition does not seem to have been advertised in the press.

51. It was advertised in *Allgemeine musikalische Zeitung* on 4 June 1806.

52. *A Catalogue of Instrumental and Vocal Music, London, Clementi, Collard and Collard*, 1823, British Library, Mus. Mic. A 2054. The catalogue is discussed in David Wyn Jones, 'Some aspects of Clementi's career as a publisher' in *Muzio Clementi compositore, (forte)pianista, editore*, ed. by Bianca Maria Antolini and Costantino Mastroprimiano (Lucca: Lim Editrice, 2006), pp. 3–19 and Rudolf Rasch, 'Muzio Clementi: The Last Composer-Publisher' in *Muzio Clementi. Studies and Prospects*, ed. by Roberto Illiano, Luca Sala and Massimiliano Sala (Bologna: Ut Orpheus Edizioni, 2002), pp. 355–66.

The sonata dedicated to Madame Moreau referred to in Clementi's letter had already been the subject of correspondence between the composer and dedicatee. On 1 November 1803 Haydn had written to Madame Moreau,[53] agreeing to write a new work for her. Landon comments that 'Haydn, of course, did not dream of composing a new Sonata for her or anyone else, and gave her a copy of the pianoforte Trio No. 41 in E flat minor (1795), without the 'cello part'.[54] The work, in the form dedicated to Madame Moreau, was eventually published by Clementi & Co. in 1821 (registration at Stationers' Hall, 1 February 1821) and around the same time by Naderman in Paris.

The other works mentioned in Clementi's letter of 4 August 1804 to Collard, the Canons that comprise the so-called Ten Commandments, were finally published six years later – sadly not before the composer's death, as Clementi had hoped. Artaria advertised them on 28 March 1810 and Breitkopf on 25 July of the same year.[55] Clementi & Co. followed shortly after, advertising them in *The Morning Chronicle* on 29 August and entering them at Stationers' Hall two days later. The fact that the London publication details were both advertised and entered at Stationers' Hall (which was not so for many of the works published in the previous few years) is almost certainly the result of the more meticulous approach to business practice that followed Clementi's return to England sometime in the previous two months.

A further work that was published by both Clementi & Co. and Breitkopf & Härtel, but which is not mentioned in Clementi's letter of 4 August 1804, is the String Quartet op. 103. The Breitkopf & Härtel edition appeared in 1806, with the Clementi edition – and others by André and Artaria – being published at around the same time.

Among the works by Haydn that Clementi & Co. published after 1810 are the last twelve symphonies arranged for piano trio and *The Seasons*, which was eventually published in vocal score in 1813.[56] In addition, when Longman & Broderip was sold in November 1798, the plates of the hundred or so Haydn works that they had published earlier were divided between their two successors, Longman, Clementi & Co., and Broderip & Wilkinson. Although the former firm reprinted more works than the latter, neither publisher had a monopoly on any particular genre, largely because of the way in which the publishing assets had been divided in 1798. A list of *Musical Publications Selected from the Catalogue Published by Broderip and Wilkinson, Lately Purchased, and Now Sold by Preston* [1811][57] gives some idea of the works that

53. *Collected Correspondence and London Notebooks*, p. 221.
54. Landon, *Haydn: Chronicle and Works*, V, 269, n. 4.
55. Hoboken, *Werkverzeichnis*, II, 304, 305.
56. See Landon, *Haydn: Chronicle and Works*, V, 199.
57. London, British Library, Hirsch IV.1113.(10.).

Broderip & Wilkinson inherited from Longman & Broderip. We can be fairly sure that the quartets, trios and sonatas originally came from Longman & Broderip, but it is possible that other works had been acquired by Broderip & Wilkinson from other publishers:

- A Symphony in D (possibly Hob.I:86)
- The string quartets Hob.III:1, 57–59 and 60–62
- The Trios Hob.XV:3–5, 14 and 27–29
- The Piano Sonatas Hob.XVI:27–32 and 37
- A few other arrangements of orchestral works, as well as some ballads and canzonets.

Longman, Clementi & Co. took over a similarly diverse list with perhaps a slightly higher proportion of more recent music than Broderip & Wilkinson. The works that were reprinted by both firms were mostly, though not exclusively, those that Longman & Broderip had originally published in the late 1780s and 1790s. By far the most popular genres were string quartets and piano trios. Seventeen string quartets were reprinted along with twelve piano trios. As we have seen, nine new quartets by Haydn were published by Longman, Clementi & Co. and their successors Clementi & Co. from 1799. The market was therefore saturated with chamber works by Haydn, particularly quartets, so it is no wonder that Clementi turned down similar works by other composers. In a letter of 26 December 1799,[58] Gyrowetz had written personally to Clementi offering him the publication rights to some new quartets. The letter refers to some previous discussion between the two men about Haydn's quartets, so Gyrowetz must have been aware that his request was being considered against tough competition and probably explains why he asked for such a reasonable price. The letter reveals that the 'usual' price for quartets (how many quartets is not specified, but it might be assumed to be three) was thirty guineas, but that Gyrowetz would be happy if Clementi offered him twenty-five. However, because the composer was so keen to have his quartets published, he was willing to receive twenty guineas, for which price he would also throw in a nocturne. The much higher price (£75 for three quartets) that Haydn could command under the Hyde contract, and the fact that so many quartets by Haydn were available in Broderip & Wilkinson's and Clementi & Co.'s catalogues, shows how popular these works must have been in England during the early years of the nineteenth century.

A curiosity of the division of Longman & Broderip's assets between the two new firms is the fact that the first works to be published under the terms of Hyde's contract with Haydn, the piano trios dedicated to Therese Bartolozzi (Hob.XV:27–29), were taken into Broderip & Wilkinson's catalogue, not the catalogue of Longman,

---

58. See *Correspondence*, ed. Rowland, pp. 40–42.

Clementi & Co, where Hyde was a partner. As we have seen, these were the only works to be published under the terms of the contract for almost three years after it was signed. How or why this came about is unknown, but it represents a similarly curious parallel to the way in which a significant amount of Clementi's own piano music – albeit, predominantly his earlier works – also passed into the hands of Broderip & Wilkinson.[59]

In addition to publishing new music by Haydn and re-issuing works previously owned by Longman & Broderip, Clementi & Co. also published some of Haydn's music formerly in the possession of other London publishers. The first English edition of the Piano Trio Hob.XV:30 had been published by Corri, Dussek & Co. in 1799 (within the period of the 'exclusive' contract between Hyde and Haydn). That firm was in difficulties at the time and was finally (and ironically) bought out by Corri himself in 1801.[60] At some point Clementi & Co. must have acquired the publishing plates for the Trio, because Clementi & Co. used them for its own re-issue of the work, just as they did with a number of other works first published by Corri, Dussek & Co.[61] Other works by Haydn that had been printed for the composer by Corri, Dussek & Co. and later published by Clementi & Co. were the first set of six Canzonettas (Hob.XXVIa:25–30). This time, however, Clementi & Co. re-engraved the works. Perhaps in this instance Clementi negotiated the ownership of the rights directly with Haydn and engraved them on fresh plates rather than buy the old ones from Corri & Dussek.

This study reveals strong connections between Clementi, his publishing circle, and Haydn extending over many years. At least some of the business that was transacted arose from the personal friendship and respect that existed between Clementi and Haydn, which lasted into the latter's final years. Since Clementi spent so much time in Vienna during the first decade of the nineteenth century it seems extremely likely that the two men met there, and even after Haydn's death Clementi remembered him with affection. At the end of Clementi's own life his business partners were anxious to present him with something special in order to acknowledge his departure from the firm. Clementi finally withdrew from the partnership of his company on 24 June 1830 and just a few months previously, on 8 September 1829 Frederick William Collard had written to Artaria:[62]

---

59. Information about the way in which Clementi's works were divided between the two companies can be found in a footnote to Charles Clementi's letter of 20 January 1824 (see *Correspondence*, ed. Rowland, pp. 309–10, n. 103) and in David Rowland, 'Clementi as Music Publisher' in *The Music Trade in Georgian England*, ed. by Michael Kassler (Farnham: Ashgate, 2011), pp. 159–91.
60. Rowland, 'Dussek in London's Commercial World', p. 102.
61. Rowland, 'Clementi as Music Publisher', p. 168.
62. See *Correspondence*, ed. Rowland, pp. 359–60.

We now beg to ask a favor of you and shall feel very thankful if you can oblige us – it is to get us if you possibly can a musical autograph of Haydn & Beethoven – we want it for a particular purpose and feel assured that you will endeavour to comply with our wishes.

Artaria must have responded positively to the request since, in an undated letter that was probably written a few months later, Clementi wrote to Collard:[63]

I believe I told you I am in possession of something autograph of Beethoven and Haydn, much at y[ou]r service.

---

63. See *Correspondence*, ed. Rowland, p. 380.

Haydn's 'British Music Library'

WHEREAS HAYDN'S PERSONAL COLLECTION OF BOOKS has already been the subject of a certain amount of scholarly scrutiny,[1] the composer's collection of music manuscripts and editions has received rather less attention. It is true that manuscripts and editions of his own works from his personal library have raised great interest and have been carefully studied by the editors of the *Joseph Haydn Werke* on account of the special significance they undoubtedly hold; nonetheless the extent to which Haydn's collection of other composers' works has been overlooked seems surprising. A comparison with a great contemporary may prove telling. Wolfgang Amadeus Mozart's rather tiny music collection has been lost apparently ever since his death. There is, nevertheless, a substantial published catalogue dedicated to it, which includes considerable guesswork about which pieces we should suspect behind the surviving catalogue entries.[2] By contrast, the better

I am much indebted to the editors of this volume for several useful comments regarding both style and content of this article, as well as to Loukia Drosopoulou for her scrupulous description of the sources I could not access in Budapest. At the time of revising this article, the author was supported by a Bolyai Research Fellowship of the Hungarian Academy of Sciences.

1. Maria Hörwarthner, trans. by Kathrine Talbot, 'Joseph Haydn's Library: An Attempt at a Literary-Historical Reconstruction', in *Haydn and His World*, ed. by Elaine Sisman (Princeton: Princeton University Press, 1997), pp. 395–462.
2. *Allzeit ein Buch: Die Bibliothek Wolfgang Amadeus Mozarts*, ed. by Ulrich Konrad and Martin Staehelin, Ausstellungskataloge der Herzog August Bibliothek, 66 (Weinheim: VCH, Acta humaniora, 1991).

part of Haydn's vast music library has survived and his collection of other composers' works is virtually complete – nonetheless, this precious material has never been properly described, let alone carefully studied in its entirety.[3]

Admittedly, this omission should not be blamed on Haydn scholars alone: there were other, very practical reasons which contributed to this neglect. A few years before his death the composer made arrangements with his long-time patrons, the Esterházy family, for his music collection to be bought from his estate for the Esterházy archives. Thus, in contrast to Mozart's music library, Haydn's collection remained together, and became part of the princely archive, which was one of the richest of its kind even before this unique accession.[4] Even though the role of music at the Esterházy court decreased significantly after the death of Prince Nicolaus II in 1833, this change nonetheless ensured the safe survival of the music collection into the following century. The First World War and the ensuing political turmoil brought about some significant developments, however: in an effort to protect the collection through those uncertain times, the greater – and more valuable – part was taken from Eisenstadt to another of the family's palaces in Hungary. Hence this part of the Esterházy collection survived the Second World War in the Buda castle (Tárnok Street) and was nationalized by the Hungarian state after it fell under Communist rule in 1948. As a consequence, the music sources – including the overwhelming majority of Haydn's own library – now form part of the Music Collection of the National Széchényi Library.

Until the middle of the twentieth century, therefore, the collection was in private ownership and it was not easy for scholars to have access to primary source material relating to musical life at the Esterházy court.[5] In this respect, the nationalization

3. My interest in Haydn's personal music collection was raised in 2001 by Katalin Szerző, then Head of Music in the National Széchényi Library, Budapest. Due to my being abroad studying for nearly six years, I could not resume my research into this topic until 2009; the present text is thus but an early fruit of an extensive project that in a few years will hopefully result in a monograph about Haydn's music collection in general. I should clarify that, notwithstanding my use of the comprehensive term 'library', this essay ignores the composer's books and deals exclusively with printed and manuscript music.

4. In addition to the vast collection built during Haydn's active years as Kapellmeister, after 1800 Prince Nicolaus II also bought the musical legacies of three major composers: Franz Xaver Süssmayr, Michael Haydn and Johann Georg Albrechtsberger.

5. This situation changed only in the 1990s, when two large-scale exhibitions ('Bollwerk Forchtenstein' in 1993 and 'Die Fürsten Esterházy' in 1995) prompted the opening of the Esterházy private collections. The newly founded Esterházy Privatstiftung has since sponsored research into the music archive as well: James Armstrong has for a decade been preparing a catalogue of the church music sources; this work was extended by the National Széchényi Library in 2008 to ensure complete coverage of the former Esterházy collection, rather than only of the sources held in Eisenstadt. Another grand project has already been completed: Josef Pratl examined the documents of the Esterházy finance archives in Forchtenstein and has presented

of the collection undoubtedly brought change for the better: proper cataloguing of the material began in the early 1950s and the Haydn celebrations in 1959 prompted a number of publications, some of which remain useful tools today.[6] Unfortunately, however, these promising first steps did not become the basis of a new school of Haydn studies in Hungary.[7] In addition, despite public ownership of the collection, many scholars abroad were able at best only to have access to the material via microfilm.[8] Unsurprisingly, only the most important sources related to Haydn's own works seemed to deserve such effort and perseverance; Haydn's own collection of works by other composers therefore escaped serious attention altogether.

Taken as a whole, Haydn's collection of other composers' works included more than two hundred scores; approximately three-quarters of these are printed, the rest are in manuscript. Two different contemporary lists of this material survive. One was drawn up for Haydn by Johann Elssler during the composer's lifetime around 1805 (the so-called *Haydn Bibliothekverzeichnis*, HBV), and may have been prompted by the composer's desire to sell the collection to Prince Esterházy. The other was assembled after Haydn's death as part of the catalogue of his estate (the so-called *Haydn Nachlassverzeichnis*, HNV), and is, understandably, much less scrupulous than the former.[9] Elssler's list is especially important for it may to a

5. *Cont.*

a general overview as well as a rich sample of this material in *Acta Forchtensteiniana: Die Musikdokumente im Esterházy-Archiv auf Burg Forchtenstein*, Eisenstädter Haydn-Berichte, 7 (Tutzing: Hans Schneider, 2009). This publication sheds welcome light on musical life at the princely court from the late seventeenth to the mid-nineteenth century – a topic that has all too often been discussed with an exclusive focus on Haydn's activities.

6. *Haydn Compositions in the Music Collection of the National Széchényi Library, Budapest*, ed. by Jenő Vécsey, Publications of the National Széchényi Library, 48 (Budapest: Hungarian Academy of Sciences, 1960); Dénes Bartha and László Somfai, *Haydn als Opernkapellmeister: Die Haydn-Dokumente der Esterházy-Opernsammlung* (Budapest: Ungarische Akademie der Wissenschaften, 1960).

7. While László Somfai kept publishing important studies even after his leaving the National Széchényi Library for the Bartók Archives, his remained rather lonely efforts. At a later stage, Katalin Komlós also contributed to Haydn research at an international level, but her work was not particularly concerned with the primary sources held in the National Library.

8. The Joseph Haydn-Institut in Cologne received a full set of microfilms soon after its foundation in 1955; it was this acquisition that made the new complete edition *Joseph Haydn Werke* possible in the first place.

9. The Elssler list is now held by the British Library (Add. MS 32070); the list prepared posthumously exists in two copies, one held by the Wiener Stadt- und Landesarchiv (catalogue reference 'Persönlichkeiten 4/2 der Verlassenschaftsabhandlung'), the other by the Österreichische Nationalbibliothek (Musiksammlung, cat. S. M. 4843). Both lists encompass the composer's entire collection (including sources of his own works) and are transcribed in Landon, *Haydn: Chronicle and Works*, V, 299–317 (esp. pp. 303–14) and 392–403 (esp. pp. 395–98, 401–02).

certain extent reflect the order in which the collection was stored on the shelves in Haydn's house. If so, it is intriguing that the list of printed music opens with no fewer than ten volumes of music by Mozart. Nine of these, however, belong to Breit-kopf & Härtel's posthumous 'complete' edition published around 1800, so unfortunately they tell us little about which Mozart compositions Haydn might have been familiar with in his active years (he apparently stopped writing music altogether in 1803). Furthermore, it is likely that Haydn did not actively collect the Mozart edition himself: the publisher may have sent these volumes unbidden, in an effort to interest him in launching a similar series of his own works. Hence this substantial collection of Mozart's music may not even reflect any particular interest in obtaining music by Haydn's esteemed colleague.

Indeed, this example should serve as a general caveat to those hoping to glean a wealth of new information about possible influences on Haydn's works from his own music collection. First of all, the overwhelming majority of the scores that can be dated with any precision appears to have been acquired after around 1780. They therefore give little information about Haydn's formative, early years when one would expect him to have been most impressionable to outside influences. Moreover, a significant portion of the collection obviously consists of complimentary copies which Haydn might have paid little attention to after taking a polite glance at the first page or two when receiving them. If so, several items may tell us more about those other composers who thus felt eager to express their admiration towards him than about Haydn's own musical interests, and might rather suggest the influence of Haydn on them rather than the other way around. Haydn was flattered by such gestures, apparently, for the *Bibliothekverzeichnis* lists the works dedicated to him at the beginning, immediately after the ten Mozart scores (the tenth of which happens to be none other than the first edition of the six quartets dedicated to Haydn by Mozart).

For the present purposes, Haydn's 'British Music Library' may be defined as those editions of his music collection that were published in Britain, together with the few manuscripts which he demonstrably obtained there. While it is impossible to trace the acquisition history of each item, it seems reasonable to assume that the overwhelming majority of these would have come into Haydn's possession during his London visits in the early 1790s, and that he took them back to Vienna himself (even if in theory he could have received further items from his London contacts after he had returned to Austria). In dealing with this material, one must first of all note that this portion is different from the bulk of Haydn's collection in two important respects. First, while the composer's printed music collection in general includes instrumental and vocal works in approximately equal numbers, in the British material the predominance of vocal music is conspicuous. Second, the scores acquired by Haydn in England apparently include a mere three manuscripts – a much lower ratio than with the rest of his collection.[10]

On that note, let me begin with a brief discussion of these three items. Among all the manuscripts listed in Haydn's own *Bibliothekverzeichnis* the very first item by another composer is a tiny song 'When from thy sight', which Haydn described on the first page as follows: 'This lied is by Mistress Hodges, the most beautiful woman I have seen in my life, a great clavier player. Text and music composed by her.'[11] A few years later, after receiving news in Vienna of Mrs Hodges's death, Haydn annotated the manuscript in a trembling hand: 'Requiescat in pace.' Unfortunately, this manuscript appears lost today – the description here derives from copies made by Carl Ferdinand Pohl in the nineteenth century (see number **41** among the manuscripts in the appendix to this article).[12]

Haydn's second manuscript of English provenance listed in the *Bibliothekver-zeichnis* is a full score entitled 'Invocation of Neptune' (**200**); it includes an anonymous setting of a jingoistic poem that appeared as preface to Marchamont Nedham's translation of John Selden's *Mare Clausum, seu de Dominio Maris*.[13] This source is of special importance, for it was apparently given to Haydn by Lord Abingdon in an effort to persuade him to set the same text himself. Haydn indeed started work on the project but only two movements were completed, probably because Abingdon was imprisoned after a libel case in 1795 and so his commission lost relevance for the composer.[14] The composer of this work, not named in the manuscript in Haydn's possession, might have been either Johann Christian Fischer or Ignaz Pleyel (or possibly the two in cooperation).[15]

10. The whole collection consists of about 160 printed items and over 60 manuscripts.
11. 'Dieses Lied ist von M[is]tris Hodges, daß schönste Weib, so ich zeit lebens gesehen, eine grosse Clavier spielerin. Text und Music von Ihrer Composition.' With respect to the music there is no reason to doubt Mrs Hodges's authorship. The text, however, proves to be an excerpt from one of the *Love Elegies* by James Hammond (1710–42), dedicated to Miss Dashwood:

    'When from thy sight I waste the tedious day,
    A thousand schemes I form, and things to say;
    But when thy presence gives the time I seek,
    My heart's so full, I wish, but cannot speak'.

12. The appendix includes bibliographic descriptions of each item from Haydn's 'British Music Library', using the numeration of the *Bibliothekverzeichnis*. For convenience these numbers have been inserted in bold in the main text of the article whenever a specific manuscript or printed item is discussed.
13. John Selden, *Opera omnia*, 3 vols (London: [n. pub.], 1725), II, 1179.
14. For details of the two movements which Haydn completed, see Arthur Searle's article at pp. 212–32 below.
15. See my 'New Light on Haydn's Invocation of Neptune', *Studia Musicologica Academiae Scientiarum Hungaricae*, 46 (2005), 237–55.

Finally, the third manuscript listed in the *Bibliothekverzeichnis* that Haydn certainly received in England is a lavishly bound copy of Handel's so-called Brockes Passion (**225**). As the catalogue prepared after his death explains (probably transmitting the account of Haydn's copyist and servant Johann Elssler): 'The original [of this work] is preserved at the University of Oxford. In beautiful binding, presented [to Haydn] by the Queen of England. A great rarity.'[16] That the queen would have found it appropriate to give Haydn an oratorio by Handel is intriguing. This 'great rarity' was an early work in German that was virtually unknown in comparison with Handel's later English oratorios. Although Haydn was yet to write *The Creation* and *The Seasons*, the British apparently already considered him a worthy successor to Handel, their greatest 'nationalized' composer of German descent.

That the majority of the printed volumes from Haydn's British collection represents vocal music might surprise some, given that Haydn has long been celebrated primarily as a key figure in the history of instrumental music: the 'father of the symphony' and, one might also say, of the string quartet. Nonetheless, a good half of Haydn's oeuvre is vocal music. It might be, therefore, that while his trips to England evidently influenced his instrumental style (see, for example, the ambitious keyboard writing in his sonatas and trios written for London), he may have been rather more interested to explore the strong British tradition of genres such as the oratorio, the partsong or the canon, which he himself had contributed to but sparingly earlier on. Be that as it may, Haydn was evidently more concerned to obtain music which he could read and play for himself: to collect symphonies or string quartets – which were typically published in parts rather than full score – would have made little sense to him. Hence the majority of the instrumental music he acquired features keyboard sonatas, including so-called 'accompanied sonatas' that called for the participation of a violin, sometimes also a cello.

About half of these scores are explicitly dedicated to Haydn on their title-pages in rather similar terms. The typical phrase was 'composed and dedicated to Doctor Haydn'; this is printed, for example, on Benoît Auguste Bertini's *Three Grand Sonatas*, op. 1 (**16**), or (slightly varied: 'to J. Haydn, M. D.') on Miss Cecilia Barthélemon's *Sonata*, op. 3 (**12**) (see Fig. 1). Some – including Thomas Haigh (**15**) – emphasized that they 'humbly' dedicated their work to the Master. Others drew attention to the fact that they had studied with him (like Johann Georg Graeff [**11**]: 'composed and dedicated to Dr. Haydn, by his late pupil'). Still others underlined that their dedication was endorsed by the composer: 'composed and dedicated, by

---

16. 'Das Original wird an der Universität zu Oxford verwahrt. In schöner Band, regalirt von der Königin aus England. Eine große Seltenheit.' Today the autograph is lost and no manuscript copy is known to have survived in Oxford: see *Händel-Handbuch*, 4 vols (Kassel: Bärenreiter, 1978–86), II, ed. by Bernd Baselt (1984), 60.

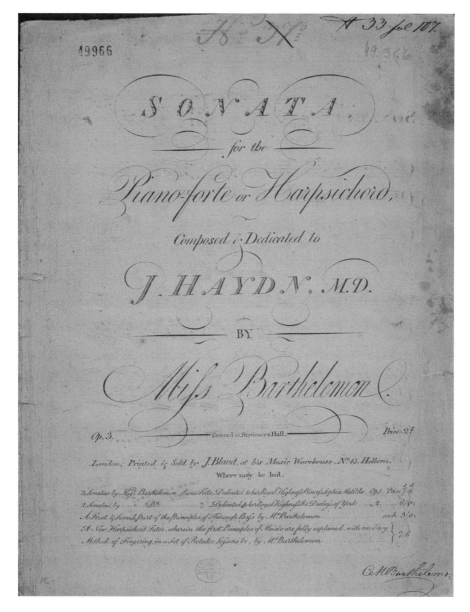

Fig. 1. Title-page of Miss Cecilia Maria Barthélemon's *Sonata for the Piano-forte or Harpsichord*, op. 3. Besides the printed dedication to Haydn, the copy also bears the author's signature ('CMBarthelemon') in the lower right corner. The reference '[Z] 49.966' that appears at the top both in pencil and stamped is the present-day shelf-mark in the Music Collection of the National Széchényi Library. On entering the shelf-mark of the 1858 Esterházy catalogue ('No. 33 fol. 107') in the top right corner, the earlier number 'No. 37' (in the middle, in pencil) became obsolete and was crossed out with the same ink. The figure '12' that corresponds to Haydn's own catalogue of his personal library is written in pencil in the lower left corner.

permission, to Mr. Haydn' (this last phrase appears on the title-page of Christian Ignatius Latrobe's *Three Sonatas* [**21**]).[17]

In most of the above cases, we also have other evidence that these composers – some of them no more than able musical amateurs – did come into personal contact with Haydn during his trips, so that it is likely that the copies that survive in his library were presented to him soon after their publication. By the same token, some of the other scores not explicitly dedicated to the composer were probably also received as complimentary copies: both volumes of sonatas by Franz Tomich (**114, 115**), the *Three Sonatas* (1791) by Miss Barthélemon (**120**), as well as the *Three Sonatas*, op. 28, by Muzio Clementi (**121**) belong in this category. If so, one should again be rather careful in taking Haydn's library as a reflection of his personal musical interests: much of what he 'collected' may tell us more about his manifold social contacts during his London years than his private artistic preferences. The fact that he owned a volume of organ pieces by Thomas Sanders Dupuis (**42**) and a fugue for the organ by Joseph Diettenhofer (**91**) – with both of whom he was on friendly terms – may only confirm this assessment.

Finally, I should mention a curious group of publications by Johann Samuel Schroeter comprising three collections of sonatas (**85, 86, 87**), two volumes of keyboard concerti (**88, 89**) and two keyboard quintets (**90**), all of which were presumably received together and were apparently shelved so in Haydn's house later on as well. To be sure, Schroeter, who had been Master of the King's Music and died a mere three years before Haydn's arrival in London, was by no means forgotten yet. Still, it would be mistaken to ascribe Haydn's acquisition to his avid interest in his dead colleague's music: Schroeter's widow, Rebecca, became an intimate friend – and possibly the lover – of Haydn. Thus this group of music, again, possibly reflects the composer's personal, rather than professional, interests.

Moving on to the vocal part of the collection, it seems appropriate to divide this material into a number of smaller categories. Haydn owned two volumes of French songs, both signed by their authors: Rothe Nugent (**116**) and Samuel Webbe (junior) (**107**). His collection also features an English song by Webbe (**77**), an *Ode on St Cecilia* (**97**) and a glee (**84**) by his father, Samuel Webbe (senior), as well as *A Collection of Vocal Music* featuring works by both father and son (**109**). All of this strongly suggests that the relationship between Haydn and the Webbe family may

---

17. Latrobe's letter to Vincent Novello dated 22 November 1828 confirms that Haydn explicitly encouraged him to publish the sonatas: see Landon, *Haydn: Chronicle and Works*, III, 58. It is also noteworthy that the dedication refers to Haydn as 'Mister' rather than 'Doctor'; the publication obviously predated the award of the composer's doctoral degree which he received from Oxford University in July 1791.

have been considerably closer than hitherto assumed (the name Webbe is as good as absent from the Haydn literature).[18]

The rest of the solo song repertory includes three volumes of national songs, namely *A Selection of the Most Favourite Scots-songs, Chiefly Pastoral* (**142**), David Sime's *Edinburgh Musical Miscellany: a Collection of the Most Approved Scotch, English, and Irish songs* (**153**), and a volume of *Twelve Songs* by the Edinburgh organist Alexander Campbell (**27**). The presence of these Scottish song collections is of particular relevance, since Haydn himself was persuaded to arrange such folk melodies. His first collection was published by none other than William Napier, publisher of the above 'chiefly pastoral' volume, which might have been presented to the composer as a tactical first step to raise his interest in this then popular genre. A fourth Scottish collection by George Jenkins (**111**) includes dances rather than songs and is noteworthy for its inclusion of *Jenkins's Compliments to Dr. Haydn* and *Haydn's Strathspey* (the latter genitive certainly not implying Haydn's authorship but at best his fondness for the piece).

Another genre that Haydn contributed to during his London years was opera (although his *Orfeo ed Euridice* remained unperformed in the composer's lifetime). In this light the two thick anthologies of opera arias he acquired during his stays are particularly interesting. One of these (**61**) includes excerpts from works by Lampugnani, Galuppi, Perez and Hasse (all of which were played in London in the 1750s), while the other (**59**) features an even older repertory: arias from operas by Bononcini, Mancini, Alessandro Scarlatti, Francesco Conti and Handel (all performed and published in London in the 1710s). Intriguingly, this latter volume was commented on in Haydn's own catalogue, the *Bibliothekverzeichnis*, as being 'most highly recommended by Kapellmeister Haydn', which suggests that comparison of his *Orfeo ed Euridice* with some of this old repertory deserves perhaps further research.[19] Speaking of Handel, it is also worth mentioning that Haydn owned a British edition of the oratorio *Jephtha* (**76**), incidentally – or rather, symbolically –

---

18. A set of variations by Samuel Webbe Junior on 'The favorite air Adeste fideles' (London: Chappel's Musical Circulating Library, [*c.* 1840]) may to some extent confirm this assessment. As the title-page explains, the composition is 'harmonized as a Quartet for Two Violins, Tenor and Bass, after the manner of Haydn's celebrated Hymn to the Emperor' (i.e., the slow movement of op. 76 no. 3).

19. 'Äuserst empfohlen von Herrn Kapellmeister Haydn'. In this context it is worth mentioning Giovanni Carlo Clari's *Sei Madrigali* (**119**), another volume presenting an 'ancient' Italian vocal repertory. Haydn may have received the score from Henry Harrington, who appears to have been the moving spirit behind its mid-1760s reprint (whose Advertisement on p. ii is signed *H. H.*). I am currently tracing the possible impact of several such publications on Haydn's own oeuvre.

the last of his great predecessor's oratorios.[20] Haydn's collection also included a 'musical drama' by Thomas Attwood entitled *The Adopted Child* (**108**). Attwood has of course been making frequent appearances in Mozart biographies as a favourite pupil, but this score, as well as his longer sojourn in Vienna earlier on, suggests that he may have been on friendly terms with Haydn as well – as was the case with Lord Abingdon, whose *Representation of the Execution of Mary Queen of Scot's* for chorus and orchestra (**139a**), a curious set of musical illustrations to seven engravings, rounds off the category of theatrical music.

Yet another interesting thematic group in Haydn's 'British Music Library' is what one might loosely term sacred choral music. The most intriguing item of this category is a copy of *Three Hymns and Three Anthems* by the composer's close friend Mrs Maria Barthélemon[21] (**110**) – a publication whose subscribers' list includes both 'Haydn Dr.' and 'Haydn Mrs.' (see Fig. 2). Given the volume's religious content it is possibly no coincidence that the composer decided to enter subscriptions for this particular publication in his wife's name as well as his own: while Mrs Haydn's devout Catholicism has mostly been commented upon sarcastically in the literature, this item may suggest that the composer himself was capable of attentive gestures towards her, their far from perfect marriage notwithstanding. The single copy of *Three Hymns and Three Anthems* that survives in Haydn's library bears the author's signature on its title-page; the same holds true for Lord Abingdon's *Selection of Twelve Psalms and Hymns* (**139b**, bound together with his *Representation* mentioned above), which undoubtedly came from the Earl as a present. A magnificent volume featuring *The Psalms of David for the Use of Parish Churches* (**143**) may also fall into this category, for its editor Dr Samuel Arnold was assisted by another close friend of Haydn's, John Wall Callcott. Besides this volume Haydn also owned Callcott's small dictionary of musical terms (**78**) but the whereabouts of his copy (which his catalogue misleadingly lists as printed music) are unknown. Since not one book from Haydn's library can be traced in the National Széchényi Library, a possible explanation for the absence of Callcott's dictionary is that it may have been stored with other books, rather than with the rest of the music. However, it is also possible

---

20. In his *Introduction to Harmony* (London: Robinson, for the author, 1800), William Shield reports that Haydn gave him a manuscript score of his *Ritorno di Tobia*, a friendly gesture which Shield returned by presenting the composer with a score of *Jephtha* – possibly the very copy that survived in Haydn's library. See Landon, *Haydn: Chronicle and Works*, III, 83–84.

21. Haydn appears to have been close with three members of this outstandingly musical family. Miss Cecilia Maria Barthélemon, author of the *Three Sonatas for the Piano-Forte*, op. 1 (**120**), and the *Sonata*, op. 3 (**12**), mentioned above, was daughter of Mrs Maria Barthélemon, née Polly Young, who pursued a moderately successful career as singer earlier on. The father, François-Hyppolite Barthélemon, was a professional violinist and composer; a glee by him also survives in Haydn's collection (**127**; see below).

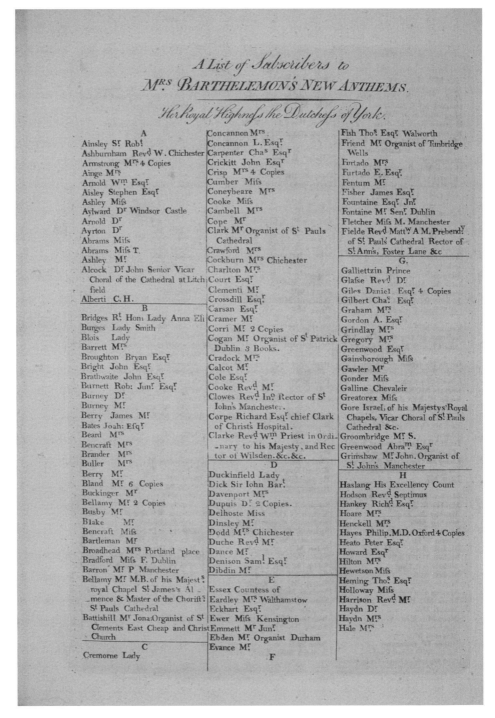

Fig. 2. Alphabetical list of subscribers from Mrs Maria Barthélemon's *Three Hymns and Three Anthems*, op. 3, featuring in the lower right corner both Haydn and his wife.

that it could have been stored among the volumes of music in pocketbook format, for all the items that Haydn's catalogue describes as 'in Taschenformat' appear to be lost, the precise explanation for which awaits further study.[22] In any case, the *Improved Psalmody in Three Parts* (**155**), edited by William Tattersall, was also of pocketbook size and is also missing in the Budapest collection – a loss all the more painful in that this publication includes six pieces by Haydn himself.[23]

Haydn in fact owned a third volume related to Callcott, which brings me to the final group of scores in his 'British Music Library', the considerable size of which may warrant some explanation. The composer owned over a dozen volumes of secular vocal music for two or more parts. Some of these might again have come from composer friends whose names have in part already been mentioned above: *The Professional Collection of Glees for Three, Four and Five Voices* (**40**; signed by Callcott on the title-page), Samuel Harrison's *Never Till Now* (**75**), the two glee publications by the Webbes (**84, 109**) and François-Hyppolite Barthélemon's *Glee for the Anniversary of the Philanthropic Society* (**127**) belong in this category. By the same token, both the twelve canonic canzonets by Charles Burney[24] (**137**) and the collection of glees by the late Dr Benjamin Cooke (**66**) must have arrived as complimentary copies, for the one bears the note 'from the Author' on its title-page, while the other features a handwritten dedication to Haydn by its editor Robert Cooke (son of the composer himself) (Fig. 3). Still, even if several of these copies were received as personal presents from the respective authors, the number of publications of pieces such as catches and glees in Haydn's collection suggests that these genres particularly intrigued him.[25] Indeed, if one assumes that *The Ladies Collection of Catches, Glees, Canons,*

---

22. In a personal communication, László Somfai has suggested that these volumes might have shared the fortune of some of the Esterházy collection's libretti of similar size: received wisdom suggests that the latter were used as 'stuffing' to insulate the windows of the Tárnok Street palace during the Second World War. On Callcott's volume and its acknowledgement of Haydn's friendship and professional advice, see Otto Biba, 'Joseph Haydn und John Wall Callcott: Eine Miszelle zu Haydns Londoner Bekanntenkreis', *Haydn Yearbook*, 20 (1996), 54–56.

23. See Hoboken, *Werkverzeichnis*, II, 181.

24. The presence of Burney's canzonets in Haydn's collection may help us interpret an undated autograph note by the latter, in which he asks his friend to send him 'a copy of that canzonetta, because I can recall neither the melody nor the text of it'. While both Robbins Landon and Dénes Bartha assumed that the piece in question was one of the twelve 'original canzonettas' by Haydn, the composer's ignorance of text and melody suggests that he could rather have meant a piece by Burney. If so, the signed copy of twelve *Canzonetti* that survives in Haydn's library might easily have been Burney's friendly gift in response to Haydn's query. See *Gesammelte Briefe und Aufzeichnungen*, p. 304; *Collected Correspondence and London Notebooks*, p. 145.

25. The title-page of Lord Abingdon's *Twelve Sentimental Catches and Glees*, which states 'the accompaniments for the harp or pianoforte [...] by Dr Haydn', illustrates the degree of interest that he took in these specific British genres.

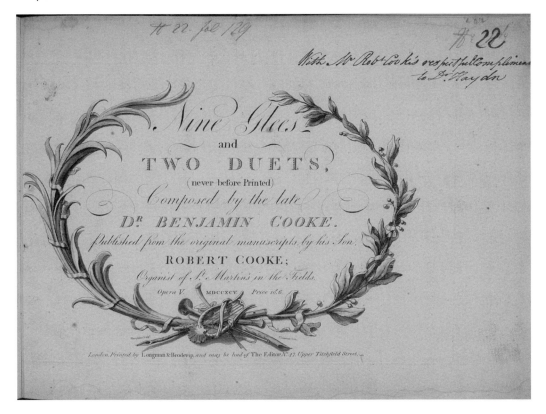

Fig. 3. Title-page of Dr Benjamin Cooke's *Nine Glees and two duets*, op. 5 (London: Longman & Broderip, 1795), with handwritten dedication by the composer's son: 'With Mr Robt Cooke's respectful Compliments to Dr. Haydn'.

Canzonets, Madrigals (**94, 95, 96, 140**), a collection of *Notturni, Duetts, Terzetts, Canzonets, Rondo's, Catches and Glees* (**141**) and another anthology of *Catches, Canons, Glees, Duetts* (**62, 63, 64**) may also have been presents, they were likely given to Haydn by their respective publishers (Bland and Corri) who may have picked these very items from their catalogues with Haydn's apparent predeliction for catches and glees in mind. All of this seems in harmony with the all too rarely stressed fact that the uniquely developed British vocal culture did not simply prompt Haydn to try his hands at the genre of oratorio along Handel's lines but evidently also played a crucial role in his turning with special interest towards the partsong and the canon in his post-London years. In neither genres are we aware of works by Haydn before his trips to England – a couple of years after his return to Vienna, however, he started to compose his impressive series of *Mehrstimmige Gesänge* and by the end of his life he considered his personal collection of canons one of the most valuable parts of his music library.

With that in mind I would suggest that possibly the most intriguing question is whether direct stylistic links may also be established between the British sources of inspiration and Haydn's own compositions.[26] Now that Haydn's personal music collection – including his 'British Music Library' – has been rediscovered, as it were, for scholars, such investigations may proceed on much firmer ground than before.

Appendix: items of British provenance in Joseph Haydn's music collection

The items are listed according to their numbers in the composer's own catalogue, the so-called *Haydn Bibliothekverzeichnis* (HBV).

The three further numbers given for each item are as follows:

HNV	*Haydn Nachlassverzeichnis*, list of the composer's estate
EA	Esterházy Archives, *Inventarium* compiled in 1858[27]
H Bn	National Széchényi Library, Budapest

Manuscripts

41. Hodges, M[is]tris [Ann Mary]: 'When from thy sight...'
HNV: 537   EA: No. 68 fol. 135

H Bn: –

> For voice and keyboard. The original manuscript appears lost but copies prepared by Carl Ferdinand Pohl survive. One is preserved in the Gesellschaft der Musikfreunde (shelf-mark: VI. 23.054) and transmits Haydn's autograph remark 'Requiescat in pace. J: Haydn'. Another, less scrupulous, copy is owned by the Österreichische National-bibliothek (Mus. Hs. 28.757), while a third one (on which Pohl's copying is not stated) is kept in the Staatsbibliothek zu Berlin (Mus. ms. 9963/5).

200. 'Invocation of Neptune, And his attendant Nereids, To Britania on the Dominion of the Sea, prefixed to Marchmont Needhams Translation of Selden's Mare Clausum, and now for the first Time set to Music'.
HNV: 556   EA: No. 86 fol. 49
H Bn: Ms. mus. IV. 523

> For soloists, chorus and orchestra. Full score.

---

26. For the plausible impact of the British repertory on Haydn's partsongs and canons, see my 'Between Tradition, Innovation and Utopia: Haydn's *Mehrstimmige Gesänge*', *Studia Musicologica: An International Journal of Musicology of the Hungarian Academy of Sciences*, 51 (2010), 179–91.
27. Often mentioned as the 'Zagitz catalogue' after its compiler Carl Zagitz, then director of the court orchestra. The numbers of this *Inventarium* are provided here since as a rule they also appear on the scores themselves.

225. Handel, G[eorge] F[rideric]: 'Der für die Sünde der Welt gemarterte und sterbende Jesus. In gebundener Rede vorgestellet und Musikalisch verfertiget'.

HNV: 564   EA: No. 88 fol. 49

H Bn: Ms. mus. IV. 517

> For soloists, chorus and orchestra. Full score. On the spine: *Passione di G. F. Handel.*

Editions

In addition to the HNV, EA and **H** Bn numbers used above for manuscripts, in this category the figures from Series A/I of the *Répertoire International des Sources Musicales* (RISM) are also provided.

11. Graeff, J[ohann] G[eorg]: *Three Quartetts for a Flute, Violin, Tenor, and Violoncello. Composed & Dedicated to Dr. Haydn, by his Late Pupil. Op. 8.* London: F. Linley, [*c.* 1794–5].

HNV: 207   EA: No. 47 fol. 91

H Bn: —   RISM: G 3285

> Four parts. These items were apparently removed from the Esterházy collection by Carl Ferdinand Pohl, from whose bequest they came into the possession of the Gesellschaft der Musikfreunde (shelf-mark: XI. 71.401).

12. Barthélemon, Miss [Cecilia Maria]: *Sonata for the Piano-forte or Harpsichord, Composed & Dedicated to J. Haydn, M. D. Op. 3.* London: J. Bland, [1794].

HNV: 211   EA: No. 33 fol. 107

H Bn: Z 49.966   RISM: B 1074

> Title-page signed in the lower right corner: 'CMBarthelemon'.

15. Haigh, T[homas]: *Three Sonatas for the Piano-Forte, Composed & humbly dedicated to Dr. Haydn. Op. VIII.* London: Printed for the Author, & sold by Preston & Son, [*c.* 1795].

HNV: 217   EA: No. 11 fol. 103

H Bn: Z 41.132   RISM: H 1779

16. Bertini, Augustus [Benoît Auguste]: *Three Grand Sonatas, for the Piano-forte (with or without additional keys) With an Accompaniment for a Violin. Composed and Dedicated to Doctor Haydn. Op. I.* London: Printed for the Author, & sold by Longman & Broderip, [1795].

HNV: 218   EA: No. 28 fol. 105

H Bn: Z 41.129   RISM: –

Two parts. Keyboard part signed at the bottom of page two: 'ABertini'.

21. Latrobe, C[hristian] I[gnatius]: *Three Sonatas for the Pianoforte. Composed & Dedicated, by Permission, to Mr. Haydn. Op. III.* London: Printed for the Author, by J. Bland, [1791].

HNV: 226	EA: No. 31 fol. 107
H Bn: Z 41.212	RISM: L 1082

27. Campbell, Alexander: *Twelve songs Set to music by – Organist Edinburgh.* London: Printed for the Author, [after 1785].

HNV: 234	EA: No. 15 fol. 129
H Bn: Z 41.146	RISM: C 616

Date and signature at the bottom of the title-page: '25 Jany 1791. Alex. Campbell'. In an effort to honour Haydn with a specially dedicated work a mere few weeks after his arrival in London, Campbell took a copy of this earlier publication and had a page of manuscript dedication bound in it right after the title-page: 'From the mountains of Scotland. The Author of this little work presents it with his best Wishes to Signior Giuseppe Haydn of Vienna Whose divine Compositions have been heard with rapture & studied with Enthusiasm, even in this inclement country.'

40. Callcott, [John Wall] – Cooke, [Robert] – Danby, [John] – Hindle, [John] – Stevens, [Richard John Samuel] – Webbe, [Samuel the Elder]: *The Professional Collection of Glees, for Three, Four, and Five Voices.* London: Printed for the Authors, sold by Longman & Broderip, [1791].

HNV: 251	EA: No. 19 fol. 129
H Bn: Z 41.333	RISM: B/II/2, p. 292

Full score. Title-page signed in the lower left corner: 'JWCallcott'.

42. Dupuis, Tho[ma]s Sanders: *Pieces for the Organ or Harpsichord, Principally intended for the use of Young Organists. Op. VIII.* London: Preston & Son, [1794].

HNV: 254	EA: No. 23 fol. 105
H Bn: Z 41.620	RISM: D 3909

59. [Inscription on the spine:] *6 Operas viz. Rinaldo, Etearco, Hydaspes, Almahide, Pyrrhus, Clotilda.*

HNV: 261	EA: No. 29 fol. 121
H Bn: Z 41.126	

This item colligates the following six vocal scores.

[59a] Hendel [Handel, George Frideric]: *Arie dell' Opera di Rinaldo.* London: J.

Walsh & J. Hare, [1711].

RISM: H 278–279

[59b] [Bononcini, Giovanni Battista]: *Songs in the Opera of Etearco.* London: J. Walsh & J. Hare, [1711].

RISM: B 3586

[59c] [Mancini, Francesco]: *Songs in the new Opera, Call'd Hydaspes.* London: I. Walsh & I. Hare, [1710].

RISM: M 297

[59d] [attributed to Bononcini, Giovanni Battista]: *Songs in the new Opera, Call'd Almahide.* London: I. Walsh & I. Hare, [1710].

RISM: B 3554

[59e] [Scarlatti, Alessandro]: *Songs in the new Opera, Call'd Pyrrhus and Demetrius.* London: I. Walsh & I. Hare, [1709].

RISM: S 1176

[59f] [Conti, Francesco Bartolomeo]: *Songs in the new Opera, Call'd Clotilda.* London: I. Walsh & I. Hare, [1709].

RISM: C 3510

61. [Six full scores bound together.]

HNV: 275   EA: No. 33 fol. 131

H Bn: Z 41.128

[61a] Lampugnani, [Giovanni Battista]: *The Favourite Songs in the Opera Call'd Siroe.* London: I. Walsh, [1755].

RISM: L 515

See also **[61f]**.

[61b] Galuppi, [Baldassare]: *The Favourite Songs in the Opera Call'd Ricimero.* London: I. Walsh, [1755].

RISM: G 286

The first aria is by 'Sig[no]r [Leonardo] Leo'.

[61c] Perez, [Davide]: *The Favourite Songs in the Opera Call'd Ezio*. London: I. Walsh, [1755].

RISM: P 1330

Includes music by Hasse as well (see RISM H 2251 and B/II/2, p.176).

[61d] *The Favourite Songs in the Opera Call'd Ipermestra*. London: I. Walsh, [1754].

RISM: H 2255

Includes two arias by Hasse and four by Lampugnani.

[61e] [Hasse, Johann Adolf]: *Four Songs in the Opera Call'd Il Demofonte Sung by Sig[no]ra Mingotti*. London: To be had at Sig[no]r De Giardini's Lodgings, Mr. Cox's Music Shop and Mr. Smith's Music Shop, [1755].

RISM: H 2248

Includes music by Nicolò Jommelli as well (see RISM J 586).

[61f] [Lampugnani, Giovanni Battista]: *The Two favourite Songs in the Opera call'd Siroe, sung by Sign[o]ra Mingotti*. [London: J. Cox], [1755].

RISM: L 516

See also **[61a]**.

62, 63, 64. *A Collection of Catches Canons Glees Duetts &c. Selected from the Works of the most Eminent Composers Antient and Modern*. Vols. 2, 3, 4. Edinburgh: J. Sibbald and Corri & Sutherland, [1780?].

HNV: 276[a, b, c]   EA: No. 12 fol. 127

H Bn: Z 41.325/2, 3, 4   RISM: B/II/2, pp. 62–63

Full scores.

66. Cooke, Dr. Benjamin: *Nine Glees and two duets, (never before Printed) Composed by the late —. Published from the original manuscripts by his Son, Robert Cooke; Organist of St. Martin's in the Fields. Opera V*. London: Longman & Broderip, 1795.

HNV: 282   EA: No. 22 fol. 129

H Bn: Z 41.168   RISM: C 3556

Full score. Dedication in the upper right corner of the title-page: 'With Mr Robt Cooke's respectful Compliments to Dr. Haydn'. Page one signed in the lower right corner: 'Robt Cooke'. The list of subscribers includes 'Giuseppe Haydn, Mus. D. Ox'.

75. Harrison, Mr. [Samuel]: *Never till now. A Favorite Glee for four Voices as sung with the greatest Applause at Harrison & Knyvett's Vocal Concerts Willis's Rooms, Harmoniz'd.* London: J. Dale, [1794].

HNV: 291   EA: No. 25 fol. 129

H Bn: Z 41.133   RISM: H 2134

For soloists, chorus and orchestra. Full score.

76. Handel, [George Frideric]: *Jephtha an Oratorio.* London: I. Walsh, [1752].

HNV: 260   EA: No. 66 fol. 45

H Bn: Z 41.136   RISM: H 578

Full score. Does not include the secco recitativo and choral numbers.

77. Webbe, S[amuel] Jun[io]r: *Address to the Thames.* London: J. Bland, [n. d.].

HNV: 288[b]   EA: No. 26[b] fol. 129

H Bn: Z 41.316   RISM: —

For voice and keyboard.

78. Callcott, I[ohn] W[all]: *Explanation of the Notes, Marks, Words &c., used in Music.* London: Printed for the Author, [1792].

HNV: 293   EA: No. 52 fol. 149

H Bn: —   RISM: B/VI/1, p. 197

In view of its content this item should have been catalogued among Haydn's books.

84. Webbe, Samuel [the Elder]: *The favorite Glee of Hence all ye Vain Delights.* London: J. Bland, [n. d.].

HNV: 288[c]   EA: No. 26[c] fol. 129

H Bn: Z 41.314   RISM: W 350

Full score.

85. Schroeter, J[ohann] S[amuel]: *Six Sonatas for the Piano Forte or Harpsichord with Accompanyments for a Violin and Bass. Opera II.* London: Ganer, [c. 1772].

HNV: 299   EA: No. 18 fol. 105

H Bn: Z 41.255   RISM: S 2166

Three parts.

86. Schroeter, J[ohann] S[amuel]: *Six Sonatas for the Piano Forte, or Harpsichord, with an Accompanyment for a German Flute or Violin. Opera 4.* London: Longman & Broderip, [*c.* 1775].

HNV: 301   EA: No. 78 fol. 113

H Bn: Z 41.258   RISM: S 2184

     Two parts.

87. Schroeter, J[ohann] S[amuel]: *Three Sonatas for the Piano Forte or Harpsichord With Accompaniments for a Violin and Violoncello. Opera VI.* [added in ink:] '2^d Set'. Edinburgh: Corri & Co., [*c.* 1785].

HNV: 303   EA: No. 75 fol. 111

H Bn: Z 41.256   RISM: S 2197

     Three parts.

88. Schroeter, J[ohann] S[amuel]: *Six Concertos for the Harpsichord or Piano Forte, with Accompanyments for Two Violins, a Tenor and Bass. Opera V.* London: J. Dale, [*c.* 1775].

HNV: 302   EA: No. 74 fol. 111

H Bn: Z 41.305   RISM: S 2189

     Five parts.

89. Schroeter, J[ohann] S[amuel]: *Six Concertos for the Harpsichord, or Piano Forte; With an Accompanyment for Two Violins, and a Bass. Opera III.* London: J. Dale, [*c.* 1774].

HNV: 300   EA: No. 77 fol. 111

H Bn: Z 41.306   RISM: S 2173

     Four parts.

90. Schroeter, J[ohann] S[amuel]: *Three Quintetto's for the Harpsichord or Piano Forte, Flute, Violin, Tenor, and Violoncello, one by G[aetano] Pugnani, and two by –.* London: Will[ia]m Napier, [*c.* 1778].

HNV: 298   EA: No. 17 fol. 105

H Bn: Z 41.332   RISM: B/II/2, p. 297 (see S 2161)

     Five parts.

91. Diettenhofer, [Joseph]: *The celebrated canon: Non nobis Domine, adapted as a Fugue for the Organ.* London: Preston & son (for the author), [*c.* 1785].

HNV: 304	EA: –
H Bn: –	RISM: D 3022

Based on a canon attributed to William Byrd.

94, 95, 96. *The Ladies Collection, of Catches, Glees, Canons, Canzonets, Madrigals, &c. Selected from the Works of the Most Eminent Composers. By John Bland.* London: Bland, [*c.* 1790].

HNV: 277[a]	EA: No. 15[a] fol. 119
H Bn: ZR 796/3, 2, 4	RISM: B/II/2, p. 214

Full scores. Nos 27 (pp. 262–71), 26 (pp. 252–61) and 30 (pp. 292–301) of the series. See also **140**.

97. Webbe, S[amuel, the Elder]: *Ode, on St Cecilia, for Six Voices.* London: Printed for the Author, [*c.* 1795].

HNV: 288[a]	EA: No. 26[a] fol. 129
H Bn: Z 41.315	RISM: W 285

Vocal score. Title-page signed in the lower right corner: 'S. W. 18[?]2'.

107. Webbe, S[amuel] Jun[io]r: *Six French Ariettes, newly arranged for the Voice and Piano-Forte.* London: Longman & Broderip, [n. d.].

HNV: 289	EA: No. 24 fol. 129
H Bn: Z 41.313	RISM: –

Title-page signed in the lower right corner: 'S. W'.

108. Attwood, Tho[ma]s: *The Adopted Child, A Musical Drama in Two Acts, As performed at the Theatre Royal, Drury Lane.* London: Longman & Broderip, [1795].

HNV: 312	EA: No. 79 fol. 113
H Bn: Z 41.616	RISM: A 2676

Vocal score. Title-page signed in the lower right corner: 'Thoˢ Attwood'.

109. Webbe, Sam[ue]l, Sen[io]r & Jun[io]r: *Ninth Book. A Collection of Vocal Music, In two, three, four and five parts.* London: Printed for the Authors, and sold by Longman & Broderip, [1792].

HNV: 290	EA: No. 23 fol. 129
H Bn: Z 41.312	RISM: W 304

Full score.

110. Barthélemon, Mrs. Maria: *Three Hymns, and Three Anthems. Op. 3.* London: Printed for the Authoress, to be had of J. Bland, [1795].

HNV: 209   EA: No. 13 fol. 119

H Bn: Z 41.143   RISM: B 1133

> With keyboard accompaniment. Title-page signed in the lower right corner: 'MBarthelemon'. The printed list of subscribers includes both 'Haydn Dr.' and 'Haydn Mrs.'

111. Jenkins, George: *New Scotch Music, Consisting of Slow Airs, Strathspeys, Quick Reels, Country Dances, and a Medley on a New Plan with a Bass for a Violoncello or Harpsichord.* Bloomsbury [i.e. London]: To be had of the Author, [1794].

HNV: 313   EA: No. 64 fol. 111

H Bn: Z 41.192   RISM: J 526

> Keyboard reduction. Also includes as separate appendices *The Prince of Wales Medley*, *Jenkins's Compliments to Dr. Haydn* and *Haydn's Strathspey*.

114. Tomich, F[rancesco] [Tomeš, František Václav]: *Three Sonatas for the Piano Forte or Harpsichord with an Accompaniment for a Violin or Flute ad libitum. Op. 3.* London: Printed for the Author, sold by Longman & Broderip, [n. d.].

HNV: 315   EA: No. 66 fol. 111

H Bn: Z 41.685   RISM: T 946

> The title-pages of both parts are signed in the lower right corner: 'Tomich'.

115. Tomich, Francesco [Tomeš, František Václav]: *A Sonata for the Piano-forte, with Accompaniments for a Violin & Violoncello.* London: Printed for the Author, [*c.* 1795].

HNV: 314   EA: No. 65 fol. 111

H Bn: Z 41.686   RISM: T 945

> Three parts. The title-page of the keyboard part is signed in the lower right corner: 'Tomich'.

116. Nugent, Rothe: *Six French Romances, and one Italian Arietta, for the Harpsichord or Piano-Forte, with an Accompaniment for the Violin to the Italian Arietta.* London: Printed for & to be had of the Author, and at R[ober]t Birchall's, [1794].

HNV: 316   EA: No. 40 fol. 131

H Bn: Z 41.265   RISM: N 813

> Title-page signed in the lower left corner: 'R Nugent'.

119. Clari, Gio[vanni] Carlo Maria: *Sei Madrigali, Mesi in Musica. Tom I–II.* London: Robert Bremner, 1740 (vol. 1) and 1742 (vol. 2).

HNV: 317   EA: No. 43 fol. 131

H Bn: ZR 651   RISM: C 2561 or C 2562

For two to three voices with basso continuo. Two full scores, lacking title-page, containing four madrigals (the third volume of 1745, featuring two further pieces, is absent). The composer was unidentified in both HBV and HNV. Even RISM lists the **H** Bn copy as anonymous under AN 1625 but comparison of the first pages establishes its identity to the Clari publication with certainty.

120. Barthélemon, Miss [Cecilia Maria]: *Three Sonatas for the Piano-Forte, or Harpsichord. The Second with an Accompaniment for the Violin. Opera Prima.* [London]: To be had of the Author, [1791].

HNV: 210   EA: No. 32 fol. 107

H Bn: Z 41.142   RISM: B 1072

Full score (no separate violin part). Title-page signed in the lower right corner: 'CMBarthelemon'. The list of subscribers includes 'Sig. J. Haydn'.

121. Clementi, Muzio: *Three Sonatas for the Piano Forte or Harpsichord with accompaniments for a Violin and Violoncello. Op. XXVIII.* London: Preston & Son, [1792].

HNV: 319   EA: No. 68 fol. 111

H Bn: Z 41.166   RISM: C 2978

Three parts.

127. Barthélemon, F[rançois] H[ippolyte]: *Glee for the Anniversary of the Philanthropic Society, as Perform'd on that Occasion.* London: Printed for the Author by R. Wornum, [n. d.].

HNV: 208   EA: No. 17 fol. 129

H Bn: Z 41.141   RISM: B 1094

Full score. Title-page signed in the lower right corner: 'F. H. Barthelemon'.

137. Burney, Carlo [Charles]: *XII Canzonetti a due voci in Canone. Poesia dell Abate Metastasio.* London: Longman & Broderip, [1794].

HNV: 327   EA: No. 42 fol. 131

H Bn: Z 41.127   RISM: B 5048

Inscription in the upper-right corner of the title-page: 'From the Author'.

139. [Two full scores bound together.]

HNV: 329   EA: No. 36 fol. 131

H Bn: Z 41.103

[**139a**] Abingdon, [Bertie Willoughby] Earl of: *A Representation of the Execution of Mary Queen of Scot's in Seven Views. The Music Composed for and adapted to each View.* London: Tebaldo Monzani, [1791].

RISM: A 153

For chorus and orchestra.

[**139b**] Abingdon, [Bertie Willoughby] Earl of: *A Selection of twelve Psalms and Hymns, Set to Music according to the Rules laid down for the Church, both Cathedral and Parochial, and with a View to promote the Established Religion of the Country, to which is prefixed a Print, as taken from the Revelations of St. John, and adapted to the purpose.* London: Monzani, [1793].

RISM: A 148

For soloists, chorus and orchestra.

140. *The Ladies Collection, of Catches, Glees, Canons, Canzonets, Madrigals, &c. Selected from the Works of the Most Eminent Composers. By John Bland.* London: J. Bland, [c. 1787].

HNV: 277[b]   EA: No. 15[b] fol. 119

H Bn: ZR 796/1   RISM: B/II/2, p. 214

Full score. Vol. 2 of the series, including Nos 13–24 (pp. 122–241). See also **94, 95, 96**.

141. *Select Collection of the Most Admired Songs, Duetts &c. From Operas in the highest esteem, And from other Works, in Italian, English, French, Scotch, Irish, &c. In Four Books. – Volume 3^d Consisting of National Airs, Notturni, Duetts, Terzetts, Canzonets, Rondo's, Catches & Glees In the Italian, French, English, Scotch and Irish Languages.* London: Corri, Dussek & Co., [1795?].

HNV: 278   EA: No. 7 fol. 119

H Bn: –   RISM: B/II/2, pp. 105–06

142. *A Selection of the most Favourite Scots-Songs Chiefly Pastoral. Adapted for the Harpsichord, with an Accompaniment for a Violin, by Eminent Masters.* [Vol. 1.] London: Will[ia]m Napier, [1790].

HNV: 279 and 280   EA: No. 14 fol. 127

H Bn: Z 41.335   RISM: B/II/2, p. 107

> Full score. The two HNV numbers are due to the fact that, as HBV clarifies, Haydn owned two copies.

143. *The Psalms of David for the Use of Parish Churches. The Words selected by the Rev. Sir Adam Gordon Bart. M. A. The Music selected, adapted, and composed, by Dr. [Samuel] Arnold, Organist and Composer to His Majesty, Assisted by J[ohn] W[all] Callcott, M. B. Organist of St. Paul, Covent Garden.* London: John Stockdale and George Goulding, [1791].

HNV: 281   EA: No. 13 fol. 127

H Bn: Z 41.108   RISM: A 2409

> For 1 to 4 voices and figured bass. Full score.

153. Sime, D[avid]: *The Edinburgh musical miscellany: a Collection of the most approved Scotch, English, and Irish songs, Set to music.* Vols 1–2. Edinburgh: Printed for W. Gordon, T. Brown [etc.], 1792–93.

HNV: 339   EA: No. 16 fol. 145

H Bn: –   RISM: –

> Neither HBV nor HNV clarifies which volume Haydn owned. Remark in HBV: 'In Taschenformat gebunden'.

155. Tattersall, William Dechair: *Improved psalmody, in three parts, printed separately for each voice: Or, a poetical version of the psalms, originally written by the late Rev. James Merrick.* London: Rivingtons [etc.], 1795.

HNV: 341   EA: No. 45 fol. 133

H Bn: –   RISM: –

> Three parts. Remark in HBV: 'In Taschenformat gebunden'.

A Newly Discovered Libretto Edited by Haydn

OTTO BIBA

E VEN THOUGH, at the present time, Haydn's operas are not yet firmly established in the performance schedules of the international opera world and their
staging is still a fortuitous exception not to be taken for granted, it is clear that for
Haydn composing operas was no mere duty but something that was central to his
compositional activity. About his two operas *L'isola disabitata* and *La fedeltà premiata*
he wrote confidently to his publisher Artaria on 27 May 1781: 'I assure you that a
comparable work has not yet been heard in Paris' – which was then the capital of
modern opera – 'and perhaps not in Vienna either'.[1] Further, Haydn considered it
to be his misfortune that he lived in the country, where his operas were first
performed, and not in a hub of musical life.

This 'countryside' was the opera house of the Esterházy princes, part of the pala-
tial complex of Eszterháza – today called Fertöd – which was not small. The audience consisted mainly of courtiers and servants of the prince. Haydn had, however,
an excellent ensemble of singers, a superb court orchestra and a generous budget at
his disposal. Even Empress Maria Theresia valued the performances above those of
the Viennese Court Opera, saying that she had to travel to Eszterháza if she wanted

---

1.   'Dann ich versichere, daß dergleichen Arbeith in Paris noch nicht ist gehört worden und vielleicht
     ebenso wenig in Wien, mein Unglück ist nur der Aufenthalt auf dem Lande', *Gesammelte Briefe
     und Aufzeichnungen*, p. 97.

to hear a good opera.[2] All this is worth remembering in the light of the greater fame and recognition Haydn has subsequently received as the composer of string quartets, oratorios and symphonies.

Since the publication in 1959 of Dénes Bartha and László Somfai's book *Haydn als Opernkapellmeister*, it has become more and more generally acknowledged that Haydn did not only compose operas himself, but also rehearsed and directed operas by other composers, often – as was customary at the time – editing them for his opera house. In his youth in Vienna, Haydn was already composing *Singspiele*, and as early as 1762, one year after his appointment as Esterházy Vice Kapellmeister, he composed his first opera, *Acide*, for that court. From then until 1776 Haydn wrote at least a further five operas, and possibly others which have not survived. During this period, Haydn was an opera composer who rehearsed his own works and performed them in the palace at Eisenstadt on a stage constructed for the occasion.

When, however, the opera house built by Prince Nicolaus I in the summer palace of Eszterháza was opened in 1776, an opera ensemble was established and Haydn assumed the duties of music director. The opera ensemble remained in existence until 1790, which meant that Haydn gained nearly fifteen years' experience in that role. The repertory consisted exclusively of Italian operas, serious and comic.

During this period, there were eighty-eight premières and six new productions of previously performed operas. Ten further operas were rehearsed by Haydn, but – for one reason or another – not brought to performance.[3] (For comparison, within the same time period, the Viennese Court Opera could scarcely match this number of Italian opera premières.) Hence in these fifteen years Haydn was occupied professionally with almost a hundred operas, only six of which were his own compositions.

It appears, though, that Haydn was not only music director but managed much else to do with the performance of opera at Eszterháza. He selected the works to be performed and discussed his choice with Prince Nicolaus, who made the final decisions. (Mozart's *Le nozze di Figaro* and Salieri's *Axur*, for example, were rejected.) It was also part of Haydn's task to cast suitable singers – indeed, he was responsible for putting the ensemble together – and to engage new singers when vacancies arose. In short, he fulfilled all the duties of an opera manager.

Evidence has recently emerged, however, that Haydn was not only music director and manager of opera at Eszterháza, but also edited the libretto for dramatic

2. 'Wenn ich eine gute Oper hören will, gehe ich nach Esterház', as reported by Carl Ferdinand Pohl, *Joseph Haydn*, 3 vols (Berlin, etc.: Sacco, etc., 1875–1927), II/1 (Leipzig: Breitkopf und Härtel, 1882) p. 62.
3. Dénes Bartha and László Somfai, *Haydn als Opernkapellmeister* (Budapest: Schott, 1960), pp. 63–165.

Fig. 1. Title-page of the libretto of Marco Coltellini, *Piramo e Tisbe*
(Vienna: Kurzböck, 1777)

purposes too. Until now, all known documents pertaining to Haydn's arrangements of operas by other composers have dealt with purely musical issues: cuts, changes and additions made to scores to suit the ensemble of singers available, adding or losing arias in order to adjust the balance between them, according to the strength of their personality, vocal or otherwise.

Recently, however, the archive of the Gesellschaft der Musikfreunde in Wien purchased a printed libretto containing textual corrections and additions in Haydn's handwriting. Such a document had hitherto been unknown, and it opens an entirely new perspective on Haydn's work for the Esterházy court opera house.

The document in question is the libretto by Marco Coltellini to Venanzio Rauzzini's 'azione tragica per musica' entitled *Piramo e Tisbe*, printed in Vienna by Joseph Kurzböck in 1777, when the work was performed at the Vienna Court Opera (Fig. 1).[4] Another copy of this libretto has survived, along with other Viennese libretti of the same period, in the Esterházy collection of librettos, as described by Harich.[5] They are found here because the family had its own box both in the Vienna Court Opera Theatre and in the Kärntnertor Theater; whenever they were in Vienna, they would, where possible, have attended performances. The new document that has come to light was clearly Haydn's personal copy. We may imagine that Prince Nicolaus Esterházy liked the opera in Vienna and instructed Haydn to plan its production at Eszterháza.

Haydn's first, preparatory step, then – regardless of whether he had become acquainted with the opera in Vienna or not – was to work through the textbook in great detail. The annotations there show Haydn as editor of the drama. They are in no way concerned with the music, only with the verbal text, correcting its dramatic weaknesses and problems. A number of examples may illustrate this.

The first act begins with Tisbe's entrance, in a 'sala' which the libretto does not describe more clearly. She is searching for Piramo. The audience does not know where she is, or where she hopes to find him. In a recitative she sings, 'I seek you; oh God, but all that my anxious soul can find of its lost contentment is a sad and painful memory.'[6] What memory? The memory of Piramo in general or one particular memory? Haydn helps the audience and supplies clarification by adding a short description. After 'I seek you; oh God', he added, 'in the sweet place where I was once happy'.[7] Now the audience knows that this is a place where this woman was, for one day, happy and content with her Piramo; for her, this is a place of sweet memories. This fact is extremely important for the understanding of the further action because it is precisely here, in the 'sala', that she does, in fact, find her Piramo.

4.　Archiv der Gesellschaft der Musikfreunde in Wien, Joseph Haydn, Briefe und Aufzeichnungen, 9.

5.　Johann Harich, *Esterházy-Musikgeschichte im Spiegel der zeitgenössischen Textbücher*, Burgenländische Forschungen, 39 (Eisenstadt: Burgenländisches Landesarchiv, 1959), p. 44.

6.　'Ti cerco; oh Dio, ma non ritrova che del perduto ben l'alma affannosa qualche trista memoria, e tormentosa.'

7.　'Ti cerco; oh Dio, [Haydn's insertion:] in questo dolce albergo de' miei contenti un di; [end of Haydn's insertion] ma non ritrova che del perduto ben l'alma affannosa qualche trista memoria, e tormentosa.'

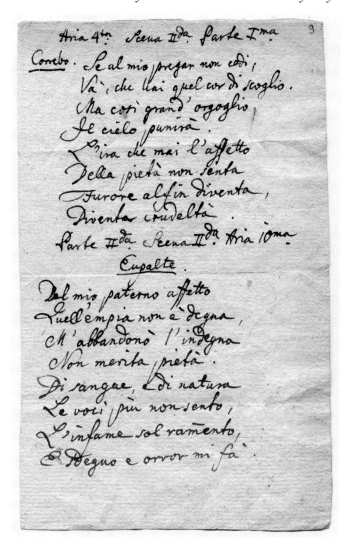

Fig. 2. Marco Coltellini, *Piramo e Tisbe*: verses added in Haydn's autograph.
Gesellschaft der Musikfreunde in Wien.

Another example may be cited from the second scene of Act I. The lovers have
fled together because they cannot expect their parents' agreement to their marriage.
In an aria, Correbo, a friend of Tisbe's father, Eupalte, asks the latter to permit
Tisbe's marriage to Piramo in spite of the fact that Piramo comes from an enemy
family and although Tisbe eloped with him.

In a very conventional manner, Correbo adds a warning to his request: 'If you do
not hear my plea [on behalf of your daughter], then your heart is as stone; if you are

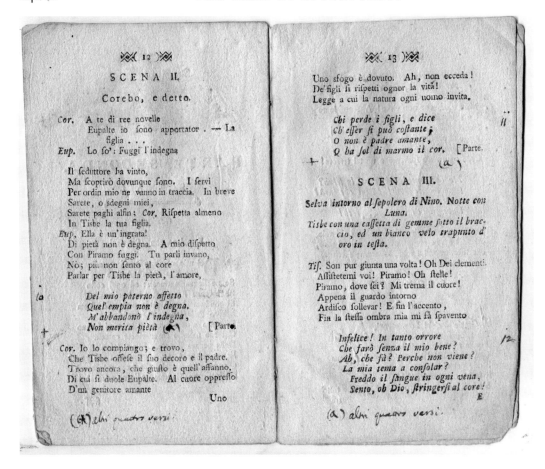

Fig. 3. Marco Coltellini, *Piramo e Tisbe*, annotated by Haydn to indicate
the placing of the extra verses he has supplied.
Gesellschaft der Musikfreunde in Wien.

so proud, the heavens will punish you.'[8] These are hollow operatic clichés. Haydn
recognizes this weakness and adds four lines of poetry, following the seven syllables
per line and rhyming pattern used by Coltellini (Fig. 2): 'The anger that blinds one
to compassion will turn ultimately to rage and cruelty.'[9] This is his warning to

8.   'Se al mio pregar non cedi,
   Và, che hai quel cor di scoglio.
   Ma così grand' orgoglio
   Il cielo punirà.'

9.   'L'ira che mai l'affetto
   Della pietà non senta
   Furore alfin diventa,
   Diventa crudeltà.'

Eupalte, a warning against the momentum engendered by uncontrolled emotion. Haydn brings to life characters from mythology with human feelings familiar to his audience.

In another example, from the second scene of Act II, Correbo tries in vain to moderate Eupalte's anger at his daughter. In his aria, Eupalte declares, 'This impious one is not worthy of my fatherly affection. The unworthy one who has abandoned me does not deserve compassion.'[10] Coltellini's phrases are, once again, rather trite and feeble. Here, too, Haydn adds four lines in verse to elevate the emotional content (Fig. 2): 'I no longer hear the voice of my blood, nor the voice of Nature. I only think of the impious one. I feel humiliation and horror.'[11] Yes, Eupalte is angry but he is also suffering. Haydn aims to make the anger comprehensible. Eupalte suffers from the shame inflicted on him by his daughter's running away; he sees this as humiliation, and he is horrified. All this overrides his paternal emotions, which he can no longer feel. Naturally, the audience's sympathies remain with the lovers; but Haydn's extra lines show the father not merely acting woodenly in the manner of an archetypal opera villain, but also moved by the authentic emotions of pain and shame.

A last example may be cited from the third scene of Act II. Eupalte goes offstage, according to Coltellini in a rage, according to Haydn also full of pain. Correbo remains and reflects – in Coltellini's text – rather tritely and woodenly on what he has just witnessed. Correbo declares in a recitative, 'I pity him. I think that Tisbe has injured both her honour and her father. I also think that Eupalte is right to feel tormented. The oppressed heart of a loving parent needs release. But it must never become excessive. Everyone must respect the lives of their children. It is a law which Nature invites all men to obey.' In the ensuing aria, Correbo continues, 'He who loses a child and declares he is unaffected is either not a loving father, or has a heart only of marble.'[12]

10.   'Del mio paterno affetto
        Quell'empia non è degna,
        M'abbandonò l'indegna
        Non merita pietà.'

11.   'Di sangue, e di natura
        Le voci più non sento,
        L'infame sol rammento,
        E sdegno e orror mi fa.'

12.   'Io lo compiango; e trovo, che Tisbe offese il suo decoro e il padre. Trovo ancora, che giusto è
        quell'affanno, di cui si duole Eupalte. Al cuore oppresso d'un genitore amante uno sfogo è dovuto.
        Ah, non ecceda! De'figli si rispetti ognor la vita! Legge a cui la natura ogni uomo invita.' [Aria:]

        'Chi perde i figli, e dice
        Ch'esser si può costante;
        O non è padre amante,
        O ha sol di marmo il cor.'

This time Haydn adds four lines of an almost pastoral nature which are striking in their emotional contrast: 'The wild beasts of the forest love their offspring and even the mute plants seem to feel love.'[13] Here the dramatic editor is naturally thinking of the composer. When forests, animals and plants are contrasted to the heart of stone, the composer is literally able to speak with different voices. Haydn the librettist is setting up opportunities for a wealth of contrasting musical imagery.

These small but telling examples demonstrate that the creation of authentic characters on the opera stage was clearly of primary concern to him. Hence – and this is the most important insight that this new source affords us – Haydn's arrangement of operas by other composers might begin by reviewing the libretto and editing it where necessary. Though he might begin with the text and not the music, however, these initial editing activities would of course give rise to significant musical consequences: music from Rauzzini's existing arias could not simply be repeated or re-arranged to accommodate the new text. Since, as we have seen, the new words often explored new and contrasting emotions there would be a corresponding need to convey these with new music which suitably expressed and reflected these new feelings and situations.

This leads to another question which will have to concern us in the future. In many of the operas that Haydn brought to performance in Eszterháza, he cut arias and inserted new ones which he had composed himself. We know that he often did this to accommodate singers or for other musical reasons. But now, with the example of this copy of the libretto of *Piramo e Tisbe* before us, it is appropriate to ask how often these changes might have arisen for purely dramatic reasons, such as, as we have seen, character portrayal, for which the necessary starting point was the words themselves. In the past such questions have not been much considered but perhaps, now, the operas which Haydn adapted for performance under his direction ought to be re-examined for evidence that they demonstrate the work of Haydn the dramatist.

Despite Haydn's work on the libretto, this opera was not performed in the Eszterháza opera theatre under his management. One can only speculate as to why this was. Ultimately, as we have seen, the decision on this point would have rested with Haydn's employer, but perhaps it was felt that, even with Haydn's proposed improvements, Coltellini's text could not attain the dramatic heights of Ovid's *Pyramus and Thisbe*, or Shakespeare's *Romeo and Juliet* and *Midsummer Night's Dream*. Coltellini's narrative simply relates – neither originally nor dramatically – the story

13.   'Amano tra le selve
        I figli lor le belve,
        E fin le mute piante
        Sembran sentire amor.'

of two lovers who want to remain together in spite of parental opposition. Neither, evidently, did this inspire Haydn to abandon Rauzzini's music completely and write a new opera on the underlying libretto himself.

If we assume that Prince Esterházy saw Rauzzini's opera in Vienna and encouraged Haydn to perform the work also in Eszterháza, for which reason Haydn would then have studied the libretto, the fact that the opera failed to come to performance throws a significant light on Haydn's position. There is no indication in the Esterházy Archive that a score was acquired.[14] It appears therefore that Haydn's judgement as to the viability of the work as an opera was on the basis of examining the libretto alone. No doubt he would draw on his own experience as an opera composer who similarly had to consider the musical and dramatic potential of any words he was considering setting. Without reference to Rauzzini's score, Haydn evidently attempted to improve Coltellini's libretto but ultimately found the opera unusable. If this was truly the case, it suggests that even if the prince had the last say as to which operas were selected for performance, on this occasion at least he appears to have deferred to Haydn the opera manager, music director and dramatist. The libretto in the possession of Prince Esterházy may have indicated the prince's interest, and that interest led Haydn to explore the possibility of revision and performance in the prince's opera house, but no performance in fact took place, for whatever reason.

As to when these annotations were made by Haydn, one can surmise that they were prompted by the performances of the opera that were given by Katharina Schindler's company in the Kärntnertor Theater at the end of 1776 (28 and 31 December) and early 1777 (twelve performances in January and February[15]), and were made soon after. In any event, they are likely to predate Nunziato Porta's appointment as director of opera at Eszterháza in July 1781. In addition to determining the repertory, Porta was also experienced in writing and adapting libretti, so it is unlikely that Haydn would have concerned himself with improvements to the verbal text after Porta's arrival. Dating this activity to some time after February 1777 also accords with the contemporary practice of presenting at Eszterháza operas which had been well received in Vienna. This practice continued through Porta's years at Eszterháza (to 1790), but was less common after 1786.

Is it possible that Haydn did not compose the new texts himself, but instead copied them from someone who did? This question is less important with respect to prose than it is with respect to the verses expanding the three arias. All insertions are in Haydn's handwriting: the one prose passage is added directly into the printed

14. Bartha and Somfai, *Haydn als Opernkapellmeister*, pp. 177–378.

15. Bibliothek der Gesellschaft der Musikfreunde in Wien, MS, Leopold von Sonnleithner, 'Materialien zu einer Geschichte der Oper und des Balletts in Wien', I, 1776–90; Pohl, *Joseph Haydn*, II, 377.

libretto and the verses expanding the arias are written on a separately inserted page. All the handwritten text on the libretto – the new prose and verses for the recitatives and the arias, the numbering of printed texts for the arias and ensembles, and the occasional correction of a word of phrase – appears to have been written by Haydn in ink[16] as part of a single process. Is it possible that Haydn did not seek assistance from others in the addition of these textual improvements, but undertook this role himself? If so, then this annotated libretto of *Piramo e Tisbe* is unexpected evidence of Haydn's skill as a poet in the Italian language.

16.   The only exception is in Act I, scene 1 where Haydn has changed three words in red crayon.

The First Performers and Audiences of Haydn's Chamber Music

INGRID FUCHS

I N 1791 the appearance of Haydn's String Quartets op. 64 in print was announced in the *Wiener Zeitung* as follows:[1]

> Until now there have been general complaints about the extraordinary difficulties experienced in the performance of Haydn's works. Mr. Haydn has resolved this [problem] in these 6 quartets [by showing] that he knows how to combine art, playfulness and good taste with the simplest facility in such a manner that both artist and mere amateur will be completely satisfied.

This notice – obviously promotional in purpose – was intended to convince Viennese music lovers that in these quartets Haydn had tempered his compositional skill to ensure the works were easily playable yet satisfied the needs of a discerning audience. This advertisement, exactly like another for the first edition of Mozart's last three string quartets (K575, 589, 590),[2] identifies a certain class of performers

---

1.   'Bisher beschwerte man sich allgemein über die ausserordentliche Schwere, mit welcher Haydns Werke exequirt werden konnten. Dieses hat Herr Haydn in diesen 6 Quartetten vermieden, […] und gezeigt,] dass er Kunst, Tändeley und Geschmack mit der leichtesten Ausführung zu verbinden gewusst hat, dergestalt, dass sowohl der Künstler, als der bloße Liebhaber vollkommen befriediget seyn wird.' *Wiener Zeitung*, 23 February 1791, quoted by Horst Walter, 'Zum Wiener Streichquartett der Jahre 1780 bis 1800', *Haydn-Studien*, 7 (1998), 289–314 (p. 306).

2.   *Wiener Zeitung*, 28 December 1791, quoted in *Mozart: die Dokumente seines Lebens*, ed. by Otto Erich Deutsch (Kassel: Bärenreiter, 1961), p. 376.

Fig. 1. Chamber music performance as depicted in print by Daniel Chodowiecki, 1774.

who are not only 'amateurs' but also 'artists'. In other words, the potential buyers and performers of these quartets will be 'connoisseurs'.

But who, then, were these skilful amateur performers who constituted the market for chamber music in the second half of the eighteenth century? Who was the audience for whom not only Mozart but also his contemporaries composed their quartets, trios, sonatas, etc? And where, indeed, were these works played? Today the term 'chamber music' is generally used to indicate the size of the performing group (usually one to a part), rather than the location of the performance, since today all such pieces may be performed in concert halls with a large audience. Originally, though, the term was used specifically to denote the performance venue: *musica da camera* and *Kammermusik* indicated music for the 'chamber' as opposed to the church, theatre or even military occasion. These performances usually took place in aristocratic circles, but in the second half of the eighteenth century, with the rise of the bourgeoisie, they became more and more prevalent in the homes of the upper middle class in Vienna, and indeed became a veritable status symbol of bourgeois culture. This private or sometimes semi-public music-making by both nobility and bourgeoisie took place in music rooms and salons, venues which were ideal for ensembles of solo players (Fig. 1), whereas public concerts of music needing more performers were accessible to anyone upon purchase of an entrance ticket, and took place in Vienna in halls rented for the purpose, or in theatres when these had no performances. There were, as yet, no special concert halls in Vienna.[3]

At that time, making music at home, whether for one's own pleasure, for the family circle or for some larger social occasion, had come to play a large role in all levels of society.[4] Frequently the performers were from the nobility themselves, since musical training was part of every young aristocrat's education. If a court orchestra was engaged, its musicians might be supplemented by other servants from the household, many of whom would have been appointed on account of being able to play a musical instrument in addition to having the necessary domestic skills.[5] Particularly in smaller aristocratic residences, bourgeois music lovers were also, at times, invited to join the nobility in making chamber music. In the second half of the eighteenth century, music became a fashionable element of bourgeois education too, as the middle class strove to imitate the aristocracy. This increasingly musical bourgeoisie consisted of well-to-do civil servants (sometimes in due course elevated to the lower ranks of the nobility), academics from various disciplines, and prosperous landowners, merchants and tradesmen. 'You will hardly find a good house in which the young lady does not tinkle on the piano, or the young master plays with great importance upon his violin' was the slightly malicious description by Johann Baptist Mittrowsky[6] in 1802.[7] Similarly, an unidentified writer in the *Neueste Sittengemählde von Wien* of 1801 stated that:[8]

3. On this subject see Otto Biba, 'Grundzüge des Konzertwesens in Wien zu Mozarts Zeit', *Mozart-Jahrbuch*, 1978/79 (1979), 132–43; Mary Sue Morrow, *Concert Life in Haydn's Vienna: Aspects of a Developing Musical and Social Institution* (Stuyvesant, NY: Pendragon, 1989); Dexter Edge, 'Review Article: Mary Sue Morrow, Concert Life in Haydn's Vienna', *Haydn Yearbook*, 17 (1992), 108–66.

4. See Walter Salmen, *Haus-und Kammermusik: privates Musizieren im gesellschaftlichen Wandel zwischen 1600 und 1900* (Leipzig: Deutscher Verlag für Musik, 1982); Dorothea Link, 'Vienna's Private Theatrical and Musical Life, 1783–92, as Reported by Count Karl Zinzendorf', *Journal of the Royal Musical Association*, 122 (1997), 205–57.

5. See Otto Biba, 'Die adelige und bürgerliche Musikkultur: das Konzertwesen', *Joseph Haydn in seiner Zeit* (Eisenstadt: Amt der Burgenländischen Landesregierung, 1982), 255–63.

6. 'Sie finden vielleicht nicht ein gutes Haus, in welchem nicht das Fräulein auf dem Klavier klimperte, oder der junge Herr mit vieler Wichtigkeit auf seiner Violine […] spielte.' [Johann Baptist Mittrowsky], *Ueberblick des neuesten Zustandes der Litteratur, des Theaters und des Geschmacks in Wien* (Vienna: Doll, 1802), p. 25.

7. See Julius Wilhelm Fischer, *Reisen durch Oesterreich, Ungarn […] in den Jahren 1801 und 1802* (Vienna: Doll, 1803), p. 136: 'Die Musik also […] macht allerdings einen wesentlichen Theil auch der männlichen hiesigen Erziehung aus.' / 'Music thus […] forms a significant part of the education of males as well here.'

8. 'In jeder nur etwas bemittelten Familie, werden die Kinder, besonders die Töchter in der Musik

In every family of even modest prosperity, the children, especially the daughters, are taught music, piano playing and singing being a fundamental part of what is regarded as good education here [… There are] without doubt truly great artists amongst the dilettantes, male and female, on all kinds of instruments […] who are able to perform the most difficult pieces masterfully.

The so-called dilettante, the 'music lover', did not – unlike the professional musician – earn a living making music, but had received a solid enough musical education to enable him or her to play chamber music with kindred spirits and even possibly to perform together with professional musicians at private or semi-public occasions. In 1784, Friedrich Nicolai wrote:[9]

In Vienna, there are many keen lovers of music and also not a few who are connoisseurs and can almost be regarded as virtuosi.

From the 1780s, the fortepiano became established as the favourite instrument for ladies, the study of which became the most intensively cultivated after singing, not only in aristocratic circles, but also increasingly amongst the bourgeoisie, in whose musical salons the mistress of the house or her daughters would take centre stage at the piano.[10] Among the extremely large number of female pianists, those with very modest skills would naturally play only within the close family circle. Many others, however, were capable of acquitting themselves well at larger social occasions, whilst some were even up to performing in semi-public and public concerts. Countless piano pieces composed in this era take into consideration this level of skill. Indeed, in 1801 Karl Gottlob Küttner writes:[11]

---

8. *Cont.*

    unterrichtet, Klavierspielen und Singen gehört wesentlich zu dem, was man hier gute Erziehung nennt [… Es gibt] unstreitig sehr große Künstler unter den Dilettanten und Dilettantinnen auf allen Arten von Instrumenten […], welche die schwersten Stücke meisterhaft auszuführen im Stande sind.' *Neuestes Sittengemählde von Wien* (Vienna: Pichler 1801), pp. 160–61. However, doubts are expressed whether 'die Unterweisung der weiblichen Jugend in der Musik nicht einen beinahe zu großen Raum in der gewöhnlichen bürgerlichen Erziehung einnimmt' / 'the musical education of young females does not take too large a place in the ordinary bourgeois education.' [Joseph Rohrer], *Neuestes Gemählde von Wien* (Vienna: Doll, 1797), p. 99.

9. Friedrich Nicolai, *Beschreibung einer Reise durch Deutschland und die Schweiz im Jahre 1781* (Berlin: [n. pub.], 1784), p. 553: 'Es giebt in Wien viel eifrige Liebhaber der Musik, und auch nicht wenige, die Kenner sind, und mehr oder weniger für Virtuosen gelten können.'

10. See Ingrid Fuchs, '"…spielt das Fortepiano mit vieler Empfindung und Präzision" – Damen im musikalischen Salon um Joseph Haydn', *Phänomen Haydn 1732–1809. Eisenstadt: Schauplatz musikalischer Weltliteratur* (Eisenstadt: Schloss Esterházy Management, 2009), pp. 144–53.

11. 'Es giebt Clavierspielerinnen […], die man, wenn sie von der Profession wären, in den Rang der Virtuosen setzen würde.' [Karl Gottlob Küttner], *Reise durch Deutschland, Dänemark, Schweden, Norwegen* […] (Leipzig: Göschen, 1801), p. 489.

There are female pianists [...] who, if they were professional, would have to be given the rank of virtuoso.

Evidently therefore there were musicians, particularly among the piano-playing ladies – the dilettantes – of the musical salon, who were so superbly trained that they were certainly equal, in both technical skills and musicianship, to the demands made by the sophisticated compositions of Mozart or Haydn.

What role, then, did the ladies of the musical salon play in the life of Joseph Haydn, whether in terms of their personal relationship with him, or as possible dedicatees or sources of commissions? First to mention in this regard are the sisters Katharina and Marianna Auenbrugger to whom the *Claviersonaten* (as Haydn called them in his letters) Hob.XVI:35–39 and 20 were dedicated. Haydn expressed his high esteem towards the two young pianists as follows:[12]

> The approval of the *Desmoiselles* von Auenbrugger is most important to me, for their way of playing and genuine insight into music equal those of the greatest masters.

The excellent pianist and singer Marianne von Genzinger, for whom Haydn felt particular admiration and friendship until her death in 1793, is another lady from the Viennese musical salons who was of especial significance to him. In 1789, Marianne von Genzinger had arranged movements from one of his symphonies for piano – a remarkable achievement for a non-professional musician – and sent these 'piano transcriptions' to the composer with a request for corrections.[13] During the winter months, while Prince Esterházy and his court were in Vienna, Haydn had the opportunity to attend various social events and musical entertainments in a number of different houses. In the home of the music-loving Genzinger family with their five children, Haydn himself arranged private concerts in which other music lovers also participated.[14] Haydn dedicated his Piano Sonata in E flat major Hob.XVI:49 to Marianne Genzinger who liked it 'exceedingly well'.[15] She did, however, ask the composer to simplify the passage in the Adagio where the left hand crosses the right: in spite of all her remarkable musical capabilities she was, after all, not a professional pianist.

12. *Gesammelte Briefe und Aufzeichnungen*, p. 90; *Collected Correspondence and London Notebooks*, p. 25.

13. *Gesammelte Briefe und Aufzeichnungen*, pp. 215–16; *Collected Correspondence and London Notebooks*, pp. 90–91.

14. *Gesammelte Briefe und Aufzeichnungen*, p. 226: 'Berichte Euer Gnaden, wie daß zu der, an künftigen freytag zwischen uns verabgeredten kleinen quartetten Music alle Anstalten getroffen sind. Herr von Häring schätze sich glücklich mir dissfals dienen zu könen.' / 'I report to Your Honour that all arrangements have been made concerning the little quartet music planned on the coming Friday. Herr von Häring was very pleased to be able to serve me in this matter.'

15. *Gesammelte Briefe und Aufzeichnungen*, p. 245; *Collected Correspondence and London Notebooks*, p. 108.

Another dedicatee of Haydn's piano compositions was Barbara Ployer, a pupil of Mozart's and an excellent pianist: not only did Mozart dedicate two piano concertos to her (K449 and K453), but also a manuscript copy of Haydn's Piano Variations in F minor (Hob.XVII:6) has survived bearing a dedication to Ployer in the composer's autograph. It dates from 1793 – that is, the period between Haydn's two visits to London.[16] She was no mere dilettante of the musical salons but was rather more of the stature of the superb pianist Therese Jansen whom Haydn mentions, with twelve other famous female pianists, in his first London Notebook.[17] Therese Jansen was a pupil of Muzio Clementi in London and an exceptionally successful piano teacher herself. Important composers such as Jan Ladislaus Dussek, as well as Clementi, dedicated several works to her, as did Haydn. Haydn evidently thought very highly of her and named her as dedicatee of two piano sonatas (Hob.XVI:50 and 52)[18] and three piano trios (Hob.XV:27–29). Jansen married Gaetano Bartolozzi, the son of the well known engraver Francesco Bartolozzi, on 16 May 1795. Even though Therese Jansen, as is documented in Haydn's handwritten dedication, was a 'famous' pianist, there is no proof that she ever performed in public concerts. For a long time it was believed that a third piano sonata (Hob.XVI:51) 'composed in England for a lady who kept the original manuscript'[19] was written for Therese Jansen too. The simpler style of writing, however, suggests that it was intended for someone less accomplished.

A few years ago Thomas Tolley was able to identify this pianist.[20] A letter written by Haydn in English[21] and now held in the Archive of the Gesellschaft der Musikfreunde in Wien (see Fig. 2) played a significant role in this discovery. During his

16. See Hoboken, *Werkverzeichnis*, I, 791–93, and further in particular Landon, *Haydn: Chronicle und Works*, III, 438–39, and A. Peter Brown, *Joseph Haydn's Keyboard Music. Sources and Style* (Bloomington: Indiana University Press, 1986), p. 46. Michael Lorenz demonstrates in 'New and Old Documents Concerning Mozart's Pupils Barbara Ployer and Josepha Auernhammer', *Eighteenth-Century Music*, 3 (2006), 311–22 (p. 313) that Haydn composed the Variations in F minor not for Barbara Ployer, but for Antonia von Ployer, née von Spaun, the wife of her uncle Gottfried Ignaz von Ployer – a dedicatee who must be numbered among the piano-playing ladies of the musical salon.
17. For the following see especially Landon, *Haydn: Chronicle and Works*, III, 439–43 and Brown, *Haydn's Keyboard Music*, pp. 50–52.
18. For the complicated history of the printing of the sonatas Hob.XVI:50–52 see Landon, *Haydn: Chronicle and Works*, III, 441–42 and Hoboken, *Werkverzeichnis*, I, 775–80.
19. See among others Georg Feder, 'Vorwort', in Joseph Haydn, *Werke* (Munich: Henle), XVIII/3: *Klaviersonaten (3. Folge)*, ed. by Georg Feder (1966), p. VIII, and Hoboken, *Werkverzeichnis* I, 776, 778.
20. Thomas Tolley, 'Haydn, the Engraver Thomas Park, and Maria Hester Park's "Little Sonat"', *Music & Letters*, 82 (2001), 421–31.
21. Letter from Joseph Haydn to [Thomas] Park, 22 October 1794, Archiv der Gesellschaft der Musikfreunde in Wien, Briefe Joseph Haydn, 6.

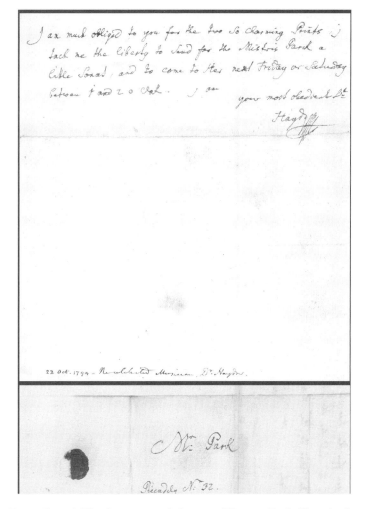

Fig. 2. Joseph Haydn, autograph letter to Thomas Park, [London],
22 October 1794. Gesellschaft der Musikfreunde in Wien.

second stay in London, Haydn wrote this letter to the engraver Thomas Park to thank him for two 'charming prints' (these can be identified in the inventory of his property left on his death). Further, Haydn – as he himself writes – took 'the liberty to send for the Mistris Parck a little Sonat' and announces his intention to call on her. This 'little Sonat', simpler in compositional style than the 'grand' sonatas for Therese Jansen, must clearly be the third English sonata Hob.XVI:51, intended by Haydn for the engraver's wife Maria Hester Park, who was a talented amateur pianist, as a token of gratitude for the two engravings.

When two of the compositions which Haydn composed for and dedicated to Therese Jansen, the Piano Trio Hob.XV:31 mentioned above and the Piano Sonata

Hob.XVI:52, were published in Vienna,²² they were dedicated to Magdalena von Kurzböck. She was an exceptionally gifted musician²³ and, like Jansen, also a pupil of Muzio Clementi, so they may have had similar performance styles. Like Josepha Auernhammer, who is known to us from her dealings with Mozart, Magdalena von Kurzböck was equally at home performing in public as in the salon. They are cited alongside the two professional musicians Ludwig van Beethoven and Joseph Wölfl in an article about the most famous female and male pianists in Vienna²⁴ which appeared in 1799 in the Leipzig *Allgemeine musikalische Zeitung*. In the same edition of the *Allgemeine musikalische Zeitung*²⁵ a review of the printed edition of the sonata dedicated to Magdalena von Kurzböck described it as being 'really for connoisseurs' and thus not to be compared, with respect to its difficulties, to his earlier sonatas. In other words, Haydn's dedicatees Jansen and Kurzböck are examples of the 'connoisseurs' for whom, along with music lovers, his piano sonatas were intended.

In addition to ladies from the upper middle class and lower nobility, the female representatives of the higher nobility proved themselves to be great lovers and patrons of music too. First to mention in Haydn's circle were the spouses of his respective employers. Barely a year after her wedding to the future Prince Nicolaus II Esterházy in 1783, the first edition of Haydn's Piano Sonatas Hob.XVI:40–42 was published with a dedication to Maria Josepha Hermenegild Esterházy, née Princess Liechtenstein. Her husband became the reigning prince in 1794 and the following year the Piano Trios Hob.XV:21–22 were also dedicated to her.²⁶ The piano compositions dedicated to the princess were certainly intended for her own music-making, and Haydn would of course have taken into consideration – as in all similar works – the capabilities of his aristocratic dedicatees. Among these were the Princess

22. Respectively by Traeg in 1803 and Artaria in 1798.
23. See *Jahrbuch der Tonkunst von Wien und Prag. Faksimile-Nachdruck der Ausgabe Wien 1796*, with epilogue and index ed. by Otto Biba (Munich: Katzbichler, 1976), pp. 38–9: 'Kurzbeck, Magdalene v., eine unserer vorzüglichsten Klavierspielerinnen […]; dabey hat sie ein besonderes, ihr eigenes Talent in der Fasskraft und Gedächtniß, so, daß, wenn sie ein Stück, es sey nun in großer Instrumentirung, wie z.B. eine Symphonie, oder auch auf dem Klavier, welches ihr gefällt, ein paarmal höret, sie im Stande ist, es sehr genau auf dem Fortepiano nachzuspielen.' / 'Kurzbeck, Magdalene v., one of our most excellent female pianists […]; she also has a special, particular, talent of understanding and memory, so that if she hears a piece a few times which she likes, whether for large orchestra, such as a symphony, or just for the piano, she is able to reproduce it very precisely afterwards on the fortepiano.'
24. 'Die berühmtesten Klavierspielerinnen und Klavierspieler Wiens', *Allgemeine musikalische Zeitung*, Leipzig, 15 May 1799, pp. 523–24.
25. *Allgemeine musikalische Zeitung*, Leipzig, 15 May 1799, p. 520.
26. While none of the six late masses is actually dedicated to the princess, at least three of them ('Theresienmesse', 'Schöpfungmesse' and 'Harmonienmesse') were composed specifically for her nameday.

Maria Anna Esterházy, née Countess von Hohenfeld, the young widowed second wife of Prince Paul Anton Esterházy, and the Countess Marianne Witzay (Viczay), née Countess Grassalkovich (a relative of Prince Esterházy who lived with her husband near Eszterháza), to each of whom Haydn dedicated a set of Piano Trios (Hob.XV:18–20 and Hob.XV:6–8).

The interest in and demand for piano trios had risen steadily in Vienna since the beginning of the 1780s[27] and was closely related to the increasing popularity of music-making in the private salon, where the piano-playing lady in the spotlight was often joined by companions from her social circle, most often male, for music-making. As a rule, violin and cello functioned as accompaniment, as is clearly indicated by the customary title of the piano trios '[…] pour le Clavecin ou Pianoforte avec Accompagnement de Violon et Violoncelle' / 'for harpsichord or pianoforte with accompaniment of violin and cello'.[28] Countless compositions, even large-scale works, were arranged and published in this increasingly popular format. Many of Haydn's symphonies, for example, reached domestic musicians via this route.

The piano trio also played an important role in piano teaching, since the piano parts in these works were generally less demanding than the solo piano sonatas, and as such were very suited to those who were not highly skilled or professional musicians. This is reflected in the dedications of the editions: while the majority of piano sonatas are dedicated to important female pianists who, as performers, had stepped beyond the purely private sphere of the musical salon (Auenbrugger, Ployer, Jansen, Kurzböck), the majority of Haydn's piano trios[29] – which in their originality and masterly composition are far superior to those composed in great quantity by some of his lesser contemporaries – were dedicated to less proficient female pianists, whether of the nobility or upper middle classes.[30]

Whereas the dedicatees and intended performers of Haydn's piano sonatas and piano trios were almost exclusively women, the sponsors and dedicatees of the string quartets, and their potential interpreters, were exclusively male. String instruments, with a very few exceptions in the case of the violin, were played only by men; but here, too, the range of proficiency of performers ranged from the amateur to the connoisseur and the professional artist.

In its origins, the string quartet was private in character. In eighteenth-century Vienna, it was played principally in the houses of the bourgeoisie and the palaces of the nobility, either for private pleasure or as part of larger social occasions. The

27. See Katalin Komlós, 'The Viennese Keyboard Trio in the 1780s: Studies in Texture and Instrumentation' (unpublished doctoral dissertation, Cornell University, 1986), pp. 33–43.
28. See Ludwig Finscher, *Joseph Haydn und seine Zeit* (Laaber: Laaber Verlag, 2000), pp. 441–44.
29. Many were composed without dedication.
30. Haydn made more virtuosic requirements of the piano parts in those piano trios that were dedicated to Therese Jansen-Bartolozzi (Hob.XV:27–29).

circumstances under which Haydn's first string quartets came into being are remark-able and indicative of how they came to be written. As Haydn himself reports, he wrote his first quartets at a very young age (before 1760) at the request of the noble Karl Joseph Weber von Fürnberg, who lived in a castle in Lower Austria and was looking for music that could be performed by his priest, his steward, Haydn and Johann Georg Albrechtsberger as cellist.[31] These early string quartets were followed several years later by the first set of six quartets, known as op. 9, which Haydn com-posed between 1768 and 1771; at this time, he was already Kapellmeister to Prince Nicolaus Esterházy and the quartets were presumably composed for his employer's court musicians, with the first violin part possibly intended for Luigi Tomasini, the Esterházy concert master.

There is interesting evidence, too, about the provenance in private circumstances of the second set, op. 17, composed in 1771. An inscription on the flyleaf of the cover of the autograph now in the archives of the Gesellschaft der Musikfreunde in Wien[32] states that the autograph is a 'gift from the Neuwirth family in Vienna, in whose house Haydn played the viola in *Quartettübungen*'. It was Haydn's biographer Carl Ferdinand Pohl who wrote this comment, based on the relevant documents in the archives of the Gesellschaft der Musikfreunde. August Neuwirth was a doctor, music lover and collector of sheet music and instruments who was friendly with Haydn.[33] What is interesting is the term 'Quartettübungen', which suggests more an informal play-through for the benefit and enjoyment of the performers alone rather than any public performance. What is further remarkable is the fact that the Quartets op. 20, composed in 1772 and not published in Vienna until 1800 (by Artaria), were also dedicated by Haydn to a Viennese music lover: Nikolaus Zmeskall von Domanowetz, who is known to us also from his friendship with Beethoven. He was a civil servant in the Hungarian chancellery and an excellent amateur cellist; quartets were apparently played at his house every Sunday, according to a letter from the doctor and music lover Amand Wilhelm Smith to a nobleman in Eastern Hungary:[34] 'apud posteriorem [= Zmeskall] omni die dominica hora

---

31. Georg Feder, *Haydns Streichquartette: Ein musikalischer Werkführer* (Munich: Beck, 1998), p. 34. Regarding the following remarks about the string quartet see also Walter, 'Zum Wiener Streichquartett', pp. 289–314.

32. Archiv der Gesellschaft der Musikfreunde in Wien, Autograph A 149: 'Geschenk der Familie Neuwirth in Wien, in deren Haus Haydn bei den Quartettübungen die Viola zu spielen pflegte.'

33. Constant von Wurzbach, *Biographisches Lexikon des Kaiserthums Oesterreich*, 60 vols (Vienna: Zamarski, 1856–91), XX (1869), 308.

34. Letter from Amand Wilhelm Smith to Emerich Horváth-Stansith, Vienna, 5 June 1787, in Levoča (Slovakia), Štátny oblastný archív, Fonds Emerich Horváth-Stansith, Correspondence 1785–1801. See also Ingrid Fuchs, 'W. A. Mozart in Wien: Unbekannte Nachrichten in einer zeitgenössischen Korrespondenz aus seinem persönlichen Umfeld', *Festschrift Otto Biba zum 60. Geburtstag*, ed. by Ingrid Fuchs (Tutzing: Schneider, 2006), pp. 187–207 (p. 190).

secunda [...] habemus parvum quartetto, cui etiam intersum.' / 'At the latter's [= Zmeskall] we play a little quartet every Sunday at 2, in which I, too, participate.'

Haydn's taking part in informal, domestic music making was not restricted to the Neuwirth and Genzinger families, however. He also performed with Mozart. The diaries of Vincent Novello, which draw on the first-hand accounts of Abbé Maximilian Stadler, reveal that before Haydn travelled to England in 1790, he took part in a private performance of Mozart's great String Quintets (K515, 516 and 593) with the composer of those works himself. The two of them took turns playing the first viola part, with Stadler playing second viola.[35] In the reminiscences of Michael Kelly, we read about a glittering occasion in June 1784 when Haydn, Dittersdorf, Mozart and Vanhall met at the home of Stephen Storace, who was then living in Vienna, to play quartets together.[36] The subsequent remarks clearly describe the social character of such a 'quartet party', as Kelly calls it:[37]

> after the musical feast was over, we sat down to an excellent supper, and became joyous and lively in the extreme.

An increasing number of documents have survived from about 1780 which show how Haydn himself became active in the promotion of his compositions, both in print and handwritten copy. He was now offering music lovers numbered subscription manuscript copies for sale before publication of the printed edition. For example, he wrote in respect of the Quartets op. 33 to Prince Kraft Ernst von Oettingen-Wallerstein and Johann Christian Lavater 'since there are many gentlemen amateurs and great connoisseurs and patrons of the musical arts in Zurich [and] Winterthur', showing a telling awareness of the type of person to whom these pieces would appeal.[38] As evidenced by the number of printed editions and the positive contemporary reviews, the op. 33 set was a great success, its popularity further demonstrated by the fact that several arrangements for other instrumental combinations were published. The first edition, published by Artaria, is dedicated to

---

35. *A Mozart Pilgrimage. Being the Travel Diaries of Vincent & Mary Novello in the year 1829*. Transcribed and compiled by Nerina Medici di Marignano, ed. by Rosemary Hughes (London: Novello, 1955), pp. 170–71, p. 347, n. 123: 'Quintets of Mozart – 1st Violin Schmidt, 2nd Stock, 1st Viola either Haydn or Mozart in turn, 2nd Viola Abbé Stadler – Bass he could not recollect.'

36. 'Storace gave a quartett party to his friends. The players were tolerable, not one of them excelled on the instrument he played; but there was a little science among them, which I dare say will be acknowledged when I name them: The First Violin – Haydn, The Second Violin – Baron Dittersdorf, The Violoncello – Vanhall, The Tenor – Mozart.' Michael Kelly, *Reminiscences*, 2 vols (London: Colburn, 1826), I, 240–41.

37. Kelly, *Reminiscences*, I, 241.

38. *Gesammelte Briefe und Aufzeichnungen*, p. 106: 'Dass in Zürich, Winterthur viele Herrn Liebhaber und grosse Kenner und gönner der Tonkunst sind'; *Collected Correspondence and London Notebooks*, pp. 32–33.

Haydn's employer Prince Nicolaus Esterházy, possibly indicating that the works
were intended for the prince's court. When Czar Paul I visited Vienna with his
music-loving wife, one of these brand-new quartets was performed for the illustrious
visitors at a private concert on Christmas Day 1781.

From correspondence of Amand Wilhelm Smith of April 1787 we also learn
about the Quartets op. 50, later designated the 'Prussian', that[39]

> [Here in Vienna] new quartets by Haydn are being played, but these will only be
> generally accessible in a year's time; Prince Esterházy had them made for himself.

These words demonstrate more clearly than any other source that, first, Haydn
was commissioned by his employer to compose string quartets and, second, that the
music so composed could not be published for a year to allow Prince Nicolaus a
period of private enjoyment. A similarly significant statement with respect to
Haydn's string quartets can be found in the same correspondence, in the spring of
1793, when Smith writes:[40]

> My friend Förster writes to me in detail and reports that Haydn has written 6
> new quartets for Count Apponyi.

Most of the early editions of the Quartets op. 71 and 74 include a dedication to
the Hungarian Count Anton Apponyi. There is, of course, a fundamental distinction
between a dedication and a commission, and the lines above furnish proof, hitherto
unnoticed,[41] that these quartets were not only dedicated to Count Apponyi, but

39. 'Quartetta nova dantur ab Hayden. sed haec tantum publico comunicabuntur post annum. Comes
Esterhazy pro se fieri jussit.' Letter from Amand Wilhelm Smith to Emerich Horváth-Stansith,
Vienna, 24 April 1787, Levoča (Slovakia), Štátny oblastný archív, Fonds Emerich Horváth-
Stansith, Correspondence 1785–1801. See also Ingrid Fuchs, 'Haydniana in einer
altösterreichischen Adelskorrespondenz', *Internationales musikwissenschaftliches Symposion
'Dokumentarische Grundlagen in der Haydnforschung'*, ed. by Georg Feder and Walter Reicher
(Tutzing: Schneider, 2006), pp. 55–76 (pp. 63–64).
40. 'Accurate mihi scribit meus Förster, et mihi refert, quod Hayden 6 nova quartetta Comiti Apponi
fecerit'. Letter from Amand Wilhelm Smith to Emerich Horváth-Stansith, Käsmark, undated
[sorted before 4 May, 1793], Levoča (Slovakia), Štátny oblastný archív, Fonds Emerich Horváth-
Stansith, Correspondence 1785–1801. It is very regrettable that this letter is not dated, for
otherwise the date of composition of the Apponyi Quartets could be more precisely determined.
Since Haydn only wrote the year 1793 on the autograph of each quartet (Hoboken,
Werkverzeichnis, I, 422–23), one could assume spring 1793 to be the date by which the quartets
had to have been completed, since Smith (as reported by the composer Emanuel Aloys Förster,
who lived in Vienna from 1779) speaks of their composition in the past tense.
41. Until now, there was only indirect evidence that these quartets could have been commissioned by
a nobleman, viz. a letter from Count Rasumowsky to Prince P. A. Subow, probably dating from
1795, which relates that Haydn is selling his newest quartets (most probably opp. 71 and 74),
composed two years previously and as yet unprinted, for 100 ducats, offering the owner exclusive
enjoyment of the quartets for one year. Count Apponyi is, however, not mentioned by name: 'J'ai

also commissioned by him. This letter by Amand Wilhelm Smith proves conclusively that Joseph Haydn had received a commission from Count Apponyi to compose six quartets by the spring of 1793. This confirms the supposition that the 'Apponyi' Quartets are indeed commissioned works, like the later 'Erdödy' Quartets op. 76[42] and the 'Lobkowitz' Quartets op. 77,[43] for which documentation of this circumstance was already known. Like the Quartets op. 71/74, the op. 76 and op. 77 sets were not published until a year or two after their composition, to allow their sponsors an initial period of exclusive enjoyment.[44]

Unlike Mozart's 'Prussian' Quartets, in which the cello part was made particularly demanding in consideration of the cello-playing dedicatee, King Friedrich Wilhelm II, Haydn's op. 50, which was also dedicated to the king when it was published by Artaria in December 1787, shows no such consideration. This is because the original commission came not from the dedicatee of the quartets but from Prince Esterházy, as is proved by the letter from Smith in 1787 quoted above. The 'Apponyi', 'Erdödy' and 'Lobkowitz' Quartets were initially only performed by musicians in the respective courts. Only when, later, copies and printed parts were made could the pieces be performed by other music lovers.

However, as we learned from the quotation about the Quartets op. 64 mentioned at the beginning of the article, music lovers had certain difficulties with Haydn's chamber music, and the quartets by Mozart were regarded as being even more

41. *Cont*

bien de regret, que les six derniers quatuors de Haydn que j'ai entendus avec le plus grand plaisir, ne se trouvent pas à acheter. Ayant été composés, il y a deux ans, pour quelqu'un, qui en paya 100 ducats la jouissance exclusive pendant la premiere année.' See Boris Steinpress, 'Haydns Oratorien in Russland zu Lebzeiten des Komponisten', *Haydn-Studien*, 2/2 [1969], 77–112 (p. 83) and especially Georg Feder's preface to Joseph Haydn, *Werke* (Munich: Henle), XII/5: *Streichquartette 'Opus 64' und 'Opus 71/74'*, ed. by Georg Feder and Isidor Saslav (1978), pp. VII–VIII.

42. Haydn spielte 'mir auf dem Clavier vor, Violinquartette, die ein Graf Erdödi für 100 Ducaten bei ihm bestellt hat und die erst nach einer gewissen Anzahl von Jahren gedruckt werden dürfen'. / Haydn played 'for me on the piano, violin quartets which had been ordered from him by one Count Erdödi and which might only be printed after a certain number of years.' Letter from F. S. Silverstolpe, 14 June 1797, quoted by C.-G. Stellan Mörner, 'Johan Wikmanson und die Brüder Silverstolpe' (unpublished dissertation, Stockholm, 1952), p. 318; quoted by Hoboken, *Werkverzeichnis*, I, 434.

43. Die Quartette, 'die Haydn für Lobkowitz komponiert hat, sind des letzteren Privateigenthum und Haydn wird gut dafür bezahlt'. / The quartets, 'which Haydn composed for Lobkowitz are the latter's private property and Haydn is paid well for them'. (Georg August Griesinger, quoted by Hoboken, *Werkverzeichnis*, I, 438).

44. Likewise, the Apponyi Quartets, whose autograph is marked 1793, were only printed in 1795, which further supports the evidence now furnished that the quartets were commissioned.

difficult. In this context let us mention just one other short quote from the above-mentioned contemporary correspondence:[45]

> The quartets by Mozart are very beautiful, they exceed even those by Haydn, but they are difficult to play. All four [players] must be very good.

Whereas in Vienna the string quartet was, according to Heinrich Christoph Koch, the 'favourite piece for small musical parties'[46] and Abbé Stadler said it would 'need entire books to record all those who performed quartets in their homes, particularly in the time of Emperor Joseph II',[47] in London string quartets had been transported to the concert hall much earlier than in Vienna, where they were performed by professional musicians.

On 2 February 1789, one of the Quartets op. 54/55, published in 1789 by Longman & Broderip, was performed in a 'Professional Concert' in the Hanover Square Rooms in London.[48] In the years 1791 and 1792, during Haydn's stay in London, a quartet was included in practically every Salomon concert in the Hanover Square Rooms.[49] These concerts had a more or less fixed sequence of genres in which the string quartet was placed either within or at the end of the first part of the concert. Along with quartets by other composers, for example Gyrowetz, Cambini and Paul Wranitzky, quartets by Haydn were performed during 1791 and 1792 which were designated as 'new'. Most probably, these were from the op. 64 set, not yet known in London, which were subsequently published there by Haydn's friend John Bland as op. 65 with the remark 'performed under his [Haydn's] direction, at Mr. Salomon's concert, the Festino Rooms Hanover Square'. The performers were always the same: Johann Peter Salomon (first violin), Damen (second violin), Hindmarsh (viola) and Menel (cello), and all were, naturally, professional musicians. When Haydn came to London for the second time in 1794, he brought his Quartets op. 71 and op. 74 with him, which were also performed in Salomon's concerts. This time, Fiorillo

---

45. 'Quartetta de Mozart sunt pulcherrima, praecellunt adhuc Haydeniana, sed difficulter producenda. omnes quatuor boni esse debent.' Letter from Amand Wilhelm Smith to Emerich Horváth-Stansith, [undated, but after 17 August 1786, death of Friedrich II, the Great], Levoča (Slowakia), Štátny oblastný archív, Fonds Emerich Horváth-Stansith, Correspondence 1785–1801. See Fuchs, 'W. A. Mozart in Wien', p. 204.

46. Heinrich Christoph Koch, *Versuch einer Anleitung zur Composition*, 3 vols (Leipzig: Böhme, 1793), III, 325: 'das Lieblingstück kleiner musikalischer Gesellschaften'.

47. Abbé Maximilian Stadler, *Seine 'Materialien zur Geschichte der Musik unter den österreichischen Regenten': Ein Beitrag zum Historismus im vormärzlichen Wien*, ed. by Karl Wagner (Kassel: Bärenreiter, 1974), p. 164.

48. Hoboken, *Werkverzeichnis*, I, 413–14.

49. Landon, *Haydn: Chronicle and Works*, III, *passim*. See also Mary Hunter, 'Haydn's London Piano Trios and His Salomon String Quartets: Private vs. Public?', *Haydn and His World*, ed. by Elaine Sisman (Princeton, NJ: Princeton University Press, 1997), pp. 103–30.

Fig. 3. Chamber music performance as depicted in a coloured print
by Johann Söllerer, Vienna, 1793.

played the viola and Damen junior played cello (the two violinists remained un-
changed). The Quartets op. 71 and 74 evidently contained certain difficulties even
for the professional quartet musicians in London, as the review in the *Morning Herald* of 7 March 1794 relates:[50]

> [Haydn] has lately produced a manuscript Quartetto of the most complex
> harmonies, but blended with all flowing beauties that melody can bestow: – so
> difficult, however, is this piece in point of execution, as to require all the powers
> [of the interpreters].

In 1801, the *Allgemeine musikalische Zeitung* in Leipzig writes about Viennese
musical culture as follows:[51]

> Cultivated people love what is good, […] less cultivated people love what is new.
> […] Among the composers who are played most often and esteemed most highly

50. *The Morning Herald*, 7 March 1794, quoted by Landon, *Haydn: Chronicle and Works*, III, 236,
     footnote 1.
51. 'Neuer Versuch einer Darstellung des gesammten Musikwesens in Wien', *Allgemeine musikalische
     Zeitung*, Leipzig, 3 (1801), p. 639.

by the more cultivated people, Haydn, [whose] quartets are never heard better […] performed than in Vienna, rightly occupies first place.

Apart from the compliment to Haydn and to Vienna, this quotation characterizes how chamber music was developing at the turn of the century in the city: the original concept of chamber music performed by connoisseurs and music lovers in the salons of the bourgeoisie and aristocracy salons was now producing increasingly demanding works, pre-eminently in the form of string quartet, that required players of the highest quality, ones who could promote a sense of discrimination. These works would satisfy the best amateur musicians performing in private domestic situations, as well as professional musicians performing in public concerts.

Publishing Practice in Haydn's Vienna: Artaria and the Keyboard Trios Op. 40

RUPERT RIDGEWELL

A bibliographical anomaly

IN 1946 the British Museum Library acquired the library of Paul Hirsch (1881–51), the German industrialist, collector and amateur musician who had settled in Cambridge after escaping Nazi Germany ten years earlier.[1] Hirsch's library was widely regarded as one of the finest private collections of music in the world, especially rich in important early editions of music by major composers of the classical canon, notably Mozart, Beethoven and Schubert. Its acquisition for the sum of £120,000 – a significant outlay in the immediate aftermath of the Second World War[2] – considerably enhanced the British Museum's existing holdings of German and Austrian editions of the eighteenth and nineteenth centuries, and complemented its extensive collection of printed music published in the UK during the same period. Hirsch nevertheless left a number of important gaps which curators of the music collection that now forms part of the British Library have sought to fill. This is true especially of Haydn's music, owing perhaps to the relative scarcity of first editions of some of his music (such as symphonies published in parts), and because Hirsch may have ceded precedence in this area to the Haydn scholar and

For their helpful comments and suggestions concerning this essay, I am grateful to Péter Barna, Nick Chadwick, Loukia Drosopoulou, Oliver Neighbour, Arthur Searle and David Wyn Jones.

1. A. H. King, 'Paul Hirsch (1881–1951): some Personal Recollections', *Monthly Musical Record*, 82 (1952), 98–100.
2. The sum was largely raised by special grants from the Treasury and from the Pilgrim Trust.

collector Anthony van Hoboken.[3] Notable acquisitions since 1946 include first editions of the sets of keyboard sonatas published as op. 30 (Artaria, 1780), op. 37 (Bossler, 1784), and op. 54 (Artaria, 1788), as well as the six sonatas published by Kurzböck in 1774, a fine edition that may represent Haydn's first 'authorized' publication (Hob.XVI:21–26). The Library has also been able to strengthen its coverage of Haydn's chamber music, notably by acquiring first and early editions of the Piano Trios op. 57 and op. 79 (Artaria), and the String Quartets opp. 54, 55, 71 and 74 (all Artaria), and op. 103 (Breitkopf). The collection of Alan Tyson also added some ninety editions of Haydn's music not previously held by the Library when it was donated in 1998,[4] including ten lifetime editions published in Vienna, twenty-two in Paris and twenty-three in London. A very recent addition to the Library's holdings is the first edition of Haydn's Symphony no. 81, published in parts by Artaria in 1785.

The acquisition in July 1949 of an early printed violin part for three Haydn Piano Trios (Hob.XV:6–8) represents an early example of this activity (see Fig. 1).[5] At that time, the Library held two contemporary London editions of the same pieces, published by Longman and Broderip and William Forster.[6] The new edition therefore promised a useful point of comparison, even if the lack of the piano and cello parts was a serious flaw. It did, however, create a problem for the cataloguer, because the part was published without a title-page and therefore lacked any details of the imprint, or any other indication of the publisher's identity or the date of publication. The task of producing a full and reliable catalogue entry would therefore have involved a certain amount of detective work and in 1949 there were very few sources to turn to either for investigating Haydn's oeuvre or the outputs of contemporary publishers: Hoboken's catalogue of Haydn's instrumental works, for example, would not appear in print for another eight years,[7] and major collaborative efforts to collate information about music published before 1800 were undertaken only from the 1950s onwards.[8] In cataloguing an edition, a librarian's engagement with the musical

3. On Hirsch's correspondence with Hoboken between 1928 and 1950 see Nick Chadwick, 'The Hirsch Correspondence: Some Preliminary Observations', *Brio*, 45/1 (2008), 60–67 (pp. 62–63). Hoboken's collection is now held by the Musiksammlung of the Österreichische

4. See Oliver Neighbour, 'The Tyson Collection', *British Library Journal*, 24 (1998), 269–77.

5. London, British Library, g.455.i.(10.).

6. London, British Library, h.70.(3.) and R.M.17.f.12.(3.).

7. Hoboken, *Werkverzeichnis*, I.

8. These notably resulted in the publication of *The British Union-Catalogue of Early Music, Printed Before the Year 1801. A Record of the Holdings of over One Hundred Libraries Throughout the British Isles*, ed. by Edith B. Schnapper, 2 vols (London: Butterworths Scientific Publications, 1957) and *Répertoire International des Sources Musicales*, Series A/1: *Einzeldrucke vor 1800* (Kassel: Bärenreiter-Verlag, 1971–2003).

Fig. 1. Joseph Haydn, three Piano Trios Hob.XV:6–8 (Vienna: Artaria, 1786),
violin part, p. 1. BL, shelfmark g.455.i.(10.).

text is usually limited to identifying the work, or at least to validating the information given on the title-page and classifying it accordingly. One might also wish to place the edition in the wider context not only of the library's existing holdings of sources for the same work, but also in the fuller picture of the transmission of a work. It is, however, not usually necessary to examine in any great detail other aspects of an edition's make-up, such as its layout, the paper type, stylistic characteristics of the engraving, and other features that might loosely be described as components of a publisher's 'house style'. In the absence of a title-page, however, some analysis of these aspects becomes necessary since they might, through comparison with other editions from the same period, betray the publisher's identity.

Knowledge of the different practices adopted by music publishers in the late eighteenth century was hardly documented in 1949 and remains to be fully codified today. In some respects it is also not an exact science: publishers are, after all, not necessarily bound by their own conventions and departures from the norm might be forced on them by unforeseen circumstances or other factors. A librarian familiar with the period might have guessed the edition's Viennese origin from an inspection of the paper and the general characteristics of the engraving, but the only definite clue to the identity of the publisher is the plate number '75', which appears in a central position at the bottom of each plate. This was the control number used by publishers from the eighteenth century onwards for practical and administrative purposes, not least to allocate stray plates or printed sheets to the correct edition. Starting in the 1950s, the bibliographer Alexander Weinmann produced an important series of catalogues of the outputs of Viennese publishers, mostly listed in plate number order and based on the rich holdings of Viennese libraries. His work remains a crucial reference tool for librarians, dealers and musicologists today, but a librarian working in 1949 with only the violin part in front of him had to proceed in the dark.[9] In the circumstances, it is perhaps not surprising that the British Museum cataloguer got the wrong name, by identifying the publisher as Franz Anton Hoffmeister in the catalogue entry.[10] Despite the publication of the Hoboken catalogue and Weinmann's work, this error remained undetected until 2007, by which time corrections to the online version of the Library's catalogue were possible.

9.   Two important contributions to the subject of music publishers' plate numbers appeared before 1949, but neither of them would have helped to identify the publisher of the Haydn edition. These were: Richard S. Hill, 'The Plate Numbers of C. F. Peters' Predecessors', in *Papers Read by Members of the American Musicological Society at the Annual Meeting, Washington, D. C., December 29th and 30th, 1938* (Washington: privately printed by the Society, 1940), pp. 113–34; and Otto Erich Deutsch, *Music Publishers' Numbers: A Selection of 40 Dated Lists 1710–1900* (London: Aslib, 1946).

10.   The error appears in the *Catalogue of Printed Music in the British Library to 1980*, 62 vols (London, 1981–87), XXVII (1984), 312.

Hoffmeister was at least a plausible candidate, having published eleven editions of Haydn's music in Vienna after setting up a publishing business there in 1785.[11] However, we can be quite certain that he never published the op. 40 Piano Trios. The edition was instead printed by the firm of Artaria & Co., established in Vienna in 1768 and arguably the single most important publisher of Haydn's music from 1780 until his death. A total of twenty copies of the edition are known to be extant in libraries around the world.[12] Artaria published some 165 editions of Haydn's music during his lifetime, including first editions of various sets of solo keyboard works, trios, string quartets, symphonies and songs. Artaria's edition of the op. 40 Trios nevertheless diverges from the firm's usual practice in at least one important respect, making the task of identifying the imprint an even more intractable puzzle before the publication of Weinmann's Artaria catalogue in 1952.[13]

A brief survey of the firm's output brings this anomaly to the fore. The main focus of the firm's activity during the 1780s and 1790s was music suitable for amateur performance at home, notably keyboard music in various genres (sonatas, variations, minuets) and with various accompanying instruments, as well as string quartets, songs and opera excerpts. The vast majority of their editions appeared in parts intended for performance and only a very few works were published in full score. Following convention, keyboard parts were usually engraved oblong (landscape) whereas the instrumental parts for symphonies and other orchestral music were typically upright (portrait). Chamber music for string instruments alone was also normally printed upright, but piano chamber music presented the publisher with a choice: either to produce a mixed set of parts consisting of an oblong keyboard part and upright string parts, or to make all the parts fit a single format. In the case of Artaria, it is clear that the firm generally preferred to adopt a single format for all parts. That nearly always meant engraving the accompanying parts oblong to make them fit with the keyboard part. This policy allowed the firm to use the same generic title-page for each part in an edition, saving them the trouble and cost of engraving title-pages in two different formats. Thus of the sixty-three editions for keyboard

11.   These notably included the String Quartet in D minor op. 42 (plate number 32), the Piano Trio in E flat major Hob.XV:10 (plate number 33), and an arrangement for string trio of the three keyboard sonatas Hob.XVI:40–42 (plate number 173). See Alexander Weinmann, *Die Wiener Verlagswerke von Franz Anton Hoffmeister*, Beiträge des Alt-Wiener Musikverlages, ser. 2, issue 8 (Vienna: Universal Edition, 1964), 240. See also his *Addenda und Corrigenda zum Verlagsverzeichnis Franz Anton Hoffmeister*, Beiträge des Alt-Wiener Musikverlages, ser. 2, issue 8a (Vienna: Universal Edition, 1982), 12.

12.   The locations are given in RISM Series A/I, H3641 and H3642. I have been able to gather information about eighteen copies, details of which are listed in Table 1.

13.   Alexander Weinmann, *Artaria & Comp.: Vollständiges Verlagsverzeichnis*, Beiträge des Alt-Wiener Musikverlages, ser. 2, issue 2 (Vienna: Krenn, 1952; 2nd edn 1978).

Fig. 2. Joseph Haydn, three Piano Trios Hob.XV:6–8 (Vienna: Artaria, 1786),
keyboard part, title-page. F Pn, shelfmark Vm7 5478.

with accompaniments published by Artaria between 1778 and 1791, only three were presented upright: these were Zimmermann's Keyboard Concerto op. 3 of 1782 (plate number 27), Haydn's Keyboard Concerto op. 37 of 1784 (plate number 38) and a set of six violin sonatas by Boccherini of 1788 (plate number 179).[14] The only edition published with both oblong and upright parts was the Haydn Keyboard Trios op. 40: upright for the two string parts and oblong for the keyboard part. This was unprecedented in the firm's output and it explains why the violin part in the British Library lacked a title-page: the firm simply did not prepare a separate upright title-page for the two string parts, but published the edition with a single oblong title-page for the keyboard part alone (Fig. 2). The edition therefore emerges as a bibliographical oddity when viewed in relation to the rest of Artaria's output. To explain why the edition turned out in this anomalous form we need to explore the process by which Haydn's music was transmitted from manuscript to print.

14.   The edition of Boccherini's Violin Sonatas op. 5 was not an original Artaria publication, but was printed from the plates of Torricella's edition of 1781 (Rudolf Rasch, personal communication). This explains the unusual format in this particular case.

The publishing process

It is one of the key tenets of historical bibliography that the circumstances in which a source originated are crucial in shaping its text, or as James Grier puts it 'directly affect the value and significance of the source for the history of the work or works they transmit'.[15] Changes to a text, whether by accident or design, can occur at every stage in the process of publication: music engravers, for example, can introduce mistakes by misreading the text given in a *Stichvorlage* (the printer's copy, or rather, the manuscript from which an edition was engraved) or by committing errors during the process of engraving. It is in the nature of research on this subject that it is rarely possible to identify the point at which such errors occurred, or even diagnose them accurately, owing to a general dearth of musical source materials directly connected with the publication process. The op. 40 Trios are no exception: Artaria's *Stichvorlage* is not known to survive, no corrected proofs of the edition have come down to us, and only the second trio in the set survives in Haydn's autograph. Furthermore, no authentic manuscript copies of the work have been identified either.[16] Artaria's edition of the three trios therefore represents the single most important source for the music of the first and third trios and is of great value in indicating Haydn's intentions for the second as well.

Documentary evidence of the publication process is also thin on the ground, although Haydn's correspondence with Artaria at least offers some information concerning the chronology and production of several editions.[17] The extant correspondence consists of some seventy letters and related documents charting the shifting tides of the relationship between composer and publisher between 1780 and 1805. The total loss, however, of Artaria's side of the correspondence means that we can only read between the lines of Haydn's letters to guess some of the decisions the publisher made in relation to his music. As a result, there is a tendency among biographers to characterize Artaria as a merely passive agent in the dissemination of Haydn's music, rather than attempt to form a balanced view of the relationship. But publishers are never disinterested parties; rather, they are mediators between the com-

15. James Grier, *The Critical Editing of Music: History, Method and Practice* (Cambridge: Cambridge University Press, 1996), p. 39.
16. The autograph was sold at Sotheby's on 11 May 1977 (lot 206) and is currently in private ownership, but a microfilm copy is held by the British Library (MUS/RP/1431). An autograph fragment of bars 1–100 of the first movement of Hob.XV:6 was once held by the Esterházy Archive in Eisenstadt, but is now lost. See Hoboken, *Werkverzeichnis*, I, 687.
17. *Gesammelte Briefe und Aufzeichnungen, passim,* and *Collected Correspondence and London Notebooks, passim.* See also *Joseph Haydn und das Verlagshaus Artaria: nach den Briefen des Meisters an das Haus Artaria & Compagnie dargestellt und anlässlich der Zentenarfeier,* ed. by Franz Artaria and Hugo Botstiber (Vienna: Artaria, 1909).

poser and public, in a position to choose what to commission and print, based on an assessment of public demand, cost and musical value. They are usually driven by a commercial imperative to be successful in the marketplace and their decisions are made accordingly. No small part of the publishing equation is the need to ensure that editions attain a certain standard of presentation and are intelligible to the customer, otherwise they will not sell in sufficient quantities to support and promote the business as a whole. Because of its anomalous position within Artaria's output, the edition of Haydn's op. 40 Trios presents us with a good case study for investigating the publishing process with reference to Haydn's correspondence and other related pieces of evidence. The following outline summarizes the key steps in the process in relation to Artaria's practice, as far as that may be determined (it is not intended as a comprehensive description). By viewing the edition in the wider context of Artaria's musical output, we may regard it as a barometer of the firm's negotiation of the commercial and practical aspects of publishing music in 1780s Vienna.

Submission of the manuscript

Haydn had apparently promised to write a set of three 'keyboard sonatas with violin' for Artaria as early as 1782,[18] but the precise date on which Haydn submitted a manuscript of the op. 40 Trios, whether by post or in person, is not documented in his extant correspondence or in any other source. A large gap in the correspondence between 20 November 1784 and 26 November 1785 almost certainly results from the loss of individual letters from this period, rather than a break in contact. Haydn was certainly in Vienna during the early part of 1785, before the opera season at Eszterháza started in April, giving rise to the possibility that he could have submitted the manuscript in person at that point. It is more likely, however, that it was dispatched somewhat later in the year, and perhaps even as late as September or October. Whether he was paid is likewise not documented, though we may legitimately assume on the basis of his other dealings with the firm that he received a fee at the point of submission. On some occasions, Haydn also provided a security receipt to document Artaria's right to publish the works with his authorization.[19] The

18. Undated letter to Artaria, *c.* 24–25 July 1782: *Gesammelte Briefe und Aufzeichnungen*, pp. 115–17; *Collected Correspondence and London Notebooks*, p. 37. He also mentions the 'Clavier Sonaten mit einer Violin und Bass' in his letter to Artaria of 18 June 1783. See *Gesammelte Briefe und Aufzeichnungen*, p. 129; *Collected Correspondence and London Notebooks*, p. 42.

19. See Haydn's letter to Artaria dated 6 April 1789, in which he states 'Übersende die anverlangte von mir unterschriebene zwey Assicurentz Quittungen' ('I enclose the two signed security receipts which you asked for'). See also the receipt dated 7 December 1792, assigning to Artaria the rights to the Minuets and German Dances Hob.XI:11–12 for 24 ducats. *Gesammelte Briefe und Aufzeichnungen*, p. 206 (letter of 6 April 1789); *Collected Correspondence and London Notebooks*, p. 85 (letter of 6 April 1789) and p. 139 (letter of 7 December 1792).

Fig. 3. Joseph Haydn, Piano Trio Hob.XV:7: autograph, p. 1,
reproduced from a microfilm copy held by the British Library:
shelfmark MUS/RP/1431.

format of the submitted manuscript is a matter of particular interest to this investigation. Haydn's autograph score of the second Trio, Hob.XV:7, in oblong format,
offers no clue regarding the copying of the parts, apart from the composer's marginal
notation of the signs for a trill, turn and half mordent in the bottom right-hand
corner of the first page (see Fig. 3). Although it is not entirely clear that this was
written by way of clarification or instruction to a copyist, it does imply that Haydn
was especially keen to ensure that the ornaments were correctly reproduced (but see
also his letter of 10 December 1785, discussed below). Judging from a collection of
manuscripts parts that he sent to the London publisher William Forster,[20] it was
Haydn's normal practice to send chamber and orchestral music in sets of parts, rather
than in score. That collection includes parts for six Piano Trios (Hob.XV:3–5, 10,
9, 2) – of which two (Hob.XV:3–4) were in fact by his pupil Ignaz Pleyel[21] – written

20. London, British Library, Egerton MS 2379, fol. 55r–124r.
21. The case for Pleyel's authorship was first made in Alan Tyson, 'Haydn and Two Stolen Trios',
    The Music Review, 22 (1961), 21–27, on the basis of a contemporary account found in a copy of
    Pleyel's 1803 edition, which is now held by the British Library at shelfmark Tyson P.M.15.(5.).

Fig. 4. Joseph Haydn, Piano Trio Hob.XV:5, ms parts sent to Forster,
London, October 1785 (title-page). BL, Egerton MS 2379, fol. 85r.

on paper lined with ten staves in oblong format by one of Haydn's regular copyists,
Peter Rampl.[22] The words 'to be done longways' also appear on the title-page of the
manuscript for the Piano Trio in G, Hob.XV:5 (fol. 85r), presumably as an instruction
by the publisher to the London engraver (see Fig. 4). It seems reasonable to suppose
that a copyist working for Haydn prepared a similar set of oblong parts for Artaria,
although the possibility that he sent a set of upright parts on this occasion, or even
a score, cannot be ruled out.

22. See Günter Thomas, 'Haydn's Copyist Peter Rampl', in *Haydn, Mozart, & Beethoven: Studies in
the Music of the Classical Period: Essays in Honour of Alan Tyson*, ed. by Sieghard Brandenburg
(Oxford: Clarendon, 1998), pp. 85–90 (p. 88) and H. Edmund Poole, 'Music Engraving Practice
in Eighteenth-Century London: A Study of Some Forster Editions of Haydn and their
Manuscript Sources', in *Music and Bibliography: Essays in Honour of Alec Hyatt King*, ed. by Oliver
Neighbour (London: Bingley, 1980), pp. 98–131.

Preparation of the Stichvorlage

It is safe to assume that manuscripts submitted to the publisher would not usually satisfy the specific needs of a music engraver, unless copied themselves from existing printed sources. Some form of intervention and preparation was therefore necessary before the works could be engraved, but the precise sequence of events that followed the receipt of a manuscript by Artaria is largely unknown. At least from 1784 onwards, a number was assigned immediately at the point of acquisition, giving Artaria a simple method of administrative control over the management of each edition.[23] This number was later engraved on each plate of the edition, to form what we now refer to as the 'plate number'. Thereafter, in cases where the submitted manuscript consisted of a full score, it is very likely that the publisher employed a copyist to prepare a separate *Stichvorlage* for each instrumental or vocal part of the work, rather than instructing an engraver to work directly from the score. Such copyists would have presumably received instructions about the format required for each part and other details of the edition in order to produce a *Stichvorlage* that approximated the design and dimensions of the envisaged edition. Clearly, textual errors could easily be introduced at this stage in the process. Artaria's employment of a music copyist is implied in Haydn's letter of 7 October 1787, in which he accuses the individual of making an illicit copy of his op. 50 String Quartets from within the firm.[24] Where the submitted manuscript consisted of a set of parts, or a single part for a work for a solo instrument, it is equally possible that Artaria prepared a separate *Stichvorlage*, rather than passing the submitted parts directly to the engraver. Even if not, some element of preparation was probably necessary to convey the publisher's specifications to the engraver, perhaps by marking up the text with instructions concerning format, layout, the number of staves per page, and the placing of page turns. Decisions made at this stage would have had financial consequences: the number of engraving plates needed to accommodate the notation and the amount of paper required to print the edition would have implications for the cost of the whole venture and the eventual sale price. To some extent these questions would have been discussed to ensure that the edition met with the publisher's expectations regarding house style. We may assume that the firm entrusted this task to an employee with a fairly high level of musical expertise. The composer Ferdinand Kauer, for example, apparently worked for Artaria over a seventeen-year period and described his po-

23. Rupert Ridgewell, 'Artaria Plate Numbers and the Publication Process, 1778–87', in *Music and the Book Trade*, ed. by Robin Myers, Michael Harris and Giles Mandelbrote (London: British Library and Oak Knoll Press, 2008), pp. 145–78.
24. *Gesammelte Briefe und Aufzeichnungen*, pp. 179–80; *Collected Correspondence and London Notebooks*, pp. 70–71.

sition there as a 'Correcteur', a title that implies some control over proofreading, although the actual nature of his duties are unknown.[25] To a very large extent, however, responsibility for the musical text resided with the engraver, who certainly required some degree of musical knowledge to be able adequately to translate the written notation into engraved text using the tools at his or her disposal.

Engraving

Very little concrete information is available concerning the professional occupation of music engravers in Vienna or the terms under which they were employed in the eighteenth century. We can nevertheless derive some information about engraving practices by studying extant copies of the editions they produced. It is clear, for example, that there was usually a division in labour between the engraving of title-pages and music. Decorative title-pages were common in Artaria's output in the 1780s and were often commissioned from notable Viennese art engravers, no doubt adding significantly to the cost of the edition. The title-page for the Haydn op. 40 Trios is a typical example, with the text enclosed in an oval frame decorated with floral garlands and surmounted by a cupid playing the harp (see Fig. 2 above). The engraving is not signed, but it is very closely related to the title-page engraved by Sebastian Mansfeld (1751–1816) for Mozart's two piano duet sonatas, K381 and K358, published in 1783 (plate number 25).[26] When output started to grow at a faster rate in the late 1780s and 1790s, the firm generally settled for a simpler and more functional design. Responsibility for acquiring a set of 'blank' pewter engraving plates almost certainly resided with the publisher and not with the engraver, although Artaria's supplier for such plates is unknown. Each music engraver, however, worked with his own set of specially designed punches for each element of music notation, including dynamic markings and details of articulation, plus the burin for engraving certain details freehand and (in some cases) letter punches for tempo indications, movement titles and other headings.[27] Although the music for a vast majority of editions published by Artaria was engraved anonymously, at least five individuals may be identified from the engraved signatures that appear on a small

25. Eva Badura-Skoda, 'Ferdinand Kauer', in *Die Musik in Geschichte und Gegenwart*, ed. by Friedrich Blume, 17 vols (Kassel: Bärenreiter, 1958–86), VII/I, col. 739–46 (col. 740).

26. The title-page is reproduced in Gertraut Haberkamp, *Die Erstdrucke der Werke von Wolfgang Amadeus Mozart*, 2 vols (Tutzing: Schneider, 1986), II, 131.

27. For a description of music engraving practices, see Anik Devriès-Lesure, 'Technological Aspects', in *Music Publishing in Europe, 1600–1900*, ed. by Rudolf Rasch (Berlin: Berliner Wissenschafts-Verlag, 2005), pp. 63–88 (pp. 75–83) and H. Edmund Poole, 'Music Engraving Practice in Eighteenth-Century London: A Study of Some Forster Editions of Haydn and their Manuscript Sources', pp. 98–131.

number of editions before 1800: these are Johann Eberspach, Anton Huberty, Phillip Richter, Johann Schäfer and Joseph Zahradníczek.[28] Of these individuals, Zahradníczek is also known to have been an active musician, playing mandolin for the Hoftheater in the 1780s.[29]

From the pattern of their activities, it seems likely that music engravers typically worked freelance in the 1780s rather than being contracted exclusively to a single publisher. Huberty's signature, for example, appears on editions issued by at least four other Viennese music publishers in addition to Artaria during the early 1780s (he also issued his own editions in collaboration with the book publisher Joseph Krüchten), while Zahradníczek worked for Christoph Torricella and Artaria.[30] None of these engravers was involved in the production of Haydn's op. 40 Trios, but it is nevertheless possible to identify the work of two different engravers from the distinctive shapes of the punches used in the edition. Based on analysis of a copy of the earliest known state of the edition, held in Paris, it is clear that one engraver took care of the piano part, while the other was responsible for the two string parts.[31] There were good practical reasons for dividing an edition in this way, when it was possible to separate the parts. For one thing, it helped to speed up the process of publication by having two or more engravers working on an edition simultaneously. It also helped to protect the publisher's rights by making it more difficult for a work to be copied and stolen in its entirety. The practice of dividing parts between copyists was also not uncommon at that time, no doubt for similar reasons.[32] Not surprisingly, editions produced by multiple engravers became increasingly common in Artaria's output from 1786 onwards, but they nonetheless raise questions about how the publisher maintained editorial control, not least to ensure a consistent approach to matters of format, pagination and overall presentation.

Clearly, the unusual mixed format in Haydn's op. 40 Trios could have resulted from confusion at this stage in the process. A survey of Artaria's output suggests

28. For editions associated with these engravers, see *Répertoire International des Sources Musicales*, Series A/1: *Einzeldrucke vor 1800* (Kassel: Bärenreiter-Verlag, 1971–2003), XV: *Register der Verleger, Drucker und Stecher und Register der Orte zu den Bänden 1–9 und 11–14*, p. 176 (Eberspach), p. 278 (Huberty), p. 488 (Richter), p. 511 (Schäfer), and p. 629 (Zahradníczek).

29. Dexter Edge, 'Mozart's Viennese Orchestras', *Early Music*, 20 (1992), 76. According to Heinz Schuler, Zahradníczek also held an appointment as a trumpeter for the Hungarian Life Guard. See Heinz Schuler, *Mozart und die Freimauer* (Wilhelmshaven: Noetzel, 1992), p. 152.

30. For a preliminary list of Huberty's work for various publishers, see Alexander Weinmann, *Verlagsverzeichnisse Anton Huberty (Wien) und Christoph Torricella*, Beiträge zur Geschichte des Alt-Wiener Musikverlages, ser. 2, issue 7 (Vienna: Universal Edition, 1962), pp. 86–88.

31. Paris, Bibliothèque nationale de France, Vm7–5478.

32. Haydn's regular copyists Peter Rampl and Johann Elssler, for example, shared the copying of the instrumental parts for the German dances Hob.IX:12 and a copy of the full score of *The Creation*. See Thomas, 'Haydn's Copyist Peter Rampl', pp. 88–89.

that the engraver of the string parts appears to have worked for the firm only twice before, on sets of parts for Haydn's Symphonies nos 79 and 81 (plate numbers 62 and 63), and perhaps for this reason was unaware of the firm's practice regarding the format to be used for chamber music with piano; alternatively, Artaria failed to communicate it.[33] Indeed, if the engraver were active as a practising musician, it might have seemed more natural to him to present the violin and cello parts in the upright format: oblong parts are, after all, not ideal for string players, making it more difficult to view the extremities of the music when laid out on a music desk. Perhaps the inconsistent format and mixed engraving resulted from the need to re-engrave the string parts for some reason. This seems unlikely, however, since there is no documentary or textual evidence to suggest the existence of an earlier state of the edition with oblong string parts.

Printing the proof

Before 1786, commercial regulations prevented Artaria from establishing their own printing workshop, which means that the firm was obliged to engage independent printers operating in Vienna's suburbs to undertake this work on a piece-rate basis. No records relating to the employment of printers is known to survive, so we are in the dark as far as day-to-day business is concerned, although the identities of several printers operating during this period have been established.[34] Reforms introduced by Joseph II in 1786 encouraged greater freedom of competition by allowing printers to trade in books and booksellers to operate printing presses.[35] It is thought that Artaria established a printing workshop with seven presses in the early 1790s, a development that allowed the firm to gain control over the printing process for the

33. The firm went on to employ the same engraver on a regular basis and evidence of his work may be found in at least thirty-two editions published in 1786 and 1787, including shared engravings of string quartets by Pleyel and Rosetti, various editions of works by Haydn and Vanhal, and six issues in Artaria's series of Mozart keyboard variations. See Rupert Ridgewell, 'Biographical Myth and the Publication of Mozart's Piano Quartets', *Journal of the Royal Musical Association*, 135 (2010), 41–114 (pp. 96–97), where this engraver is labelled as 'Hoffmeister 1'.

34. For information about Viennese copperplate printers active in Vienna in the eighteenth century, see Peter R. Frank and Johannes Frimmel, *Buchwesen in Wien 1750–1850: Kommentiertes Verzeichnis der Buchdrucker, Buchhändler und Verleger*, Buchforschung: Beiträge zum Buchwesen in Österreich, 4 (Wiesbaden: Harrassowitz Verlag, 2008), pp. 223–33.

35. A court decree issued in November 1786 states that 'every book printer should be permitted to trade in books, and every book dealer [permitted] to establish a printing workshop', so long as they were adequately equipped. See Rupert Ridgewell, 'Music Printing in Mozart's Vienna: the Artaria Press', *Fontes Artis Musicae*, 48 (2001), 217–36 (pp. 220–22).

first time and improve productivity.[36] The task of proofing a new edition *before* 1790 now emerges as a fairly complicated matter. In the 1780s, a set of plates presumably had to be sent from the engraver to the printer for the proof to be printed and then back to the engraver for any corrections to be made, before being sent again to the printer for the first main batch of copies to be run from the press. Aside from the logistics of transporting sets of plates around Vienna, this process was no doubt time-consuming and liable to delay. The first unequivocal mention of the op. 40 Trios in Haydn's correspondence appears in his letter to Artaria of 26 November 1785, in which he requests a 'first printing', or proof copy, to check:[37]

> Please let me know, by the Monday dispatch of the Princely Hussars, if my Sonatas are already engraved, and when you intend to give them to the Countess Witzey; the reason why I would very much like to know is that, before my departure, which will be in a fortnight at the latest, I want to pay a visit to the Countess at her estate; I only waited for the first printing of the Sonatas, in order to correct them, for there is a mistake that needs to be set right. Therefore please write to me once more next Monday. I would also ask you to send me a copy of the last Lieder on this occasion; I shall pay for it with thanks. I am, most respectfully.

Your wholly obedient servant,
Haydn.

The nature of the mistake Haydn wanted to correct is not made clear in the letter: it could equally have related to the wording of the title-page as to the musical text. This former possibility is implied by the context in which Haydn's request was made: an imminent visit to the edition's dedicatee, Countess Marianne Witzay née Grassalkovich de Gyarak, whose father's estate was located at Nagylózs, some ten miles southwest of the palace of Eszterháza.[38] An administrative note on this letter indicates that Artaria responded on the 6th ('beantwortet den 6. Xbis') and we know from Haydn's next letter to Artaria, dated 10 December, that he received a proof copy on the 8th (the 'day before yesterday'). The edition must therefore have been already engraved, or at least very close to completion, by the end of November to allow time for the proof to be printed and dispatched.

---

36. An inventory of the firm's printing workshop is reproduced and described in Ridgewell, 'Music Printing in Mozart's Vienna'.

37. *Gesammelte Briefe und Aufzeichnungen*, p. 147; *Collected Correspondence and London Notebooks*, p. 50.

38. *Gesammelte Briefe und Aufzeichnungen*, p. 147, n. 2. According to Katalin Komlós, two-thirds of piano trio editions published in Vienna in the late eighteenth century were printed with dedications, nearly all of which were addressed to women pianists and aristocrats. See Katalin Komlós, 'The Viennese Keyboard Trio in the 1780s: Sociological Background and Contemporary Reception', *Music & Letters*, 68 (1987), 222–34 (p. 223).

178   T H E   L A N D   O F   O P P O R T U N I T Y

Proofreading

Haydn immediately set to work annotating the proof with corrections, either by comparing the printed parts with his score or by simply reading the parts and correcting them from memory. He may also have taken the opportunity to add details of dynamic markings or articulation that had not been notated before, or even make small adjustments to the notation. He returned the proof copy to Artaria with a lengthy covering letter dated 10 December, which outlines his analysis of the edition's failings:[39]

> The day before yesterday I received the pianoforte Sonatas, and was greatly astounded to have to see such bad engraving, and so many glaring errors in all the parts, especially in the pianoforte part. I was at first so furious that I wanted to return the money to you and send the score of the Sonatas instantly to Herr Hummel in Berlin; for the sections which are occasionally illegible, and the passages omitted or badly spaced, will bring little honour to me and little profit to you. Everyone who buys them will curse the engraver and have to stop playing, especially on page 8, and on the first page of the 3rd Divertimento, page 15, where the passage marked in red is especially badly laid out, and this really seems to be the result of complete stinginess. I would rather pay for two new plates out of my own pocket than to see such confusion. Even a professional would have to study before disentangling this passage, and then where would the dilettante be?

The composer goes on to describe in some detail the notational problems associated with the engraving, insisting that the corrections should be implemented before the edition went to press and referring to points that were marked on the proof. The letter is remarkable not only for its tone, but also for the detail in Haydn's criticism, giving a very real sense of how he thought Artaria's edition should look:

> Four notes are missing on page 18, and in the last line the engraver was too lazy to write out the whole of the bass part: such abbreviations and signs are all very well in the viola part of symphonies, but not in pianoforte parts. Moreover, most of the natural signs ♮ are so small, and occasionally so close to the note, that you can barely see them: one such case is found on page 18, at the end of the uppermost stave. There are prodigiously many wrong notes and omitted notes. On pages 6 and 8 most of the following sign ⌒ are wrongly placed, for they ought not to be put directly over the note but over the neighbouring dot, in this way: ♫ (page 6, bar 4). All the way through, the dots ought to be further away from the notes, so that the sign ⌒ comes directly over the dot. And on this very page, in the second stave, you should put instead of the sign *tr*: the following: ∿ ,

39. *Gesammelte Briefe und Aufzeichnungen*, p. 148; *Collected Correspondence and London Notebooks*, p. 51.

for the first one, as the engraver has done it, means a trill, whilst mine is a half mordent. If, therefore, the Herr Engraver doesn't know signs of this sort, he should inform himself by studying the masters, and not follow his own stupid ideas. In the 2nd Sonata he even forgot the tempo at the beginning, where the clef is. A whole bar is missing in the violin part, too. I spent the whole of yesterday and half of today in correcting, and yet I have only glanced over them.

Now, my good friend, see to it that everything is corrected, for otherwise little honour will accrue to either of us. By the way, I hope to see you personally and am, meanwhile, most respectfully,

Your wholly obedient servant,

Joseph Haydn.

It should be noted that Haydn's references in the letter to the trill, turn, and half mordent relate directly to his marginal annotation of those signs in the autograph of the second trio (see Fig. 3 above). How the firm dealt with Haydn's complaints and the extent to which it sought to bring the edition into line with his expectations is an issue that may be explored by comparing the specific points raised in his letter with extant copies of the edition. After all, it was surely in the publisher's best interests to make sure that the edition was clear, accurate and could be used in performance. Failure in this respect simply did not make good business sense, a point that was clearly not lost on Haydn himself: as he says in the letter, the faulty edition would 'bring little honour to me and little profit to you'. Any remedial work would nevertheless need to be balanced against the additional cost and delay caused by the process of re-engraving all or part of the edition.

Implementing proof corrections

We don't know how the firm responded to Haydn, or what reassurances it was able to give him. However there is one piece of evidence that should be introduced at this point because it appears to show that Artaria took immediate steps to address Haydn's complaints. This evidence comes from a rather remote and unlikely source, a letter sent by the music publisher Bernhard Schott to Canon Johann Georg Battonn (1740–1827), librarian of the Bartholomäus Stift (Monastery of St Bartholomew) in Frankfurt.[40] The letter dates from 3 January 1786, a little more than three weeks after Haydn wrote his letter of complaint, and the relevant passage is as follows: 'Artaria has asked me to repair the ruined piano trios for the Countess

---

40. For information about Battonn, see Volker Harms-Ziegler, 'Ein Mainzer in Frankfurt – Der Historiker Johann Georg Battonn', Institut für Stadtgeschichte Frankfurt, Newsletter 6 (October 2006), www.stadtgeschichte-ffm.de (accessed 21 August 2013).

Witzay. I will therefore engrave them straight away'.[41] This rather confounds one's understanding about how music was produced in Vienna during the 1780s, suggesting as it does that Artaria asked Schott to 'repair' the edition in Mainz, rather than undertaking the work in Vienna. It would seem safe to assume that Artaria's operations were based entirely in Vienna. Why then would they consider sending the edition all the way to Mainz to be 'repaired'? Was this an unusual procedure employed as a result of Haydn's strong criticisms, or was it actually common practice at the time? By way of context, it should be noted that Artaria did have commercial interests in Mainz and maintained a shop there as well as in Vienna. Indeed, we know that Francesco Artaria, who was one of the principal partners in the firm alongside his cousins Carlo and Domenico, was in Mainz at precisely this time. On 14 January 1786, the composer Franz Xaver Sterkel wrote to Artaria in Vienna offering a selection of excerpts from his opera *Il Farnace* and states that he had discussed the excerpts with Francesco during the latter's stay in Mainz a few weeks previously.[42] It is conceivable, therefore, that Francesco travelled to Mainz at some point between 10 December 1785 and 3 January 1786, with a view to engaging Schott's help with the Haydn edition; he could even have brought the engraving plates with him. Furthermore, if the edition was fully re-engraved, it might also explain the anomalous format of the string parts, since an engraver working for Schott might not be expected to be aware of Artaria's specifications. Even if Schott wasn't directly involved in the re-engraving (there is, after all, no indication that the edition was conceived as some kind of a joint publication), it is quite possible that he could have recommended a local freelance engraver, who likewise would not necessarily have been aware of the Artaria house style.

Was Artaria's edition therefore re-engraved, either in full or in part? The evidence of the extant copies suggests not, even though the plates for the string parts show no sign of being repaired and might therefore look – superficially – as if they had been newly engraved. The general complaints raised by Haydn in his letter appear to be fully satisfied in the engraving of these parts: natural signs are clearly legible

---

41. Hoboken, *Werkverzeichnis*, I, 688: 'Artaria hat mich gebeten die verdorbenen Klaviertrios für die Gräfin Witzay zu reparieren. Ich werde sie also schleunigst stechen'. Hoboken cites two other letters to Batton held by the Schott archive (see *Werkverzeichnis*, II, 52, 66), but does not give the location of this letter.

42. Letter, Franz Xaver Sterkel to Artaria, Mainz 14 January 1786: 'Vermöge der verabredung, welche ich mit S^{gr} Francesco Artaria in betreff einiger Arien Duetten und Terzetten aus meiner Italiänischen opera bey seiner anwesenheit vor einigen wochen in Mayntz getroffen, um sie bey Ihnen zum stiche zu geben, sind wir bisdahin übereins gekommen, dieselbe, so bald sie kopirt wären, Ihnen nach Wien zu übermachen.' See *Johann Franz Xaver Sterkels Briefwechsel mit seinen Verlegern*, ed. by Axel Beer and Dagmar Schnell, Beiträge zur Mittelrheinischen Musikgeschichte, 36 (Mainz: Schott, 2001), p. 41.

Fig. 5a. Joseph Haydn, three Piano Trios Hob.XV:6–8 (Vienna: Artaria, 1786), violin part, p. 5, stave 6. F Pn, shelfmark Vm7–5478.

Fig. 5b. Joseph Haydn, three Piano Trios Hob.XV:6–8 (Vienna: Artaria, 1786), violin part, p. 7, stave 12. F Pn, Vm7–5478.

and placed at a regular distance away from the note and signs indicating a turn are clearly indicated and placed directly above the dot between the notes. Haydn's only specific comment about the violin part concerns a whole bar of music that was somehow left out by the engraver, a mistake that might easily occur if the part had been engraved separately and without reference to the keyboard part. However, it seems possible to suppose that this may have been a bar's rest, which was squeezed into the engraving at the beginning of the sixth stave on page 5 (see Fig. 5a). And at least one important mistake was apparently overlooked by Haydn, or at least not corrected in the engraving: a run of four quavers in bar 2 of the penultimate stave on page 7 should, in fact, be semiquavers (see Fig. 5b).

But the anger expressed in Haydn's letter was directed not so much at the engraving of the string parts, which are hardly mentioned at all; if anything had to be repaired, it was surely the keyboard part. Artaria had employed this second engraver sporadically for about three years before this edition was published, including the production of four Haydn editions: the aria 'Or vicina a te' from Haydn's opera *L'incontro improviso*, the Keyboard Concerto in D (Hob.XVIII:11), the collection of *Menuetti Ballabili* for various instruments (Hob.IX:7), and a set of twelve keyboard minuets (Hob.IX:8). He was certainly not a beginner or an apprentice and yet the general quality of the engraving gives the impression that it was executed rather clumsily and perhaps in unusual haste. Looking at the keyboard part in relation to Haydn's comments, we find that it was not fully re-engraved, but instead corrected in at least some of the ways that the composer demanded, and mainly where it was possible to implement the corrections without disrupting the existing text to any great extent. For example, Haydn drew attention in his letter to two specific errors on page 18, relating to the end of the first movement of the third trio

Fig. 6a. Joseph Haydn, three Piano Trios Hob.XV:6–8 (Vienna: Artaria, 1786),
keyboard part, p. 18, system 5. F Pn, Vm7–5478.

Fig. 6b. Joseph Haydn, three Piano Trios Hob.XV:6–8 (Vienna: Artaria, 1786),
keyboard part, p. 18, system 1. F Pn, Vm7–5478.

in the set. His first comment relates to the last line of music, where he states the
engraver did not write out the repeated bass notes fully, but instead abbreviated
them in a way that was – in Haydn's view – appropriate in the viola part of a symphony but not in a keyboard part. Haydn was presumably referring to an abbreviation of the repeated B flat quavers in the left hand in bars 2 to 5, a passage that had
been fully adjusted by the time this copy was printed, almost certainly by re-engraving the left-hand part only (see Fig. 6a). Some evidence of the correction may be
reflected in the slightly irregular stems to some of the notes, suggesting that they
were lengthened. Haydn's second comment refers to the end of the first system of
music on the same page, where he points to the placing of a natural sign that was
so close to the note that it could hardly be seen. In this case it is safe to assume that
Haydn's point was ignored. The last bar of that system has semiquavers in the right
hand and a natural sign that nearly overlaps the preceding note, making it difficult
to distinguish part of the sign (see Fig. 6b). This seems to be the result of bad plan-
ning on the part of the engraver, judging from the lack of space available to accommodate all the notes in that bar, and it was probably deemed impossible to improve
this passage without substantial re-engraving.

    Haydn also highlighted three errors on page 6, which marked the beginning of
the second movement in the first trio of the set. Two of Haydn's comments related
to the placing of the sign for a turn, which he wanted to appear between the notes,

Fig. 7a. Joseph Haydn, three Piano Trios Hob.XV:6–8 (Vienna: Artaria, 1786),
keyboard part, p. 6, system 1. F Pn, Vm7–5478.

Fig. 7b. Joseph Haydn, three Piano Trios Hob.XV:6–8 (Vienna: Artaria, 1786),
keyboard part, p. 6, system 2. F Pn, shelfmark Vm7–5478.

rather than directly over the first note head. He mentions this specifically in relation to bar 4, by which he presumably meant the third full bar of music in the first line (see Fig. 7a). Since the turn appeared above the stave, it was possible for the engraver to remove the existing sign and punch it in the new position without disturbing the musical text below, even though some residual 'smudging' is visible where the change was made, arising from rough indentations on the surface of the plate. In the second system, Haydn states that the engraver had engraved the sign for a trill instead of a half mordent, prompting his barbed comment about the engraver's level of musical competence. This particular correction was also incorporated into the edition: the sign for a half mordent appears above the right hand in bars 3 and 5 (Fig. 7b).[43]

Haydn drew attention to two omissions in his letter. First, he states that 'four notes are missing on page 18' without going into any further detail, presumably because he marked the omitted notes on the proof. Without further information it is not possible to determine which notes were omitted: certainly, the music on page 18 appears to be fully notated, which implies that this correction was implemented.

43. For discussion of this letter in relation to Haydn's preferences with regard to ornamentation, see Bernard Harrison, *Haydn's Keyboard Music: Studies in Performance Practice* (Oxford: Clarendon Press, 1997), pp. 331–33.

Fig. 7c. Joseph Haydn, three Piano Trios Hob.XV:6–8 (Vienna: Artaria, 1786), keyboard part, p. 9, system 1. F Pn, shelfmark Vm7–5478.

The second omission was the tempo indication 'Andante' at the beginning of the second trio on page 9. This indication is present in Haydn's autograph and was evidently added to the engraving at the beginning of the movement in response to his instruction (see Fig. 7c). Like the other elements of text in the edition, the letters were engraved freehand rather than being knocked into the plate using punches, and therefore reflect the engraver's personal style. A second appearance of the word 'Andante' in the same movement (p. 11, system 2) shares the same distinctive characteristics, notably the shape of the letter 'A', offering further confirmation that the edition was the work of a single engraver. The edition is also a source of some readings that are not in Haydn's autograph of the D major Trio, notably dynamic markings. The autograph is typical of the composer's practice in being largely devoid of dynamic markings, although there are a few in the second movement. To take only one example, the *forte* marking at the beginning of the first movement is missing in the autograph, but present in the edition (see Fig. 3 and Fig. 7c above). One can only assume that Haydn added this and other dynamic markings either to the copy submitted to Artaria or in the proof.

Despite these corrections and additions, the keyboard part displays many of the problems identified in Haydn's letter, notably badly spaced passages of semiquavers and poor alignment of the treble and bass. He refers specifically to two instances where the performer would 'curse the engraver and have to stop playing' because the music was badly laid out. The first of these passages was on page 8 and may be identified as corresponding to the three bars shown in Fig. 8a. The alignment between the right and left hand is especially poor here in the syncopated passage in the first and second bars: there was apparently no attempt by the engraver to coordinate the left-hand crotchets with the off-beat notes in the right hand. The second passage Haydn specifies was on page 15, almost certainly the passage shown in Fig. 8b, where again the engraver failed to represent the off-beat right hand against the crotchets in the left hand in the spacing of the notes on the page. Faced

Fig. 8a. Joseph Haydn, three Piano Trios Hob.XV:6–8 (Vienna: Artaria, 1786), keyboard part, p. 8, system 1. F Pn, shelfmark Vm7–5478.

Fig. 8b. Joseph Haydn, three Piano Trios Hob.XV:6–8 (Vienna: Artaria, 1786), keyboard part, p. 15, system 5. F Pn, shelfmark Vm7–5478.

with this faulty engraving, a less than proficient keyboard player might be inclined to render the passage mostly as a series of unison chords. The problem is not specific to this edition, but may be found in other editions associated with this particular engraver. Similar examples may be found in editions of Haydn's Keyboard Concerto in D and Giuseppe Sarti's *Sonata caracteristica* for solo keyboard, op. 1 (see Figs 9a, 9b and 9c). This implies a pattern of behaviour that resulted not so much from 'stinginess' in laying out the music, as Haydn would have it, but a certain lack of understanding of the practical aspects of keyboard performance.

Overall we therefore gain a fairly mixed picture from comparing Haydn's letter with the sources available to us, with some errors obviously corrected in the edition and others apparently ignored, and with some details in the edition that are not found in Haydn's autograph. Even if Artaria initially considered engaging Schott's help, it is quite certain that the edition was not fully re-engraved, but was instead sent back to the original Viennese engravers for some – though not all – of Haydn's corrections to be implemented before it went to press. Despite the evidence of his letter to Canon Battonn, Bernhard Schott apparently had nothing to do with the final product.

Fig. 9a. Joseph Haydn, Keyboard Concerto in D Hob.XVIII:11 (Vienna: Artaria, 1784), keyboard part, p. 11, system 5. BL, shelmark h.655.p.

Fig. 9b. Joseph Haydn, Keyboard Concerto in D Hob.XVIII:11 (Vienna: Artaria, 1784), keyboard part, p. 11, system 4. BL, shelfmark h.655.p.

Publication and dissemination

Following the return of the plates from the engraver, it is not likely that Haydn received a second proof of the edition to check that his corrections had been taken into account. Once again, the documentary record of Haydn's contact with Artaria is sparse during the period in which the edition was corrected, owing to the loss of correspondence between the two parties between the extant letters dated 10 December 1785 and 11 February 1787. We can only assume that the plates were amended in early 1786 and the first print run was produced before the edition was advertised in the *Wiener Zeitung* on 26 April 1786. How many copies were initially printed is unknown, but the edition attracted significant interest from foreign publishers and dealers, so that Artaria's market expanded beyond the confines of Vienna and justified reprinting the edition periodically over the following months. Artaria's advertisement was, in fact, pre-empted by four days by Pierre Leduc in Paris, who advertised a set of piano trios by Haydn as 'opus 43' in the *Journal de la Librairie* on 22 April 1786. It is not entirely clear whether this was a new edition published in parallel with Artaria, or whether Leduc initially offered copies of Artaria's edition on commission. Although Leduc did indeed issue an edition 'based on the edition

Fig. 9c. Giuseppe Sarti, Sonata caracteristica per il Clavicembalo o forte-piano Op. 1 Giulio sabino ed Epponina (Vienna: Artaria, 1785), p. 9, system 5. BL, Hirsch M.1456

of Vienna' ('selon l'édition de Vienne') with the plate number 181, the exact date of publication has not yet been established and it may well have been issued only after Leduc had sold out of copies of Artaria's edition.[44] Some evidence in favour of the latter possibility is found on a copy of Artaria's edition held by the Bibliothèque nationale de France, in which the opus number has been changed on the title-page in a contemporary hand from '40' to '43'. The text of Leduc's advertisement also tends to support this hypothesis ('Sonates pour le clavecin, avec acc. de Vl. & Vlc […] Oeuvre XLIII, imprimé à Vienne').[45] Indeed, as late as 1790 Le Duc bought thirty-one copies of the edition from Artaria as part of a large consignment of material covering Artaria's output over the preceding years.[46]

Confusion over the designation of an opus number to the set is reflected in editions that were published over the following months: Boyer & Le Menu's edition was advertised as 'opus 45' on 27 May 1786, while Hummel advertised the works as 'opus 25' on 1 July 1786, Götz and Schmitt published them as 'oeuvre 41', and the firms of Longman & Broderip, Johann André and William Forster all published editions before the end of 1786 with the opus number 43.[47] In London, it is possible to document quite precisely the sequence of events from legal records unearthed by Nancy Mace. According to a receipt issued by Artaria on 4 July 1786, Longman & Broderip purchased eighty copies of Artaria's edition for the sum of £21 and 13 shillings, making it possible for Longman to place an advertisement for the edition in the *Morning Herald* on 31 July 1786. The firm also sent a manuscript copy, perhaps – as Mace speculates – as a way to validate Longman's right to publish the

44. RISM, Series A/1, H3644.
45. Hoboken, *Werkverzeichnis*, I, 688.
46. See Rupert Ridgewell, 'Mozart's Music on Sale in Vienna and Paris, 1780–1790', in *The Circulation of Music in Europe, 1600–1900: A Collection of Essays and Case Studies*, ed. by Rudolf Rasch (Berlin: Berliner Wissenschafts-Verlag, 2008), pp. 121–42 (p. 141).
47. Hoboken, *Werkverzeichnis*, I, 688–89.

works in London under his own imprint, which he formalized by registering the new edition at Stationers' Hall on 26 October 1786.[48] At the same time, William Forster prepared an edition of the same works and advertised it in the *Morning Herald* on 21 November 1786. Perhaps knowing that his entitlement to sell the edition was not secure, Forster failed to register it at Stationers' Hall and the question of the work's ownership escalated into a legal dispute between Forster and Longman & Broderip. In legal proceedings that continued until 1792, Longman tried unsuccessfully to claim sole rights to the edition, while Forster denied pirating Longman's edition directly, claiming instead (in a legal deposition dated 6 January 1792) to have used a copy of Artaria's edition purchased from Longman in July 1786.[49] Longman's registration copy and a copy of Forster's edition acquired by the Royal Music Library later entered the collections of the British Museum Library and represented the full extent of its holdings of these works until the acquisition of the Artaria violin part in 1949.

While the French, English and German editions are of no great textual significance compared to Artaria's first edition, they are nevertheless important in documenting the dissemination of Haydn's music during his lifetime and in demonstrating the wide market for his music in the late 1780s and 1790s. This explains why Artaria continued to reprint the edition in the months and years after its first publication, as the firm sought to maximize the commercial potential of their catalogue. How many copies were printed is not documented, but analysis of eighteen copies of the edition suggests it went through at least four different states (see Table 1).[50] The second state may be identified by a few minor changes to the title-page, including a change in the spelling of 'Grassalkowics' to 'Grasalkowitz', a correction to the firm's privilege statement from 'Com. Priv. S. C. M.' to 'Cum. Priv. S. C. M.' (an abbreviation of 'Cum Privilegio Sacrae Cesarea Majestatis') and the addition of the accent in 'À Vienne'. At some point thereafter, the firm also decided to amend the opus number given on the title-page, changing it from 'oeuvre 40' to 'oeuvre 45', presumably to distinguish the edition from the set of three symphonies published originally as op. 38–40 in 1785 (and later as op. 40, numbers 1, 2 and 3:

48. See Nancy A. Mace, 'Haydn and the London Music Sellers: Forster and Longman & Broderip', in *Music & Letters*, 77 (1996), 527–41 (p. 530).

49. See Mace, 'Haydn and the London Music Sellers', p. 536.

50. I am grateful to Ruthann B. McTyre, Remi Castonguay, Bozena Blechert, Michael Ladenburger and Michel Noiray for assistance in describing the copies held in Iowa, New Haven, Kiel, Bonn and Paris respectively. I have been unable to consult two further copies listed in RISM Series A/I, held in the Musashino Ongaku Daigaku (Tokyo) and in the Stift Sankt Lambrect (Austria) respectively, although they are likely to be exemplars of either the third or fourth states, with the opus number changed on the title-page to 45.

Fig. 10. Joseph Haydn, three Piano Trios Hob.XV:6–8 (Vienna: Artaria, 1786), keyboard part, p. 6, stave 1. NL Uu, shelfmark LBMUZ: RAR C Artaria 75.

Hob.I:79–81).[51] This amendment (the third state) must have taken place by the time Artaria published their sale catalogue of January 1788, in which the edition is listed as op. 45,[52] and was probably implemented around the time of the publication of 'op. 46', a set of keyboard arrangements first advertised on 9 September 1786.[53] In the fourth state, page 6 of the keyboard part was replaced with a newly engraved plate, perhaps because the original plate was damaged in some way, or because cracks on the surface of the plate intruded significantly on the clarity of the printed text. Ironically, one side effect of this substitution was the reversal of at least one of Haydn's corrections: the sign for a turn in bar 3 was placed over the first note head in the new plate, rather than between the notes as Haydn had specified (see Fig. 10).[54] While there is no guarantee that these variants represent the full publication history of Artaria's edition, they do at least show that demand for the trios was such

51. The original numbering of opp. 38–40 was added in manuscript to a passepartout title-page used for these editions; later, the title-page was adjusted by an engraver to read 'oeuvre 40', with the numbering 1–3 being added in manuscript for each of the three symphonies.

52. *Verzeichnis von Musikalien welche bei Artaria Compagnie, Kunst- Kupferstich- Landkarten-Musikalien-Händlern und Verlegern in Wien auf dem Kohlmarkt der Michaeler Kirche gegenüber zu haben sind. Im Jäner 1788* (Vienna, 1788), p. 41. The catalogue is reproduced in *Die Sortimentskataloge der Musikalienhandlung Artaria & Comp. in Wien aus den Jahren 1779, 1780, 1782, 1785 und 1788*, ed. by Otto Biba and Ingrid Fuchs (Tutzing: Schneider, 2006), pp. 243–326.

53. Joseph Haydn, *Différentes petites Pièces faciles et agréables, Oeuvre 46* (Vienna: Artaria, 1786); see RISM A/I, H 4300 and Hob.XVII: Anhang (Hoboken, *Werkverzeichnis*, I, 799). The likelihood that the first three states appeared within a short space of time in 1786 is suggested by the fact that the copies examined were printed on the same type of paper, with a watermark consisting of three crescent moons facing a crown over the letters AV.

54. Copy held by the University Library in Utrecht, shelfmark LBMUZ: RAR C Artaria 75.

State	Criteria	RISM	Exemplars
1	Title-page text: TROIS SONATES / POUR LE CLAUECIN OU PIANO FORTE / accompagnées d'un Violon et Violoncelle / Composées par / IOSEPH HAYDN / Maitre de Chapelle de S.A.S. Monseig. le Prince Esterhazy &. / Oeuvre 40me / Dediées / A MADAME LA COMTESSE / MARIANNE DE WITZAY / Neé Comtesse de Grassalkowics / par ses très humbles et très / obeis^ts. serviteurs Artaria / Com.Priv.S.C.M. A Vienne chez Artaria Compagnie Prix 3f / 75.	H3641	F Pn: Vm7 5478 (ms op. no.: 43)
2	Title-page changes: 'PIANO FORTE' changed to 'PIANO=FORTE' 'Esterhazy' changed to 'd'Esterhazy' 'Grassalkowics' changed to 'Grasalkowitz' 'humbles et' changed to 'humbles, et' 'Com.Priv.S. C. M.' changed to 'Cum.Priv.S.C.M.' 'A Vienne' changed to 'À Vienne'	H3641	A Wn-h: S.H. Haydn 722 A Wst: M23994 (ms op. no.: 41) D BNba: Slg. Grundmann D Kll (pf only): Yw 106 E Mn: M.GUELBENZU/1317(3) F Pc: A.34.344 (ms op. no.: 41) I PS (pf, vl only): B 169/20 US NH (pf only): Ma31 H32 J35 (ms op. no.: 45)
3	Title-page change: 'Oeuvre 40me' changed to 'Oeuvre 45me'	H3642	A Wn-h: S.H. Haydn 723 (pf and vln only) CZ Pnm: XXXIII F 26 US HOUr: M312 .H43 H.XV,6–8 1786
4	p. 6 of the pf part is newly engraved	H3642	NL Uu: LBMUZ: RAR C Artaria 75 US IO: FOLIO M312.H43 A8
Unknown	Copies lack title-page	H3641 and H3642	D F: Mus.pr. Q 49/216 F Pc: A.34.325 (vln and vlc only) F Pn: Vm7 6019 (vlc only) GB Lbl: g.455.i.(10.) (vln only)

Source locations

A Wn-h	Hoboken collection, Musiksammlung, Österreichische Nationalbibliothek, Vienna
A Wst	Wienbibliothek im Rathaus, Vienna
CZ Pnm	Nàrodnì museum, Prague
D BNba	Wissenschaftliches Beethoven-Archiv, Bonn
D F	Musik- und Theaterabteilung, Universitätsbibliothek Johann Christian Senckenberg, Frankfurt am Main
D Kll	Schleswig-Holsteinische Landesbibliothek, Kiel
E Mn	Biblioteca Nacional, Madrid
F Pc	Bibliothèque du Conservatoire, Bibliotheque nationale de France, Paris
F Pn	Département de la Musique, Bibliothèque nationale de France, Paris
GB Lbl	British Library, London
I PS	Biblioteca dell'Archivio Capitolare, Pistoia
NL Uu	Rariora-collectie Muziekwetenschap, Universiteitsbibliotheek Utrecht
US IO	Rita Benton Music Library, University of Iowa, Iowa City
US NH	Beinecke Rare Book and Manuscript Library, Yale University, New Haven
US HOUr	Fondren Library, Rice University, Houston

that reprints were required periodically. Another indicator of the edition's success within the firm's publishing programme is its continuing presence in Artaria's sale catalogues until at least the 1840s.[55]

Conclusion

The extent to which Haydn's piano trios were published and reprinted in the 1780s clearly reflects not only demand for Haydn's music, but also the popularity of the genre among musical amateurs in the main centres of musical activity throughout Europe. In Vienna, no fewer than seventy new editions of music for piano trio were published between 1781 and 1790, most of them from 1786 onwards.[56] In this context it should not come as a surprise that Artaria was anxious to bring the new trios to market as soon as possible. Viewed in the context of Artaria's output as a whole

55. The trios are listed in a copy of an undated Artaria catalogue held by the British Library at shelfmark R.B.23.b.784 (*Verzeichniss der Musikalien im Verlage der Kunsthandlung Artaria & Comp.*, p. 4). Judging from the contents, this catalogue probably first appeared in around 1846. The trios do not, however, appear in Artaria's 1837 catalogue: see *Verzeichniss des Musik-Verlags von Artaria & Comp., k.k. priv. Kunsthändlern* (Vienna: Artaria, 1837), British Library shelfmark Hirsch IV.1095.

56. Katalin Komlós, 'The Viennese Keyboard Trio in the 1780s: Sociological Background and Contemporary Reception', p. 224.

and in relation to the constraints under which it operated, the edition of Haydn's op. 40 Trios emerges at an important moment in the history of the firm. The imminent relaxation of printing restrictions in Vienna promised a substantial increase in productivity, but in 1786 the firm's ambition did not quite match the resources available to it. To speed up the process of preparing music for publication, the firm began to experiment with the practice of dividing an edition between two different engravers. This practice became ever more prevalent in the late 1780s and 1790s as the firm's output of new editions expanded rapidly. The edition of Haydn's trios was an early example of that experiment, which resulted in something unique in Artaria's output, an edition for piano and accompaniments with the parts in different formats: a bibliographical curiosity that nonetheless tells us much about Artaria and the practice of music publishing in Haydn's Vienna.

In terms of Haydn's relationship with Artaria, the episode might have precipitated a temporary breakdown in communications. Certainly, no letters between the two parties are extant from 1786, although this is not in itself irrefutable proof of a lack of contact. More importantly, only one other new edition was advertised by the firm in that year: the set of *Différentes petites pièces faciles et agréables*, op. 46, containing abridged keyboard arrangements of a selection of movements from symphonies and other works, together with the first appearance in print of the Adagio in F major Hob.XVII:9. It is not entirely clear whether this edition was published with Haydn's consent, although there is evidence to suggest that, together with the Adagio, at least one of the arrangements was obtained from Haydn himself.[57] Significantly, Haydn agreed a contract with William Forster to supply various sets of symphonies, divertimenti, and piano trios in 1786.[58] This signalled a new phase in his dealings with publishers, as he increasingly sought to do business with a wider range of firms in London, Paris, Vienna, and elsewhere. While his correspondence with Artaria continued during 1787, the dispute between Forster and Longman & Broderip concerning the rights to the op. 40 Piano Trios threatened to derail the relationship once again: in a letter dated 28 February 1788, he professed

---

57. The arrangement of the fourth movement of the String Quartet op. 33 no. 5 exists in Haydn's autograph, albeit with some textual differences compared with the version given in the edition. It is also quite likely that the arrangements of the second and third movements from the Symphony no. 85 were also provided by the composer himself. See Joseph Haydn, *Werke* (Munich: Henle), XII/3: *Streichquartette op. 20 und op. 33, Heft 3*, ed. by Georg Feder and Sonja Gerlach (1974), Kritischer Bericht, p. 25 and I/13: *Pariser Sinfonien 2. Folge*, ed. by Sonja Gerlach and Klaus Lippe (1999), pp. 184–85. On the subject of Haydn's arrangements of his own works, see David Wyn Jones, 'Haydn's Forgotten Quartets: Three of the 'Paris' Symphonies Arranged for String Quartet', *Eighteenth-Century Music*, 8 (2011), 287–305.
58. The contract is dated only '1786'. See *Gesammelte Briefe und Aufzeichnungen*, pp. 151–55; *Collected Correspondence and London Notebooks*, pp. 53–55.

to Forster that he would no longer do business with Artaria at all.[59] However, this particular threat was clearly designed to improve his standing with Forster and in any case proved to be mere hot air: by 22 May of the same year he had resumed his correspondence with Artaria. The relationship nevertheless continued to be problematic at times. In July 1789, for example, Haydn wrote to Artaria complaining that the practice of sending him a proof copy had fallen by the wayside:[60]

> Thank you very much for the 3 Sonatas and the Fantasia which you sent to me; I only regret that, here and there, some mistakes have crept in, which can no longer be corrected, because the works are already circulated and on sale. It is always painful for me that not a single work of mine that you have published is free from errors. Formerly you always sent me the first copy, before publication, and you acted wisely; I could not use the single copies of the Sonatas you sent me as samples, because I didn't want to soil them and was also afraid of having to do without them for such a long time, or perhaps of losing them altogether, which is always irritating to an author.

The works referred to here were a new set of three Piano Trios, Hob.XV:11–13, and the Fantasia for piano in C major, Hob.XVII:4. Once again, the commercial imperative to make popular keyboard pieces available as soon as possible seems to have overridden other concerns. Also in 1789 the composer Franz Xaver Sterkel complained to Artaria for advertising an edition of his Piano Trios op. 30 before his corrections had been received and implemented, a practice that the firm justified with reference to the need to make it available in time for the Frankfurt Book Fair.[61] This time, however, Haydn did not force the issue and in his next two surviving letters to the firm (dated 15 November 1789 and 11 January 1790) sought to give assurances that Artaria would receive preference for his works over the claims of other publishers, such as John Bland.[62] However, this did not stop Haydn from selling works to other publishers whenever the opportunity arose.

---

59. See Haydn's letter to Forster dated 28 February 1788: *Gesammelte Briefe und Aufzeichnungen*, p. 189; *Collected Correspondence and London Notebooks*, p. 76.

60. Haydn, letter to Artaria, 5 July 1789. See *Gesammelte Briefe und Aufzeichnungen*, pp. 209–10. *Collected Correspondence and London Notebooks*, pp. 86–87.

61. Franz Xaver Sterkel, letter to Artaria dated 29 September 1789. See *Johann Franz Xaver Sterkels Briefwechsel mit seinen Verlegern*, p. 45.

62. The slightly flattering tone of these letters no doubt reflects the fact that Haydn found himself in debt to Artaria for some unspecified goods or services precisely at this time. On 15 November 1789, Haydn wrote: 'since you have often shown me various kindnesses, and since I really am your debtor, you may be assured that at all times you shall have the preference for my works'; then on 11 January 1790 he offered the firm '12 new and most splendid Minuets with 12 Trios, for 12 ducats' in order to cancel his debts. See *Gesammelte Briefe und Aufzeichnungen*, p. 218; *Collected Correspondence and London Notebooks*, pp. 91, 94. It is likely that the debt related to a piano by Wenzel Schanz purchased in 1788.

Apart from a couple of signed receipts dated 22 November 1790 and 7 December 1792, no further correspondence with Artaria survives until 1799. Given that Haydn's visits to London dominated his professional activities during the first half of the 1790s, a diminution in contact seems hardly surprising, even though Artaria continued to publish his music. The seven letters to Artaria dating from 1799 and 1800 largely deal with issues related to Haydn's edition of *The Creation*, which Artaria printed and distributed at Haydn's expense, and with the publication of his String Quartets op. 76. The tone of this later correspondence suggests a greater level of maturity in the relationship between composer and publisher, especially with regard to the timing of the release of the string quartets. Indeed, the publication of the first three of the op. 76 Quartets elicited an especially positive response from Haydn on 12 July 1799: 'I am most grateful to you for the copies of the Quartets you sent me, which are a great credit to me and – because of the legible engraving and the neat title-page – to you.'[63] This clearly gave some credence to Artaria's hyperbolic announcement in the *Wiener Zeitung* that 'nothing which our house has ever published equals this edition'.[64] Haydn had also promised the quartets to the firm of Longman, Clementi & Co. in London and was at great pains to ensure that Artaria's edition of the second set did not appear first. By now, such arrangements were seemingly *de rigueur* and one can read no embarrassment into Haydn's letter of 15 August 1799 in which he spells out the situation. Indeed, he trusted Artaria implicitly to establish whether or not the quartets had appeared in London already, and relied on their 'integrity' to delay the release of their publication until receiving confirmation that the London edition had appeared. The problems of the 1780s had, by now, receded into the past. Haydn's final documented letter to Artaria is dated 17 August 1805. Employing the laconic good humour of his final years, Haydn encapsulates his long-standing dealings with Artaria by expressing the hope that 'for these twelve pieces of music the old Haydn shall have merited a small reward'.[65]

63. See *Gesammelte Briefe und Aufzeichnungen*, p. 325; *Collected Correspondence and London Notebooks*, p. 157.
64. *Wiener Zeitung*, 17 July 1799: 'noch nichts in unserm Verlage erschienen ist, was dieser […] gleich käme'.
65. *Gesammelte Briefe und Aufzeichnungen*, p. 458. *Collected Correspondence and London Notebooks*, p. 238.

Mythological Motifs
in the Biographical Accounts of
Haydn's Later Life

CHRISTOPHER WILEY

Accounts of Haydn's life hold an important position within the modern tradition of musical biography. Of the earliest full-length texts, only Mainwaring's volume on Handel (1760),[1] Forkel's on Bach (1802),[2] and a flurry of writing about Mozart's life around the turn of the nineteenth century[3] predate the first of the biographies on Haydn – and even then, their appearance was surely de-

This essay has been drawn primarily from my 'Re-writing Composers' Lives: Critical Historiography and Musical Biography', 2 vols (unpublished doctoral dissertation, University of London, 2008). My thanks to Katharine Ellis for all her invaluable input on this project, to James Dack for advice on the specific avenues of enquiry explored here, and to the Arts and Humanities Research Board for providing financial support to enable me to pursue this research.

1. [John Mainwaring], *Memoirs of the Life of the Late George Frederic Handel* (London: Dodsley, 1760).

2. Johann Nicolaus Forkel, *Über Johann Sebastian Bachs Leben, Kunst und Kunstwerke* (Leipzig: Hoffmeister, Kühnel, 1802), trans. in *The New Bach Reader: A Life of Johann Sebastian Bach in Letters and Documents*, ed. by Hans T. David and Arthur Mendel, rev. and enlarged by Christoph Wolff (New York: Norton, 1998), pp. 415–82. Also worthy of note is Bach's so-called 'Nekrolog': [C. P. E. Bach and J. F. Agricola], 'Denkmal dreyer verstorbenen Mitglieder der Societät der musikalischen Wissenschaft', in *Neu eröffnete musikalische Bibliothek*, ed. by L. C. Mizler, 4 (1754), 158–76, trans. in *The New Bach Reader*, pp. 297–307.

3. For instance, Friedrich Schlichtegroll, 'Johannes Chrysostomus Wolfgang Gottlieb Mozart', in *Nekrolog auf das Jahr 1791: Enthaltend Nachrichten von dem Leben merkwürdiger in diesem Jahre verstorbener Personen* (Gotha: Justus Perthes), II (1793), 82–112; Franz Xaver Niemetschek, *Leben des K. K. Kapellmeisters Wolfgang Gottlieb Mozart nach Originalquellen beschrieben* (Prague: Herrlische Buchhandlung, 1798; 2nd edn 1808); Friedrich Rochlitz, 'Verbürgte Anekdoten aus

layed by the fact of their aged subject's not having died sooner. Elliot Forbes has remarked on the parallels between the evolution of biographical writing on Mozart, Haydn and Beethoven, the three great composers of the Viennese Classical School: all commenced with biographical notices hastily written close to the time of death, followed by reminiscence biographies penned by authors personally acquainted with (or otherwise close to) their subject and, somewhat later, by monumental 'definitive' biographies that were subsequently revised or completed by others.[4] Historical notices aside,[5] Haydn's own biographical tradition was established by a series of valuable texts by writers who had known him, which appeared in the years immediately following his death: the concise account by Georg August Griesinger, originally published serially in the *Allgemeine musikalische Zeitung* in 1809 and subsequently revised in book form (1810); a more elaborate, but less reliable, biography by Albert Christoph Dies (1810) which appeared around the same time and retained the format of the author's series of visits to Haydn; and Giuseppe Carpani's more engaging, though less historically significant volume (1812), written in epistolary form.[6] Several decades later, the gargantuan task of writing an enduring multi-volume life of

3.   *Cont.*
     Wolfgang Gottlieb Mozarts Leben: ein Beytrag zur richtigeren Kenntnis dieses Mannes, als Mensch und Künstler' and 'Anekdoten. Noch einige Kleinigkeiten aus Mozarts Leben', published serially in *Allgemeine musikalische Zeitung*, 10 October 1798–27 May 1801; [Théophile Frédéric Winckler], *Notice biographique sur Jean-Chrysostome-Wolfgang-Théophile Mozart* (Paris: Fuchs, 1801); and [Ignaz Theodor Ferdinand Cajetan Arnold], *Mozarts Geist: Seine kurze Biografie und ästhetische Darstellung seiner Werke* (Erfurt: Henningssche Buchhandlung, 1803).
4.   *Thayer's Life of Beethoven*, rev. and ed. by Elliot Forbes, 2 vols (Princeton, NJ: Princeton University Press, 1964), I, p. v.
5.   In Haydn's case, such sources included [Johann] Simon Mayr, *Brevi notizie istoriche della vita e delle opere di Giuseppe Haydn* (Bergamo, 1809); [Nicolas Étienne] Framery, *Notice sur Joseph Haydn, associé étranger de l'Institut de France [...] Contenant quelques Particularités de sa vie privée, relatives à sa Personne ou à ses Ouvrages* (Paris: Barba, 1810); and Joachim Le Breton, *Notice historique sur la vie et les ouvrages de Joseph Haydn, Membre Associé de l'Institut de France et d'un grand nombre d'Académies* (Paris: Baudouin, 1810). Here Forbes's tripartite model is revealed to be not completely watertight, for some of these biographical notices appeared after serial publication of Griesinger's biography had begun.
6.   Georg August Griesinger, *Biographische Notizen über Joseph Haydn* (Leipzig: Breitkopf & Härtel, 1810; originally published serially in *Allgemeine musikalische Zeitung*, 12 July–6 September 1809, and revised for republication), trans. as 'Biographical Notes Concerning Joseph Haydn', in *Joseph Haydn: Eighteenth-Century Gentleman and Genius*, trans. and ed. by Vernon Gotwals (Madison: University of Wisconsin Press, 1963; 2nd edn, as *Haydn: Two Contemporary Portraits*, 1968), pp. 3–66. Albert Christoph Dies, *Biographische Nachrichten von Joseph Haydn* (Vienna: Camesinaische Buchhandlung, 1810), trans. as 'Biographical Accounts of Joseph Haydn', in *Haydn: Two Contemporary Portraits*, pp. 67–209. Giuseppe Carpani, *Le Haydine, ovvero Lettere su la vita e le opere del celebre maestro Giuseppe Haydn* (Milan: Buccinelli, 1812).

Haydn was undertaken by the music historian Carl Ferdinand Pohl, the first two instalments of which were published in 1875 and 1882; the project remained unfinished at Pohl's death and was ultimately completed by Hugo Botstiber in 1927.[7]

Historically, authors have been particularly keen to place Haydn's life side by side with Mozart's: one of Mozart's early biographers, Ignaz Arnold (1803), seized the opportunity just one year after the death of Haydn to produce a second volume (1810) that juxtaposed the lives of the two composers in Plutarchian manner, a strategy repeated some decades later by Pohl himself in his publication *Mozart und Haydn in London* (1867), the result of extensive research conducted in the British Museum.[8] However, while Mozart biography has recently been widely theorized by scholars including Maynard Solomon, William Stafford, H. C. Robbins Landon and Karen Painter, that of his greatest contemporary has received significantly less critical attention.[9] Yet the trajectories of the two composers' biographies are completely different: as I have elsewhere discussed, Haydn's long, stable and relatively uneventful life contrasts strikingly with Mozart's exceptional rate of development from precocious childhood to premature death.[10] It would therefore be a mistake simply to suppose that the study of Haydn biography sheds little new light on the overall phenomenon of writing about composers' lives. Indeed, my wider research has suggested that fresh insights into the ideologies of musical biography are gained by examination of precisely those stories connected with Haydn's later life, in terms both of the tropes – romantic views and themes nonetheless grounded in fact –

7. C. F. Pohl, *Joseph Haydn*, 3 vols (Berlin, etc.: Sacco, etc., 1875–1927); III, as Hugo Botstiber, *Joseph Haydn: Unter Benutzung der von C. F. Pohl hinterlassenen Materialien* (Leipzig: Breitkopf & Härtel, 1927).
8. Arnold, *Mozarts Geist* (cited above, n. 3); idem, *Wolfgang Amadeus Mozart und Joseph Haydn. Nachträge zu ihren Biografien und ästhetischer Darstellung ihrer Werke. Versuch einer Parallele* (Erfurt: Johann Karl Müller, 1810). C. F. Pohl, *Mozart und Haydn in London*, 2 vols (Vienna: Carl Gerold's Sohn, 1867).
9. Maynard Solomon, 'Mozart: The Myth of the Eternal Child', *19th-Century Music*, 15/2 (1991), 95–106; idem, 'The Rochlitz anecdotes: Issues of Authenticity in Early Mozart Biography', in *Mozart Studies*, ed. by Cliff Eisen (Oxford: Clarendon, 1991), pp. 1–59. William Stafford, *Mozart's Death: A Corrective Survey of the Legends* (London: Macmillan, 1991), also published as *The Mozart Myths: A Critical Reassessment* (Stanford, CA: Stanford University Press, 1991). H. C. Robbins Landon, *1791: Mozart's Last Year* ([London]: Thames and Hudson, 1988; 2nd edn 1989). Karen Painter, 'Mozart at Work: Biography and a Musical Aesthetic for the Emerging German Bourgeoisie', *The Musical Quarterly*, 86 (2002), 186–235. For a discussion of how the development of Haydn biography has itself trailed behind that of Mozart (as well as Beethoven and Bach), see James Webster, 'Prospects for Haydn Biography after Landon', *The Musical Quarterly*, 68 (1982), 476–95 (pp. 478–80).
10. Christopher Wiley, '"A Relic of an Age Still Capable of a Romantic Outlook": Musical Biography and The Master Musicians Series, 1899–1906', *Comparative Criticism*, 25 (2003), 161–202 (p. 184).

already present from their earliest accounts and of the elaborations they accumulated during their retellings in the myth-loving, hero-worshipping context of nineteenth- and early twentieth-century writings.[11]

The purpose of this essay is to investigate three of the most fascinating stories of Haydn's later life: his visit of 1795 to the monument erected in his honour by Count Carl Leonhard Harrach at Rohrau; the celebrated performance of *The Creation* in 1808; and the episode of Haydn's death the following year. Consideration of their emergent 'mythological motifs', to borrow a term used by Ernst Kris and Otto Kurz in an early experimental study of the prevalence of analogous themes in biographies of (visual) artists of a number of different epochs,[12] yields much information in two main areas: first, on the cultural significance of their perpetuation across the decades and countries, by which Haydn's claim to inclusion within the musical canon was confirmed and reinforced; and second, on the origins of certain important biographical tropes that were subsequently developed elsewhere in writings about composers' lives in the course of the last two centuries. Starting from within the framework of Haydn biography and gradually working outwards, the following discussion opens with a survey of these three episodes and the themes they embody, leading to an analysis of the ways in which those motifs relate both to one another and to parallel stories elsewhere in musical biography, and the likely reasons for their enduring cultural currency.

The first chronological story to be discussed, that of Haydn's visit to Count Harrach's monument, may actually itself be the product of the later nineteenth century. While the earlier sources such as Griesinger's and Dies's reminiscence biographies described the pyramidal monument at some length, they merely noted the composer's awareness that it had been constructed; it had also been discussed some years earlier in an article appearing in the *Allgemeine musikalische Zeitung* in 1800 (see Fig. 1).[13] It was with Carl Ferdinand Pohl, however, that a new tale appeared: that Haydn

---

11. See Wiley, 'Re-writing Composers' Lives', especially Part I, 'Mythology in Musical Biography', pp. 19–178, which comparatively examines many of the most enduring stories drawn from writings on the lives of the great composers, charting the development they exhibited in subsequent retellings and assessing the cultural significance of their various accretions and distortions.

12. Ernst Kris and Otto Kurz, *Die Legende vom Künstler: Ein historischer Versuch* (Vienna: Krystall Verlag, 1934), rev. by Otto Kurz and trans. by Alastair Laing and Lottie M. Newman as *Legend, Myth, and Magic in the Image of the Artist: A Historical Experiment* (New Haven: Yale University Press, 1979).

13. *Haydn: Two Contemporary Portraits*, trans. and ed. by Gotwals, pp. 36–37 (Griesinger); ibid., pp. 161–64 (Dies); 'Nachricht: Monumente deutscher Tonkünstler', *Allgemeine musikalische Zeitung*, 12 March 1800, cols 417–23 (cols 419–20). For a modern description of the monument, see Matthew Head, 'Music With "No Past?" Archaeologies of Joseph Haydn and *The Creation*', *19th-Century Music*, 23/3 (2000), 191–217 (pp. 191–93).

Fig. 1. The Haydn monument at Rohrau, from an engraving published
in the *Allgemeine musikalische Zeitung*, 12 March 1800.

was taken by a company of aristocrats to his birthplace, where he visited both his
monument and the house in which he grew up. Extensive research has alas not succeeded in determining the ultimate origin of this story, but it was surely uncovered
by Pohl in the course of researching for his 'definitive' biography.[14] Although Pohl
died prior to completing the volume that would have included this period of Haydn's
life, the episode entered the public domain through the article he contributed to

14. H. C. Robbins Landon's discussion of this episode implies that Pohl's biography as completed by
    Botstiber (1927) was the originating documentary source; see Landon, *Haydn: Chronicle and
    Works*, IV, 55. My own research has traced its appearance in print in England some fifty years
    earlier, but the trail seems to run dry. However, as the present discussion reveals, the implicit
    contradictions between this story and primary evidence offered by Dies suggest that Pohl must
    have had good reason for placing it in the public domain.

George Grove's groundbreaking *Dictionary of Music and Musicians* (1878) and, some decades later, in the additional volume with which Botstiber completed Pohl's unfinished biography. In Pohl's earlier account, Haydn's return to the modest dwelling in which he was born emotionally overwhelmed him, and led him to declare that his musical career had started in that very place. Pohl described the group that accompanied the composer as 'a genial party of noblemen and gentlem[e]n', led by Count Harrach himself, to which constituency Botstiber subsequently added the count's two brothers.[15] While my intentions in this study are to examine the cultural priorities that underpinned biographical myth-making rather than merely to bring to light deviations from the historical record, that the story was unquestioningly retold in Haydn biography thereafter is particularly revealing given that it was strikingly at variance with Count Harrach's own testimony. In a letter solicited by Dies and reproduced in his early biography of Haydn (surely a key source for any subsequent author[16]), Harrach wrote that having commemorated the composer in this manner, 'it was not until two or three years later that [Haydn] happened to hear that this monument in Rohrau existed *and without my knowing it went to see it*'.[17] Despite this and other discrepancies as well as the general lack of documentation for the episode, the position adopted even by modern scholarship such as Landon's landmark five-volume Haydn biography nonetheless suggests that it 'no doubt took place'.[18]

The story of the homage paid to the aged Haydn at the performance of *The Creation* given by the Viennese Society of Amateur Concerts in the University's Aula Magna on 27 March 1808 provides contrast in that it is documented in some detail in a number of contemporary sources, all of them in broad agreement; accounts of the occasion are to be found in the early biographies by Griesinger, Dies and Carpani, not to mention several periodicals.[19] As Vernon Gotwals has remarked,

15. C. F. P[ohl], 'Haydn, Joseph', in *A Dictionary of Music and Musicians (A.D. 1450–1889) by Eminent Writers*, ed. by George Grove, 4 vols (London: Macmillan, 1878–90), I (1878), 702–22 (p. 713); Botstiber, p. 97.

16. Botstiber's account, for instance, quotes Harrach's letter at length from Dies's biography (Botstiber, pp. 97–99; see Dies, *Biographische Nachrichten von Joseph Haydn*, pp. 138–41), but tellingly omits the sentence about Haydn's visiting the monument without the count's knowledge.

17. Landon, *Haydn: Chronicle and Works*, III, 201 (italics added). See Dies, *Biographische Nachrichten von Joseph Haydn*, p. 139: 'hat [Haydn] erst zwey bis drey Jahre später zufällig erfahren, daß dieses Monument zu Rohrau bestehe, *und dasselbe ohne mein Vorwissen in Augenschein genommen*'.

18. Landon, *Haydn: Chronicle and Works*, IV, 55.

19. *Haydn: Two Contemporary Portraits*, trans. and ed. by Gotwals, pp. 48–49 (Griesinger); ibid., pp. 177–78 (Dies); Carpani, *Le Haydine*, pp. 242–46. The event was also reported in at least four periodicals between March and May 1808, which may have further informed Griesinger's and Dies's accounts; see Landon, *Haydn: Chronicle and Works*, V, 364, n. 1. Given the nature of my study coupled to the longevity of influence on subsequent life-writing of major biographical sources relative to periodical reports, the above analysis necessarily privileges the former.

Carpani was known for going one better than Griesinger and Dies, both of whose texts he had consulted prior to the appearance of his own.[20] Nonetheless, in this instance, his version is accorded special significance since he was implicated in the occasion in question: *The Creation* was performed in Carpani's Italian translation, and he was also the author of a sonnet written in praise of Haydn and presented to the composer at the concert.[21] Read in tandem, the accounts depict a glorious occasion in which the guest of honour made a triumphant entry accompanied by a trumpet fanfare, whereupon the assembled crowd rose to its feet, cheering loudly as Haydn was carried to his designated place at the front of the orchestra – seated among people from the highest echelons of society including Princess Esterházy (who also commissioned the painter Balthasar Wigand to commemorate the occasion, in a miniature watercolour on the lid of a box subsequently presented to the composer, reproduced as Fig. 2; Haydn is shown seated in the centre at the front).[22] In the course of the evening, however, it became necessary for Haydn to leave prematurely, and it is here that the earliest accounts differ from their immediate successors. Neither Griesinger's nor Dies's versions yield much of a sense in which the episode was to be explicitly understood as a foreshadowing of the composer's demise, old and weak though he was; Dies even observed that it had actually revitalized Haydn to the extent that some days later, 'it was as if an electric current were flowing in [his] veins', and noted that he had been greeted by the jubilant crowd with shouts of 'Long live Haydn!'[23] Both authors had received the story from the composer himself; conversely, Carpani, in spite of his own long-standing acquaintance with Haydn, could be more independent in his retrospective retelling of an event in which he had himself played a part. While nonetheless referring to the composer as 'uomo immortale',[24] Carpani's account represented a turning-point in

20. Vernon Gotwals, 'The Earliest Biographies of Haydn', *The Musical Quarterly*, 45 (1959), 439–59 (p. 441).
21. The sonnet is reprinted in *Haydn: Two Contemporary Portraits*, trans. and ed. by Gotwals, p. 179.
22. Prince Lobkowitz was likewise in attendance, as was Haydn's pupil Baroness von Spielmann, and perhaps also Prince Trautmannsdorf who, like Lobkowitz, had sponsored the concert; Dies additionally documented the presence of the French Ambassador, Count Andreossy (*Haydn: Two Contemporary Portraits*, trans. and ed. by Gotwals, p. 177).
23. *Haydn: Two Contemporary Portraits*, trans. and ed. by Gotwals, pp. 180, 177.
24. Carpani, *Le Haydine*, p. 243. The sonnet that Carpani had presented to Haydn as part of the celebration, which he reproduced in the course of his retelling of the story (pp. 245–46), was similarly entitled 'All'immortale Haydn per la sua Creazione del Mondo' ('To the immortal Haydn for his *Creation*').

injecting into the narrative more overt indications of the composer's impending departure from the world:[25]

> Surrounded by the nobility, his friends, the artists, the poets, and the fair sex [i.e. women]; listening to the praises of God, which he imagined, and his own praises confused with those of the divinity, the good old man had to believe himself [as being] in heaven, and we ourselves, judging from the sweetness of the feelings and the music, had to believe it as much as he did.

Thereafter, the episode – complete with the exit of its protagonist mid-concert – began to resemble the now-familiar scene that Matthew Head has eloquently described as a 'dress rehearsal' for Haydn's actual death.[26] To give just one further example, Carpani's text was heavily plagiarized two years later (1814) in a French-language volume by the author and music critic Stendhal (Marie-Henri Beyle, here using the pseudonym Louis-Alexandre-César Bombet) together with some material on Mozart and Metastasio, in which form it quickly travelled to England via the Rev. C. Berry's translation (1817; other sections of the volume were translated by Robert Brewin).[27] Stendhal's glosses on the description of the scene are particularly revealing here, for he altered Carpani's words to become[28]

> Surrounded by the nobility, his friends, the artists, the charming women, all of whose eyes were fixed upon him, listening to the praises of God, which he himself imagined, *Haydn bade a fine farewell to the world and to life.*

In so doing, Stendhal implicitly extended the religious inflections present as early as Griesinger's retelling of the story (as well as, in part, that of the *Allgemeine musikalische Zeitung*), in which the audience's reaction to one especially emotive passage of the work, at the words 'E la luce fu' ('And there was light'), purportedly

25. Carpani, *Le Haydine*, p. 244: 'Circondato dai grandi, dagli amici, dagli artisti, dai poeti e dal bel sesso; ascoltando le lodi di Dio, da lui stesso immaginate, e le lodi proprie confuse con quelle della divinità, il buon vecchio ha dovuto credersi in cielo, e noi stessi a giudicarne dalla dolcezza de' sentimenti e della musica dovemmo crederlo al pari di lui.'
26. Head, 'Music With "No Past?"', pp. 215–17.
27. Louis-Alexandre-César Bombet, *Lettres écrites de Vienne en Autriche, sur le célèbre compositeur Jh. Haydn, suivies d'une vie de Mozart, et de considérations sur Métastase et l'état présent de la musique en France et en Italie* (Paris: Didot L'Aîné, 1814), trans. [by C. Berry and Robert Brewin, with additional notes by William Gardiner] as *The Life of Haydn, in a Series of Letters Written at Vienna. Followed by The Life of Mozart, with Observations on Metastasio, and on the Present State of Music in France and Italy* (London: Murray, 1817).
28. Bombet, p. 268: 'Environné des grands, de ses amis, des artistes, de femmes charmantes dont tous les yeux étaient fixés sur lui, écoutant les louanges de Dieu, imaginées par lui-même, *Haydn fit un bel adieu au monde et à la vie*' (italics added).

Fig. 2. Balthasar Wigand, reproduction of a lost watercolour depicting the performance of Haydn's *Creation* in the Aula Magna of Vienna University on 27 March 1808.

prompted the composer to point heavenwards and exclaim 'Es kommt von dort!' ('It comes from there!').[29] Griesinger's description, subsequently repeated by Carpani, of the benedictory gesture that Haydn made in extending his hand towards the musicians upon his exit from the hall was particularly significant in this respect: rather than merely echoing *The Creation*'s sacred theme, it seemed moreover to signal an ending for the music analogous to the devoutly religious composer's renowned practice of signing off his scores with phrases such as 'Fine. Laus Deo' (or 'Finis. Laus Deo').

The events that led to Haydn's actual passing in May 1809 were pieced together by Griesinger from a letter written to him by Haydn's factotum and eyewitness to the episode, Johann Elssler, together with a second, less reliable, letter from the piano maker Andreas Streicher.[30] Certain discrepancies notwithstanding, Dies's and

29. Griesinger, *Biographische Notizen über Joseph Haydn*, p. 89; *Haydn: Two Contemporary Portraits*, trans. and ed. by Gotwals, p. 49.

30. Johann Elssler to Griesinger, 30 June 1809; Andreas Streicher to Griesinger, 2 July 1809, with a postscript of 12 July (both reprinted in Botstiber, pp. 385–90; English translations are to be found in Landon, *Haydn: Chronicle and Works*, V, 385–87).

Carpani's accounts agree in their main themes with Griesinger's. For instance, all three writers strongly link Haydn's end to the second Napoleonic invasion of Austria, in that it took place against the backdrop of the incursion of French troops into Vienna that Dies described as having 'passed sentence' on the composer's life[31] – a notion that Griesinger ascribed to Haydn himself, who had reportedly often remarked that 'this unfortunate war is bringing me ever closer to the grave!'[32] Thus, in an implicitly anti-Napoleonic gesture, while Haydn biography has traditionally held the security and tranquillity epitomized by his decades of employment in the service of the Esterházy family to have been the source of the composer's longevity, war brought only his death. As the cannon shots started to fall in the vicinity of his house, Haydn was portrayed from the earliest accounts (in accordance with Elssler's letter) as having summoned his remaining strength to comfort his distressed servants, loudly proclaiming the variously rendered words, 'Children, don't be afraid, for where Haydn is, nothing [bad] can happen.'[33] Griesinger, Dies and Carpani concur that this exertion was too great for the elderly composer, and hence precipitated the first physical manifestations of his descent towards death. Before taking to his bed for the last time, however, Haydn received a pilgrimage-like visit from a French officer who sang one of his arias, widely held to have been 'Mit Würd' und Hoheit angethan' ('In Native Worth and Honour Clad') from Part II of *The Creation* – which therefore brought some closure to the story of the work's performance the previous year, Haydn's premature departure from which meant that he would not have heard an aria that appeared so late in the oratorio. In the midst of war, the patriotic Haydn had also taken to playing through the 'Emperor's Hymn' ('Gott erhalte Franz den Kaiser') at the keyboard on a daily basis; his final rendition was given particular emphasis in Dies's account, in which the composer was said to have gathered his servants around him at the instrument as if to share with them his last musical act. Likewise, Elssler's testimony stated that Haydn's servants were among those present at his bedside when he died.

Having given a brief outline of the three episodes in Haydn's later biography that are the subject of this essay, we may now proceed to a discussion of the tropes they came to exemplify and of the cultural functions that their dissemination and perpetuation might have served. Perhaps the most striking mythological motif is

31. *Haydn: Two Contemporary Portraits*, trans. and ed. by Gotwals, p. 192.
32. Griesinger, *Biographische Notizen über Joseph Haydn*, p. 91: 'Der unglückliche Krieg drückt mich noch ganz zu Boden!'; *Haydn: Two Contemporary Portraits*, trans. and ed. by Gotwals, p. 49.
33. Quoted from Landon, *Haydn: Chronicle and Works*, V, 386. Elssler's original words were 'Kinder, fürchtet euch nicht, denn wo Haydn ist kann nichts geschehen' (quoted from *Haydn: Two Contemporary Portraits*, trans. and ed. by Gotwals, p. 232, n. 70), which both Griesinger (*Biographische Notizen über Joseph Haydn*, p. 91) and Dies (*Biographische Nachrichten von Joseph Haydn*, p. 192) presented slightly differently in their own narratives.

manifested in Haydn's changed relationship with the aristocracy in his final years. In traditional accounts of Western music history, Haydn was the archetypal composer emancipated from the social constraints of patronage, ascending from his status as little more than a servant in feudal employment at the outset of his career, to that of a liberated musician able to compete freely in public arenas towards the end (reaching its pinnacle in his two visits to England of the 1790s) – and hence exemplifying a general historical trend traceable at least as far back as Bach's biography and continued through to those of Mozart, Beethoven and beyond. Taking the episode of Haydn's visit to the Rohrau monument at face value, it would appear that an aristocratic company was obliged on this occasion to the composer rather than the other way around, and this was an idea that flourished following its introduction by Pohl in Grove's *Dictionary*. Just a few years later, for example, Pauline Townsend's biography on Haydn (1884) for Francis Hueffer's 'Great Musicians' series extended Pohl's notions in implying that the nobility had waited until the composer had returned from his second visit to England in order to inaugurate the monument with its dedicatee present, while Botstiber additionally suggested that the impetus for visiting his birthplace *en route* may have even come from Haydn himself.[34] Likewise, as noted, accounts of the *Creation* concert in 1808 placed the composer in some distinguished company. Given the continuation of this trend of social ascendancy in the musical generations that succeeded Haydn coupled to the increasing visibility of the middle classes and the prevalence of anti-aristocratic feeling throughout much of the nineteenth century, such notions must have found favour both with many authors and with the readers for whom they were writing. Within musical biography, indeed, few clear precedents for anecdotes of this nature present themselves, perhaps the most obvious being that of Bach's inadvertent interruption of court activities upon his visit to King Frederick the Great of Prussia in 1747.[35]

The emphasis that Haydn biographers placed on the Harrach brothers in the story of the composer's visit to the monument is noteworthy, for their father had been the overlord for the young Haydn's household. Similarly, the appearance of members of the Esterházy family in the episode of the 1808 *Creation* concert served to illustrate Haydn's changed standing with respect to the aristocratic house he had served for much of his adult life; Princess Esterházy was even said to have lent

---

34. Pauline D. Townsend, *Joseph Haydn*, The Great Musicians (London: Sampson Low, 1884), p. 103; Botstiber, p. 97.

35. Though implicit in at least one of the contemporary reports of this episode (that appearing in the *Spenersche Zeitung*, 11 May 1747, trans. in *The New Bach Reader*, p. 224), notions of Bach's unanticipated arrival at court having prompted changes to the king's planned schedule are more fully developed in Forkel's biography (*The New Bach Reader*, pp. 429–30). Though first published over fifty years after the event, Forkel had received the story directly from Wilhelm Friedemann Bach, who had travelled with his father and was therefore a witness to proceedings.

Haydn her shawl to keep him warm, while the prince (whose presence was precluded by official court engagements) had reportedly sent his personal carriage to transport Haydn to the performance.[36] Ultimate closure to the trope of the composer's rise upwards through the social strata is brought by the role played by his own servants in the story of his final days: in calling out to comfort them during the cannon fire, Haydn assumed responsibility for their well-being (rather than their taking care of him) even though his actions were deemed to have ultimately cost him his life.[37] His servants were also present at his death, Elssler having touchingly recorded Haydn's squeezing of the hand of his loyal cook Anna Kremnitzer as his last conscious act, an evocative detail that was repeated over a century later by Botstiber.[38] Given the composer's roots in aristocratic employment, Haydn's special empathy for his own domestic staff is particularly illustrated by Dies's account of the reading of the composer's will some weeks prior to his death, which epitomized the reversed direction of his life: once essentially a servant himself, Haydn now had servants of his own, for whom he made generous provision to secure them a good future.[39]

A related trope, especially given the details of Pohl's account, is that of Haydn's pride in his humble origins. This implicit emphasis on art over wealth mirrors the plethora of stories of poverty and modest living standards found in texts on later composers such as Schubert and Brahms, as well as in those of Mozart, with whom biographical writing on Haydn, as noted, has frequently engendered comparison.[40] Such notions also intersect more widely with nineteenth-century assumptions as to the advancement of great art being a loftier aim than merely pandering to public taste in pursuit of fame and financial reward; out of all the first-rank composers, substantial tension on this point has particularly pervaded biographies of Handel, whose musical endeavours resulted in a vast accumulated fortune. Likewise, this

---

36. However, the prominence of this aristocratic family in Dies's account may have been motivated by other factors, since his biography had received the backing of Prince Esterházy, to whom it was humbly dedicated.

37. The episode's explicit casting of Haydn's servants as his 'children' (reminiscent of the description of his artistic brethren in accounts of the 1808 *Creation* concert) conveniently provided a substitute for the family that he never had, given his failed marriage — another vexed matter with which Haydn's biographers have had to contend.

38. Botstiber, p. 276.

39. *Haydn: Two Contemporary Portraits*, trans. and ed. by Gotwals, pp. 194–96. For a detailed discussion of Haydn's will, see further, Vernon Gotwals, 'Joseph Haydn's Last Will and Testament', *The Musical Quarterly*, 47 (1961), 331–53.

40. Themes of poverty in Mozart biography, which have long been deeply ingrained in Western culture, have come under particular scrutiny in modern academic discourse; see, for instance, Julia Moore, 'Mozart in the Market-Place', *Journal of the Royal Musical Association*, 114 (1989), 18–42 and Daniel K. L. Chua, 'Myth: Mozart, Money, Music', in *Mozart Studies*, ed. by Simon P. Keefe (Cambridge: Cambridge University Press, 2006), pp. 193–213.

whole line of enquiry connects to nineteenth-century social trends that witnessed the rise of the musical amateur, the public concert-goer and music-lover, and the autodidact aspiring to self-improvement – that being precisely the readership attracted to many of the populist biographies in which such novelistic stories thrived. For authors writing for these interpretive communities, then, Haydn provided a subject with whom the lay reader might readily identify, as well as an exemplar of what Peter Kivy has succinctly described as the "'just plain hard work'" picture of genius': the artist whose life story proves that greatness can flourish, even within an underprivileged environment, simply through industrious dedication to one's studies.[41] The case of Haydn further offers ideal demonstration that such a path could indeed lead to social ascendency through artistic attainment – to the extent, apparently, that Haydn ultimately achieved a reversal of the normative hierarchy of servant and aristocrat.

Of all the accretions and motifs under consideration in this essay, however, the single development with the furthest-reaching consequences for musical biography surely concerns the insertion of Haydn's famous former composition student, Beethoven, within the story of the 1808 *Creation* concert. Neither Griesinger, nor Dies, nor Carpani placed Beethoven at the occasion, though the presence of sundry other musicians was mentioned; notably, both Griesinger and Carpani named Salieri as the conductor of the performance, the latter even describing how he tenderly embraced Haydn, and took his hand, upon his entrance. Beethoven's first appearance in connection with this episode occurred instead in various other contemporary sources, including a passing mention in the entry on Haydn in the second edition of Gerber's influential *Lexikon* (1812–14), whose account of this story is generally anomalous for the information that it presents.[42] More importantly, in a poem written retrospectively in 1812 by Heinrich Joseph von Collin – who, like Carpani, had penned a laudatory verse to be presented to Haydn at the event – the younger composer was said to have kissed Haydn on the head and hand upon his departure.[43] This description, for which Collin's poem is the only contemporary source, bears

41. Peter Kivy, *The Possessor and the Possessed: Handel, Mozart, Beethoven, and the Idea of Musical Genius* (New Haven: Yale University Press, 2001), pp. 169–70.

42. Ernst Ludwig Gerber, *Neues historisch-biographisches Lexikon der Tonkünstler*, 4 vols ([Leipzig: Kühnel], 2nd edn 1812–14), II, cols 535–605 (col. 556).

43. Collin's poem is reprinted in Landon, *Haydn: Chronicle and Works*, V, 362–64. Nor were these the only two contemporary sources that explicitly placed Beethoven at this concert. Some of the periodical reports of the event also noted Beethoven's presence, including that appearing in the *Allgemeine musikalische Zeitung*, 20 April 1808, cols 479–80 (col. 479). Landon (*Haydn: Chronicle and Works*, V, 364, n. 1) suggested that this article may have been written by Griesinger, however, while its content is similar to the retelling of the episode in Griesinger's biography, the two narratives nonetheless differ in this and certain other details.

such a striking resemblance to Carpani's writing about Salieri's actions towards Haydn at the beginning of the concert that the similarity is surely not merely coincidence. Nonetheless, the interpolation became fairly standard in subsequent retellings of the story, and even as recently as 1981, Landon tells us that 'Beethoven, the tears streaming down his face, bent and kissed the hand of his former teacher.'[44]

Whether the result of a simple error on Collin's part or a deliberate attempt to embroider the scene by augmenting the role of another composer with whom Collin was acquainted, over time, the figure of Beethoven essentially came to replace that of Salieri. In many later accounts, mention of Salieri is limited to his role as conductor of the performance and as the composer who subsequently set to music Carpani's sonnet. Carpani, whose biography gave the greatest level of detail as to Salieri's involvement in proceedings, was evidently an advocate of his Italian compatriot: when the notorious theories that Salieri might have been Mozart's killer emerged in the 1820s, Carpani defended him at length in print, pointing to the absence of any actual evidence that Mozart was poisoned and even soliciting testimony from one of the doctors who had been consulted about Mozart's final illness.[45] But Beethoven was evidently the character whom music historiography ultimately favoured for inclusion within the story, as a composer of a much greater stature than Salieri and one whose posthumous reputation was unsullied by allegations of jealousy and murder. Conversely, the edging out of Salieri over time reflects the precarious position he came to occupy at the canonic periphery, as a musical figure of only minor historical importance.

The combined life stories of Haydn and Beethoven yield one further reason why this version of the story might have been held particularly dear to biographers. As a composition student of Haydn's in the early 1790s, Beethoven's relationship with his teacher was famously believed to have been an acrimonious one, and it has been the cause of substantial unease amongst biographers ever since, the continuing legacy of which is demonstrated by a systematic defence by James Webster appearing as recently as 1984.[46] Prior to the surfacing of Beethoven in the story of the 1808

44. H. C. Robbins Landon, *Haydn: A Documentary Study* ([London]: Thames and Hudson, 1981), pp. 192–93.

45. On this point see Johannes Dalchow, Gunther Dyda and Dieter Kerner, *Mozarts Tod 1791–1971: zur 180. Wiederkehr seines gewaltsamen Endes am 5. Dezember 1971* (Pähl: Verlag Hohe Warte-Franz von Bebenburg, 1971), pp. 188–239; Carpani's long letter to the journal *Biblioteca Italiana*, 35 (1824) is quoted on pp. 198–214. The letter of 10 June 1824 from Court Councillor Eduard Vincent Guldener von Lobes, which Carpani reproduced as an appendix to his own, is translated in Otto Erich Deutsch, *Mozart: A Documentary Biography*, trans. by Eric Blom, Peter Branscombe and Jeremy Noble (London: Black, 1965), pp. 522–23.

46. James Webster, 'The Falling-Out between Haydn and Beethoven: The Evidence of the Sources', in *Beethoven Essays: Studies in Honor of Elliot Forbes*, ed. by Lewis Lockwood and Phyllis Benjamin (Cambridge, MA: Harvard University Press, 1984), pp. 3–45.

Creation concert, the last chronological episode that featured the two composers together involved a chance encounter on the street around a decade after their period
as teacher and student, in which they exchanged words about *The Creation* as well
as Beethoven's ballet *The Creatures of Prometheus*. The droll remarks they made about
one another's works served only to indicate that time had failed to heal old wounds,
and the tale was thus unsatisfactory in its provision of closure to the rift that had
earlier developed between them. However, the foregrounding of Beethoven in later
accounts of the scene of Haydn's last public appearance – and, moreover, the act of
homage he supposedly paid to him – provided musical biography with the much-
cherished resolution of the problematic matter of their strained relationship, conveniently in time for Haydn's death.

Analogous themes may be identified in the evolution of biographical writing on
other great composers too. Perhaps the clearest example is a parallel episode occur-
ring close to Beethoven's own death, in which he was said to have been delighted to
receive a gift of a lithograph of Haydn's birthplace, and to have remarked on the
irony of such a great man having originated in such unassuming surroundings. The
anecdote has come down to us from Gerhard von Breuning, who as an adolescent
had visited Beethoven throughout his last illness and some decades later published
his reminiscences; most significantly, Breuning's account entered into some detail
as to Beethoven's distress at the misspelling of Haydn's name on the picture's mount-
ing, perhaps implicitly responding to reports that Beethoven deliberately rendered
Haydn's name incorrectly throughout his life.[47] Neither is the retrospective emer-
gence of a historically important junior composer within a notable episode in the
biography of a great contemporary merely limited to the case of Haydn. One more
recent example is the appearance of Schubert within the much-mythologized story
of the première of Beethoven's Ninth Symphony in 1824; this was an accretion that
originated with the work of Otto Erich Deutsch, which substantially advanced
Schubert biography in the early to mid-twentieth century.[48] Likewise, the construc-
tion of mythology surrounding the receipt of a kiss from Beethoven is itself encoun-
tered elsewhere in musical biography, in the tale of the so-called *Weihekuss* (kiss of
consecration) that Beethoven reportedly bestowed upon the young Liszt at a

47. Gerhard von Breuning, *Aus dem Schwarzspanierhause: Erinnerungen an L. van Beethoven aus meiner
   Jugendzeit* (Vienna: Rosner, 1874), trans. by Henry Mins and Maynard Solomon as *Memories of
   Beethoven: From the House of the Black-Robed Spaniards*, ed. by Maynard Solomon (Cambridge:
   Cambridge University Press, 1992), pp. 98–99. On this point see further, Landon, *Haydn: Chronicle
   and Works*, V, 359–60.
48. Otto Erich Deutsch, *Schubert: A Documentary Biography*, trans. by Eric Blom (London: Dent,
   1946), p. 345.

performance the latter had given in 1823, which, as Michael Saffle has recently shown, has similarly been a source of much disagreement among biographers.[49]

The preceding exploration of the mythological themes that materialized and developed in Haydn biography, though hardly exhaustive, has at least offered indications that retellings of stories connected with the composer's later years have historically extended and enhanced some of the tropes already present (in some guise or other) in the life-writing of canonical predecessors and contemporaries, as well as establishing other motifs that subsequently migrated into biographies of later great composers such as Haydn's Viennese successors. While comparisons with Mozart are inevitable, Haydn biography reveals itself as distinctive precisely because of the subject's longevity, and not just because it enabled the eleventh-hour *rapprochement* with Beethoven and the natural conclusion of his ascent from the servant ranks to a more liberated standing within society. Biographical theorist Paula Backscheider has written of the general expectation that 'the [subject's] death must be *explained* and dressed in momentous trappings' almost as a prerequisite of biography.[50] That may be comparatively easy to achieve when subjects are cut off in their prime (as was the case with Mozart, and a plethora of other canonical composers), but becomes much harder when faced with a life that proceeded as Haydn's did, the composer living to such a ripe age that reports of his death had been greatly exaggerated some years prior to his actual passing.[51] So where, for example, the celebrated story of the commission and composition of Mozart's Requiem dominates narratives of his demise, Haydn's life seemed to require an epitomizing tale that similarly revolved around a great last work, soon provided by the recasting of the 1808 *Creation* concert as a pseudo-death scene.[52] These instances alone reveal that episodes in the biography of a single subject may be brought into sharper focus by

49. Michael Saffle, 'Lingering Legends: Liszt after Walker', in *Musical Biography: Towards New Paradigms*, ed. by Jolanta T. Pekacz (Aldershot: Ashgate, 2006), pp. 89–110 (pp. 101–07).

50. Paula R. Backscheider, *Reflections on Biography* (Oxford: Oxford University Press, 1999), p. 91, italics in original.

51. Rumours of the composer's demise had swept across Europe as early as 1805. See, for instance, Karl Geiringer, *Haydn: A Creative Life in Music*, 3rd edn, written in collaboration with Irene Geiringer (Berkeley: University of California Press, 1982), pp. 182–83; Leon Botstein, 'The Consequences of Presumed Innocence: The Nineteenth-Century Reception of Joseph Haydn', in *Haydn Studies*, ed. by W. Dean Sutcliffe (Cambridge: Cambridge University Press, 1998), pp. 1–34 (p. 1); and, for a stimulating cultural analysis of these aspects of Haydn historiography with particular emphasis on *The Creation*, Matthew Head's 'Music With "No Past?"'.

52. Ironically, as I intend to explore in a different context, the great last work about which tales of Mozart's decline crystallized was indisputably on the theme of an end, whereas that of Haydn biography instead embraced new beginnings in terms of both its subject matter and, indeed, its early reception history.

their being knowingly read alongside parallel manifestations elsewhere in writings about composers' lives, in order to explore thematic connections between them. The future cultivation of these strategies may lead both to a more complete understanding of the emergent preoccupations of musical biography as a genre and to an enhanced recognition of the historical and cultural significance of life-writing on such presently under-theorized figures as Haydn.

'A scarce specimen of that unrivalled Master's Handwriting': Haydn Manuscripts in the British Library

ARTHUR SEARLE

THE QUOTATION COMES FROM a short note of presentation pasted on one of the binding fly-leaves of the first autograph Haydn manuscript to enter the collections of the British Museum.[1] Perhaps appropriately, the manuscript is the full score of Haydn's fragmentary attempt at an ode in the English style, a bass aria and chorus composed in 1794 (Hob.XXIVa:9), setting extracts from Marchamont Nedham's 'Neptune to the Commonwealth of England', verses published as an introduction to his translation of John Selden's *Mare Clausum seu de Domino Mares*. The surviving two numbers, probably all that was written, in effect praise Britain's supremacy at sea: the aria begins 'Nor can I think my suit is vain', the chorus 'Thy great endeavours to increase the Marine power'. The manuscript has no title-page, heading or date, and originally belonged to Lord Abingdon, from whom the idea that Haydn should set this particular text may well have come. From Abingdon it passed to the music publisher (and, like Abingdon, flute player) Teobaldo Monzani; Monzani presented it, accompanied by his little note, to the Museum in 1821.[2] Hence the beginnings of that institution's collection of autograph manuscripts of Haydn is in marked contrast to the case of Mozart: the British Museum's collection

1. London, British Library, Additional MS 9284, fol. 1.
2. For details of an anonymous setting of these words apparently given to Haydn by Lord Abingdon, and now held by the National Széchényi Library in Budapest, see Balázs Mikusi's article at p. 116 above.

of Mozart manuscripts was initiated by the composer himself when, as a nine-year-old, he visited the Museum in 1765 and presented the trustees with the manuscript of a short work written out specially for the occasion.[3]

After this late start with Haydn, however, the Museum added a good deal more to its manuscript collection as the opportunity arose. Indeed, the process of gradual accretion continued after the library departments of the Museum were established as the new British Library in 1973: three of the four 'London' Symphony autographs now held in the Library's new premises at St Pancras were acquired by gift or purchase in the 1980s, for example. As a result, today there are in the British Library a dozen substantial Haydn works in autograph; all major genres of his output are represented with the exception of the string quartet – though even this situation was remedied for a short time during and after the Second World War when the Museum gave temporary shelter to the music manuscripts from the library of the Royal College of Music.[4] Opportunities to acquire further Haydn manuscripts have occurred in more recent times and, one hopes, will continue to do so. Haydn's folk song settings may not be the most substantial pieces he produced, but if they are included in the count, the number of his works in autograph in the Library comes to over twenty. There are also a considerable number of sets of instrumental parts prepared under Haydn's own (albeit evidently often somewhat lax) supervision, as well as letters, contracts and other associated documents, many of them linked to his two periods in England.

A detailed list of sources, arranged as nearly as possible in chronological order, is given at the end of this article (pp. 228–32 below), so precise catalogue numbers and shelf marks are not given in the following account of the content and growth of the collection.

Autographs and copyists' parts dating from before 1791

Music manuscripts and associated documents relating to Haydn's years in England of course predominate. But circumstances in the later years of the nineteenth century were favourable to the acquisition of manuscripts of the great classical composers, and the Museum had the funds and the imagination to take advantage of this, possibly to a greater extent than the other great European libraries. In 1884 the trustees purchased from the dealers List & Franke a large part of the *Nachlass* of Johann

3. The motet 'God is our refuge' (K20) is now bound with the printed editions of Mozart's sonatas for keyboard and violin (K6–9) published as op. 1 and 2 in Paris the year before, and presented by the composer to the British Museum on the same occasion: British Library shelfmark K.10.a.17.(1–3.). See Alec Hyatt King, *A Mozart Legacy* (London: British Library, 1984), pp. 20–21.
4. This collection on loan contained the autograph score of Haydn's Quartet in C op. 64 no. 1.

Nepomuk Hummel. As Haydn gradually withdrew from his duties in the service of the Esterházy family, Hummel was one of those who took over the provision of music to the princely household. Among his first tasks was to put the Eisenstadt music library in order.[5] A clutch of Haydn autographs ended up in his possession. The Hummel papers in the British Library include the autograph of the E flat Keyboard Sonata of 1766 (Hob.XVI:45) – 'Divertimento per il Clavi Cembalo Solo', signed and dated beside this title in the upper margin of the first of its six leaves.[6] This sonata was published with two others (Hob.XVI.44 and 46) as op. 54 by Longman & Broderip in the late 1780s, 'engraved from the authors [sic] original manuscript', but the whereabouts of the autographs of the other two sonatas is not known.

By far the largest manuscript among the Hummel material is the full score of the first two acts, the major part, of the opera *Orlando Paladino*, composed for Eszterháza in 1782. The score of the third (and at thirty-nine folios, the shortest) act is now in the Staatsbibliothek zu Berlin, and three of the twenty-nine gatherings which make up Act II are missing from the British Library manuscript, their present location unknown. In its present state, Act II therefore comprises seventy-two folios. The missing pages contained the duet 'Quel tuo visetto amabile' (as well as parts of the preceding and succeeding numbers). As 'Quel cor umano e tenero', to words by Da Ponte, this was sung at Haydn's benefit concert in London on 4 May 1795, and according to a contemporary publication, even appears to have been inserted in a performance of Martin y Soler's *Burbero di buon cuore* in London in May 1794, presumably with Haydn's agreement if not his active collaboration.[7] These Hummel papers also include a copy of the printed libretto for the Eszterháza performances of *Orlando Paladino*, with the first cast and details of the scenery and its painter (Pietro Travaglia); on the title-page the composer's name is by far the most prominent, stating that the music is 'del celebre Sigr, Giuseppe Haiden'.

One other Hummel collection item dates from before Haydn's visits to London: the autograph of the German song 'Beim Schmerz der dieses Herz durchwühlt' (Hob.XXVIa:37). (The autograph of the first of the two parts of the duet 'Nisa e Tirsi' of 1796, as well as the partially autograph manuscripts of 'Der Sturm' and of three of the English Canzonettas, all also part of the Hummel purchase, are noted later.) The song has a rather elaborate twenty-bar solo keyboard prelude. Its date is not known, and although it is usually put at *c.* 1765–75, a modern note pencilled on the cover of the manuscript identifies the paper on which it is written (one of the three crescent-moon family of watermarks) as being the same as that used in *Orlando*

5.   Landon, *Haydn: Chronicle and Works*, V, 280.
6.   London, British Library, Additional MS 32173, fol. 35r.
7.   See Hoboken, *Werkverzeichnis*, II, 405–16 (esp. p. 411) for sources and details, and Landon, *Haydn: Chronicle and Works*, III, 254, 306.

Paladino, which may indicate that it was written in 1782, at the same time as most of his other German songs. In this manuscript Haydn has at some time corrected or clarified the musical text at two minor points, using a much darker ink.

The other significant British Library autograph from this period of Haydn's career is the full score of the F major Symphony no. 40, written in 1763. It is a manuscript of sixteen folios in upright format, and possibly the finest of the forty music manuscripts bequeathed to the Museum in 1952 by E. H. W. Meyerstein, who had been briefly an assistant in the Department of Manuscripts during the First World War.[8]

In addition to autograph material, the Hummel collection includes a small number of contemporary copyists' sets of instrumental parts of Haydn pieces: the Symphony no. 84, a group of overtures, among them *L'isola disabitata* and *Il ritorno di Tobia*, and the String Quartets op. 50 nos 1, 2 and 4–6. There are no autograph or other markings on these manuscripts. The parts sent by Haydn to his English publisher William Forster during the 1780s are of more interest, however, both because each set is 'authenticated' by the composer with a signature – sometimes rather more, in some instances amounting to a complete autograph title-page – and because they are such a powerful reminder of how popular his music was in this country long before he came here. There are parts for eleven symphonies (nos 76–78, 80, 81 and the 'Paris' Symphonies nos 82–87) and the overture *Armida*, the complete set of six String Quartets op. 50, the string-quartet version of the Seven Last Words, six piano trios (Hob.XV:2–5, 9 and 10), and the Divertimentos Hob.IV:6*–11*. The parts are written on various sizes of small 'post' paper, so they could be more easily (and cheaply) sent by mail coach from Austria to England, their pages as closely packed with staves as legibility would allow. They are covered in often clumsily written markings by the engravers in England and grimed with printers ink. In many instances the original wrappers for the parcels have been kept as well, annotated with the date of their receipt in the firm – all within the period 1784–87. (In some instances these dates were perhaps added later from documents in the firm's records not acquired by the Museum, and which are now apparently lost.) The late Edmund Poole drew attention to the importance of these manuscripts for publishing history in a groundbreaking article;[9] there he identifies Forster as, after the Viennese firm of Artaria, the most 'considerable' publisher of Haydn's music in the whole of Europe in the 1780s.

8. Meyerstein was a minor poet and novelist, but a major collector: his bequest also includes substantial autograph manuscripts of Beethoven, Schubert and Weber. He left the Department of Manuscripts in 1918 to pursue his career as a writer and collector.

9. H. Edmund Poole, 'Music Engraving Practice in Eighteenth-century London: A Study of Some Forster Editions and their Manuscript Sources', in *Music and Bibliography: Essays in Honour of Alec Hyatt King*, ed. by O. W. Neighbour (London: Bingley, 1980).

While large parts of the Forster archive do indeed appear to be lost, a small number of related papers is preserved in the British Library with the parts. These include five autograph letters from Haydn, 1787–88,[10] written in German and French, and a contract with Forster of 1786 giving incipits of the works concerned, and signed by Haydn. This contract has been later marked with a large letter D, and an endorsement records that it was shown to Haydn during his examination in the case of Forster v. Longman & Broderip. This dispute between the two London publishers over rival editions of the same works has been fully investigated by Nancy E. Mace, using papers unearthed from Chancery records in the National Archives. Among them is a detailed record of a deposition made by Haydn in 1791 in which he attests that the signature on the paper marked D (in addition to other documents) is his.[11]

A further set of parts, in the collection since its purchase from a dealer in 1891, has only anecdotal (rather than scribal) evidence for a direct association with Haydn. These parts are the principal source for the trio 'Pietà di me', for two sopranos, tenor and orchestra (Hob.XXVb:5*); they form part of a group of papers formerly belonging to Vincent Novello, a musician who could seldom refrain from annotating any document that passed through his hands. In marginal notes Novello states that he had been given the piece by the ageing William Shield (1748–1829), and that Shield had told him it had in turn been given to him by Haydn in London, expressly so that it could be sung by the popular soprano Elizabeth Billington. The parts are on small post paper in a hand similar to, if not the same, as those used in the Forster manuscripts. With them is a vocal score in a confident if rather slapdash hand, written on European paper, and a full score made by Novello from the parts. The only guide to the date of this work is its likely performance at the Professional Concert in London on 25 April 1791.[12]

1791–5

Two days before he left England for good in August 1795, Haydn signed over exclusive rights to the first six of his 'London' Symphonies, those performed during his first stay in England, 1791–93, to the impresario Johann Peter Salomon – 'die folgende specifierte Ouverturen die ich für sein Concert componiert habe'. This

---

10. The letter of 28 February 1788 was for long among the documents exhibited in the Manuscripts Saloon at the British Museum, and appears from 1878 in editions of the published *Guide to the Autograph Letters [...] Exhibited to the Public in the Department of Manuscripts*.

11. Nancy E. Mace, 'Haydn and the London Music Sellers: Forster v. Longman & Broderip', *Music & Letters*, 77 (1996), pp. 527–41, esp. p. 535.

12. Simon McVeigh, 'The Professional Concert and Rival Subscription Series in London', *RMA Research Chronicle*, 22 (1989), p. 95.

document, with musical incipits of the six symphonies apparently in Salomon's own hand, is in the British Library, part of a miscellaneous collection of letters and documents, mostly on artistic subjects. Early in 1796 Haydn gave Salomon similar rights over the remaining six symphonies, written during his second stay.[13] The set of manuscript full scores of the twelve owned by Salomon survives. At his death in 1815 it passed to William Ayrton, his musical executor. In 1847 Ayrton sold the scores to the Philharmonic Society (which in 1912 became the Royal Philharmonic Society), of which both he and Salomon had been founder members in 1813.[14] At that time the Society did not have scores of the entire set in its library, and in any case, even before buying them they had frequently borrowed these authoritative scores from Ayrton. In 1988 they were acquired by the British Library from the Society. They are bound (work apparently carried out during Ayrton's ownership) into four volumes, each containing three symphonies, and arranged in the order once traditional, and by which they were identified in the early Philharmonic concert programmes as Haydn's 'Grand' Symphonies nos 1–12.[15]

Included in these volumes are the autograph full scores of the first two symphonies to have been performed, nos 95 and 96, both signed and dated London, 1791. The score of Symphony no. 96 includes a cancelled page of sketches for the second movement, kept because the recto is part of the main text. The remaining ten symphonies are copies, written in two hands working in the two separate periods when Haydn was in London. Both hands are extremely clear. The first, in symphonies nos 93, 94, 97 and 98, is extremely fluent and professional (and was also employed in copying his London opera, *L'anima del filosofo*), whilst the second, in which symphonies 99–104 are copied, is more expansive and less professional but equally accurate. The copies were clearly made from the autograph scores, or from the instrumental parts used in the concerts, or perhaps most likely, from a combination of both. All the scores in the set, including in a few places the two autographs, are annotated with variant readings, some of them at least in Salomon's own hand. Many of these annotations contain variants otherwise found only in the sets of parts published in London by Robert Birchall; together the two sources evidently preserve something of a London performing tradition for these works. The scores were rediscovered well after the completion of Landon's complete edition of the symphonies, but he was characteristically enthusiastic and encouraging about the find. The Landon edition of course has the Birchall parts among its sources, but in 2004

13. Both documents are given in translation by Landon, *Haydn: Chronicle and Works*, III, 319.
14. See Arthur Searle, 'The Royal Philharmonic Society Scores of Haydn's "London" Symphonies', *Haydn Yearbook*, XIV (1983), 173–86.
15. Hoboken, *Werkverzeichnis*, I, 178, is a comparative table of the various numberings which have over time been given to these works.

an edition of symphonies nos 93, 94, 97 and 98 by Michael Ruhling was published drawing specifically on these manuscripts.[16]

In addition to the two autograph scores in the Salomon set, the British Library also now has the autograph full score of Symphony no. 97 of 1792, signed by the composer with 'London' and the year, like all of the 'London' Symphony manuscripts. In this instance, this appears on a title-page rather than at the top right of the first page of music, as is more usual. Following their general practice in the concerts, at the first performance Haydn was at the keyboard with Salomon as leader. The score contains above the violin line towards the end of the Trio to the Minuet movement Haydn's celebrated instruction to his fellow performer: 'in 8va Salomon Solo' with the evidently necessary adjunct 'ma piano'. This manuscript forms part of the British Library's Stefan Zweig Collection, one of a number of remarkable items added by his heirs after Zweig's death which continued and enhanced the musical element of his great manuscript assembly.

The last of the British Library's four 'London' Symphony autographs, and another which also did not form part of Salomon's own set, is that of Symphony no. 103, the 'Drum Roll'. This was in fact the first of the four symphony autographs to enter the collections, one of the enormous number of music manuscripts, of widely varying quality and interest, purchased in the mid-1880s from the omnivorous English collector Julian Marshall.[17] Marshall seems to have been an even more compulsive collector than Meyerstein; his vast collection of prints (many now in the National Art Library at the Victoria and Albert museum) was sold at auction over twelve days, and his Handel libretti were bought by Arthur Balfour and are now in the National Library of Scotland. He and his wife also contributed many entries to the first edition of Grove's *Dictionary* and were early members of the (Royal) Musical Association. In the case of the 'Drum Roll' manuscript, provenance is of more than passing interest. Haydn had given it to Cherubini when the latter visited him in Vienna in 1806, and suggested that they regard themselves as musical father and son. At the head of the first page of the score he wrote 'Padre del celebre Cherubini' and the date, underneath 'London', his original signature and '1795', the year of the work's composition. Marshall purchased the score at the sale of the Cherubini collection in Paris in 1878–79; a cutting from the sale catalogue is pasted inside the front cover. Two leaves, containing three pages of music, of Haydn's original are missing, and

16. *Johann Peter Salomon's Scores of Four Haydn Symphonies, 1791–2*, ed. by Michael E. Ruhling (Lewiston, NY: Edwin Mellen Press, 2004).

17. Perhaps the other most outstanding manuscript from the Marshall collection is the major part of Beethoven's 'Pastoral' Symphony sketchbook, Add. MS 31766. See A. Searle, 'Julian Marshall and the British Museum: Music Collecting in the Later Nineteenth Century', *British Library Journal*, XI (1985), 67–87.

have been replaced in a curiously shaky hand which in fact turns out to be a characteristic of Cherubini's writing later in life; indeed, Marshall suggested that Cherubini was the copyist in a note on an end-paper in the manuscript.[18] It is possible – though rather unlikely – that the original leaves were not present in the manuscript when he was given it by Haydn; more probably they were subsequently accidentally removed or destroyed, or given away as gifts by Cherubini himself, as precious relics of the older man. As the century progressed, Mozart's manuscripts in particular were frequently subjected to dismemberment in this way. If the 'Drum Roll' manuscript pages were removed for this purpose, then it follows, first, that it is most likely that Cherubini's replacements were copied directly from them and, second, that they may yet survive to be rediscovered at some time in the future.

During the 1792 London concert season, Salomon's rivals, the Professional Concert, invited Haydn's former pupil Ignaz Pleyel to write and appear for them, in an attempt to counter the older master's overwhelming success with the public. Pleyel wrote three symphonies during this short-lived experiment – he left at the end of that season, and the Professionals disbanded the following year – and it has recently emerged that these were the three previously unpublished works by him that, just like Salomon's 'London' Symphony scores, had found their way into the library of the Philharmonic Society, their full significance previously unrecognized. They were a gift to the Society in 1835 from William Dance. Like Salomon and Ayrton, Dance had been among the founder members of the Society in 1813, but more significantly in this context, before that he had played with the Professionals in the 1790s.[19]

The most substantial autograph manuscripts of Haydn's London years in the British Library are undoubtedly the four symphony full scores and the *Mare Clausum* fragment. But there is other material related to this period, some of it partly autograph. Besides new symphonies, there were other new works, among them the madrigal 'The Storm' (Hob.XXIVa:8), a short continuous, and highly dramatic, piece for soloists, chorus and orchestra. Composed in 1792, this was his first setting of English words, paving the way for the *Mare Clausum* aria and chorus, as well as arguably, over time, for *The Creation*. 'The Storm' was one of a number of English

18. Walter Gerstenberg, *Musikerhandschriften von Palestrina bis Beethoven* (Zurich: Atlantis Verlag, 1960), no. 88, reproduces a strikingly similar example of Cherubini's writing. Until chancing upon Gerstenberg's reproduction, I was for a long time puzzled by this strange, shaky, hand. The position put forward that the pages are not in Cherubini's hand (see my 'Haydn Autographs and "Authentic" Manuscript Copies in the British Library', *Early Music*, 10 (1982), 496, and Hoboken, *Werkverzeichnis*, I, 218) is therefore quite incorrect.
19. British Library, RPS MSS 155, 157, 158. See A. Searle, 'Pleyel's 'London' Symphonies', *Early Music*, 36 (2008), 231–42, which explains how a number of features of Haydn's 'Drum Roll' Symphony are anticipated in Pleyel's E flat Symphony (Benton 152). All three Pleyel symphonies have now been published by Heinz Anderle, Ruppersthal, Austria, 2007, 2009.

works that Haydn presented to the Viennese audience in two concerts late in 1793, between his two London visits. For the Vienna performance he recast the work, among other things with a German text and with extensive revisions to the wind parts. The British Library's Hummel collection includes a full score of this German version ('Der Sturm') in which the parts for voices and most of the strings are the work of a copyist, leaving space in the layout of the staves for the wind and timpani. These have been completed by the composer, together with much of the instrumental bass part; in addition, the last page of the manuscript, containing the concluding fourteen bars of the piece, is entirely in Haydn's hand.

Haydn's temporary return to Vienna coincided with Beethoven's arrival there, and during 1793 the younger composer studied with Haydn. Among the sources for this is the small pocket notebook which Beethoven kept that year, an astonishing testament to the relationship between those two composers, and now in the British Library Zweig Collection. The book contains a number of references to Haydn, including on one page a list of repeated payments of small sums to 'Heidn', some for coffee, some, it is assumed, for lessons.[20]

In his London Notebooks, Haydn records a number of meetings with members of the British royal family, and the cordial treatment he received from them. The Royal Music Library is now part of the British Library music collections. It contains two manuscript items associated with Haydn, both copies, but evidently derived from sources close to the composer. The first is an incomplete set of parts for the eloquent march for wind band composed, probably in 1792, for the Prince of Wales (Hob. VIII:3a). At present they are in an otherwise rather scrappily written set of part books, together with a variety of other wind band marches. But the parts for the Haydn march have clearly been inserted into the books at a later date: each of them is headed 'Mr Haydn Marcia', and they are all on the same paper and in the same hand, which is different from (and far more professional than) anything found elsewhere in the books. When the Royal Society of Musicians in turn asked Haydn for a march, he expanded this piece by omitting the serpent and adding flutes and strings to the original instruments. The autograph score, still with the Society, clearly – and remarkably – shows the two stages of composition, with the wind parts on the upper staves, and the additions below in a markedly darker ink. A comparison of the parts with this score shows a quite remarkable degree of agreement: the parts are not merely accurate in notation but also contain every dynamic, staccato and stress mark to be found in the autograph.[21]

20. British Library, Zweig MS 14, fol. 5v.
21. The late Stanley Sadie first pointed out to me the two stages apparent in the score. I am grateful to Mrs Maggie Gibb, to Colin Coleman and to the Royal Society of Musicians for generously making the score available to me.

The other set of parts of Haydn works in the Royal Music Library can more obviously be related directly to the composer because they bear his signature in a number of places. In about 1790, to a commission from King Ferdinand IV of Naples, Haydn had composed a series of delicate Notturni incorporating parts for two *lire organizzate*, instruments little used elsewhere. He arranged some of these for different instruments, in which form the pieces can be identified in Salomon's concert programmes in 1792. There they were perhaps played by a larger ensemble, but the surviving parts in the Royal Music Library for three of these rewritten Notturni (Hob.II:27*, 28*, 31*) indicate performance as chamber music, suitable for a court entertainment. In addition to Haydn's signature, there is in each set, in another hand, the date 26 April 1792. In the titles to the parts, the pieces are variously described as either 'Divertimento' or 'Notturno'.

Haydn also records in his London Notebooks his growing friendship with Mrs Anne Hunter, the widow of a distinguished surgeon and something of a poet. At around this time, Haydn wrote two sets of six English Canzonettas, published in handsome editions available from the composer and usually signed by him on the title-page.[22] The first six all set verses by Mrs Hunter; the second set includes a setting of her poem 'The Wanderer'. Among the Hummel manuscripts in the British Library are copies, apparently by Haydn's amanuensis Johann Elssler, of three of the songs from the second book: The 'Sailor's Song' (beginning 'High on the giddy bending mast', one of the most popular of Haydn's English songs), 'Sympathy' (to a translation of words by Metastasio), and the deeply moving setting of words from Shakespeare's *Twelfth Night*, 'She never told her love' (Hob.XXVIa:31, 33, 34). Minor errors in the words indicate that the copyist had some difficulty with English, whilst the words to the 'Sailor's Song' are in Haydn's own hand (Fig. 1).

Haydn's last benefit concert in London took place at the King's Theatre concert room on 4 May 1795, 'perhaps the greatest concert of Haydn's life'.[23] The British Library has a copy of the handbill, giving the programme, and with remarkable manuscript annotations by a member of the audience. This was the concert at which the Symphony no. 104 was given its first performance; it also included the duet extracted from the opera *Orlando Paladino* which is mentioned above. The 'Military' Symphony (no. 100) was also played, and is appropiately annotated as 'Grand but very noisy'.[24]

22. These works are the subject of the article by Caroline Grigson at pp. 77–91 above.
23. Landon, *Haydn: Chronicle and Works*, III, 306. Landon also transcribes the annotations to the playbill, and the upper part of it is reproduced in A. Searle, *Haydn & London* (London: British Library, 1989), p. 10.
24. This playbill was kindly lent by Mr Albi Rosenthal for display in the British Library's 1989 exhibition 'Haydn and England' and acquired for the Library in 2007.

Fig. 1. Joseph Haydn, 'Sailor's Song' from the the English Canzonettas, the words in
Haydn's autograph. British Library, Add. MS 32173, fol. 30v.

Later manuscripts

Haydn's Piano Trio in E flat minor (Hob.XV:31) apparently neatly spans the divide
between his second visit to London and his return to Vienna. The Trio is in two
movements – an Andante and an Allegro. Each is written on a different kind of
English paper, though both have a watermark date of 1794. The Andante has
Haydn's date 1795 at the head of the page, whereas the Allegro appears at first to
be undated, but closer examination reveals that text has been scratched out above
the beginning of the music. With the aid of ultra-violet light, this text can be clearly
read: 'Sonata "Jacob's Dream" by Dr Haydn', with the date 1794. In the composer's
own list of works written in London, contained in his fourth London Notebook, is
a work called 'The Dream', taking up five leaves of paper,[25] and Elssler's later

---

25. *Collected Correspondence and London Notebooks*, pp. 309–10; the significance of the title 'Jacob's
     Dream', and the circumstances of an early performance accompanied by Therese Jansen, is
     discussed by Thomas Tolley at p. 58 above.

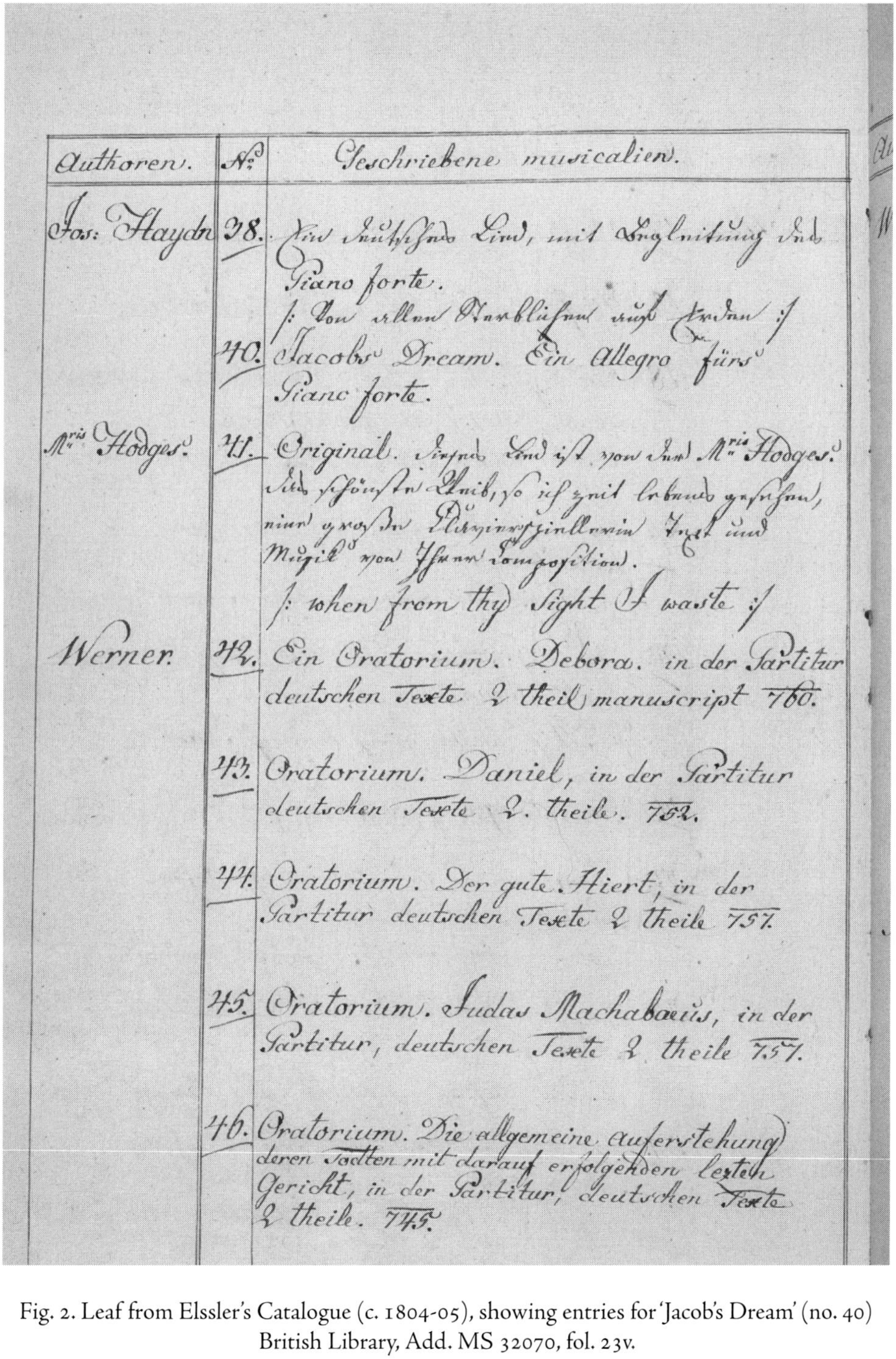

Fig. 2. Leaf from Elssler's Catalogue (c. 1804-05), showing entries for 'Jacob's Dream' (no. 40) British Library, Add. MS 32070, fol. 23v.

Fig. 3. Joseph Haydn, Theme and variation on 'Gott erhalte Franz den Kaiser',
for keyboard. British Library, Zweig MS 41 (between 1797 and 1799).

catalogue of Haydn's music library (see Fig. 2; discussed below, p. 227) includes,
under autograph manuscripts, an Allegro for piano called 'Jacobs Dream'. The Trio,
consisting of both movements, was eventually published, in Vienna, in 1803. The
complete autograph score is part of the British Library Zweig Collection, purchased
by Zweig in 1932 at the second André auction in Berlin. The reference in Haydn's
London work list to 'Jacob's Dream' alone, and the number of leaves given, makes it
clear that the two movements were not yet put together when Haydn compiled his
London list, and that the Andante must therefore have been composed and added
sometime later.

Evidence of Haydn's continued links with London is provided by the contract which
he entered into with the music publisher Frederick Augustus Hyde in the months
of July and August 1796.[26] Hyde was a partner in the firm which soon after became
Longman & Broderip. The agreement, intended to cover a period of five years, re-

26. This contract is discussed in David Rowland's article at pp. 92–111 above.

lates to specific types of music, principally instrumental (piano trios, string quartets, etc.), with a tariff of prices for each category. Hyde's signature is witnessed by Rebecca Schroeter, a devoted admirer of Haydn in London; the composer received the document in Vienna early in August and had his signature notarised before sending it back to London. That year Longman & Broderip published three piano trios, the first category in the list.

Stefan Zweig was among the greatest of twentieth-century collectors, in both the extent and the consistent quality of the manuscripts he acquired. The core of the British Library Zweig Collection consists of the items he chose to take with him when he left Austria, a fraction of all that he once owned. In addition to the Trio mentioned above, the other Haydn manuscript he brought with him to London is only part of a work, consisting of just a single leaf. It contains the theme and first variation from Haydn's own keyboard arrangement of the variations on his Imperial hymn 'Gott erhalte Franz den Kaiser' which form the second movement of his String Quartet op. 76 no. 3 (Fig. 3). The keyboard variations were published in Vienna in 1799 by Artaria whose authentication appears on the verso of the leaf. The remaining variations are on a second leaf, now in Berlin, and the two were separated long before Zweig acquired his half of the autograph. The melody was later also adopted as the German national anthem, to the words 'Deutschland über alles', from 'Das Lied der Deutschen' of Heinrich Hoffmann von Fallersleben. Zweig's collection was made up of literary and historical papers as well as music, and ten years after he acquired the Haydn he was able to add an autograph manuscript of the 'Lied der Deutschen' as well. He took great delight in such connections between items he owned.

The last significant wholly autograph music from this final period of Haydn's composing life consists of three pages of sketches for *The Creation*. They are now together in a British Museum binding with eight of the settings of British folk songs for voice and piano trio, a large number of which occupied some of his very last working years; the two manuscripts were apparently received in the Museum at the same time. The oratorio sketches are naturally the more interesting. They comprise a bifolium, the first leaf bearing an elaborate inscription in an unknown hand identifying them as a 'Heilige Relique […] aus dessen unsterbliches Werke Die Schöpfung' ('a sacred fragment […] from the immortal work The Creation'). The sketches themselves are in four or five stave score, and principally for what is possibly the oratorio's best known chorus, 'Die Himmel erzählen' ('The Heavens are telling'). The leaves are a little crumpled and have clearly been folded in half at some stage of their life.

Their provenance is in striking contrast to the patrician Zweig Collection. The sketches were purchased by the British Museum in 1871 from two sisters living in Budapest, the daughters of Anton Polzelli, who in turn was the son of Luigia

Polzelli, a singer in the service of the Esterházys and someone to whom Haydn was at one period particularly close. Young Anton was also a musician at the Eisenstadt court. With the sketches is a lithograph copy of a letter to him from Haydn addressed to 'Mein lieber Sohn', though clearly using Anton as means to convey his greetings to the entire musical establishment at court, all of whose members he thought of as his children. With it is a statement of 1813 relating to Anton's career, also a lithograph, but notarised by a Pest lawyer in 1865. In addition to these papers, incorporated into the volume in which the sketches are bound, there is in the archives of the former Department of Manuscripts a lengthy correspondence between the sisters and the Museum in which, as a final demonstration of the importance of their offer, they unhesitatingly describe themselves as the granddaughters of Joseph Haydn. A few years later the two, pleading great need, offered other Haydn relics for sale in the Viennese press, making the same claim.[27]

By the time of Haydn's visits to London, the taste for folk songs, suitably adapted for the fashionable pleasure gardens or for the drawing room, was already well established. The Edinburgh musical amateur George Thomson first commissioned arrangements for voice and piano trio from Pleyel when both he and Haydn were in London in 1791, but did not approach Haydn until after his return to Vienna. Haydn set approaching 200 Scots, Welsh and English airs for Thomson, who also commissioned similar work from other European composers, Beethoven prominent among them. The Thomson archive in the British Library includes correspondence as well as manuscript music. Earlier than any surviving letter from Haydn himself, he is mentioned grumpily in one from Leopold Kozeluch complaining that the older composer is being paid more than him, 'et je les a arrangé surement si bien com[m]e lui'.[28] In all, ten letters from Haydn, dated 1801–04, survive in the Thomson papers, along with six receipts – one in English and signed 'Dr Haydn'. The latter show just how profitable this hack work could be: in June 1803 Haydn received 120 ducats, stated as the equivalent then of £59. 3s. 5d. sterling. As with the Forster papers, a number of the wrappers in which parcels were sent to Thomson, usefully annotated on arrival, are also preserved.

The music manuscripts of the folk song settings, chiefly the work of copyists, are more problematic and indicate the ease with which this profit was earned. A volume of seventy-two mainly Welsh songs seem indeed to be the master's work, but another of Scots songs has been demonstrated by Rudolf Angermüller to be in large part the work of Sigismund Neukomm, Haydn's pupil at the time (and one who subsequently built a very successful career out of being 'elève de Haydn'). A smaller volume, today still in its contemporary binding, contains arrangements of Scots songs

27. Roland Tenschert, *Frauen um Haydn* (Vienna: Donau-Verlag, 1947), pp. 91–92.
28. British Library, Additional MS 35263, fol. 48.

in the hand of Haydn's copyist Radnitzky, and, bound in at the end, a few songs re-copied and evidently sent back to the composer with marginal requests from Thom-son for extended opening and closing 'symphonies': in the spaces duly left are brief introductory and concluding passages in Haydn's own hand. Among the copies sent to Thomson is one complete setting in Haydn's autograph, a familiar Scots tune which he has headed 'The blue Bell', signed 'Dr. Haydn' and dated 1805. The only other autograph settings in the British Library – eight arrangements all fully written out by Haydn, but with no words or titles – are those already mentioned as bound in with the sketches for *The Creation*. Though they are not mentioned in the relevant correspondence, their presence in this volume, most likely assembled by the Museum from material received at the same time, suggests that these too came from the two ladies of Budapest. They are neither signed nor dated and are of songs published in Edinburgh by William Whyte, one of the two publishers, in addition to Thomson, for whom Haydn wrote folk-song settings, and have been dated to 1802–03. Whyte began issuing the songs in 1804, and the Library also has a receipt from Haydn to him dated that year.[29]

One further enlightened nineteenth-century acquisition by the British Museum – neither autograph nor a music manuscript – relates to Haydn's final years. It is the catalogue of the composer's music library compiled for him with typical care by Elssler. It was purchased by the Museum in 1863 from the band master and com-poser Carli Zoeller. The text of this catalogue has been transcribed and published by Landon,[30] and the material acquired by Haydn in London is discussed in Balázs Mikusi's article in the present volume at pp. 112–136 above. The manuscript is divided into categories: printed music, manuscript copies of his own and other people's works, etc. The final section is 'Eigner Manuskripten', autographs of Haydn's own compositions. The entries under this heading are numbered in what is clearly a continuous series, though with breaks in the numbering where Haydn did not possess his own scores of particular works. These numbers take us back almost to where this account of the British Library's Haydn sources began: all of the manu-scripts mentioned above – those from the Hummel collection, the opera, the piano sonata, the duet, 'Der Sturm' with German words, and so on – have lightly written in the bottom left-hand corner of their first page the relevant number from Elssler's list. Intriguingly, those which have no corresponding entry in the list still carry a number fitting neatly into one of the breaks in the sequence.

When Haydn's strength began to fail towards the end of his life, he had a cele-brated visiting card printed quoting lines from his partsong 'Der Greis'

29. For the Thomson and Whyte material see Joseph Haydn, *Werke* (Munich: Henle), XXXII: *Volksliedbearbeitungen*, vols 3–5 ed. by Marjorie Rycroft and others (2001–05).
30. Landon, *Haydn: Chronicle and Works*, V, 299–320.

(Hob.XXVc:5): 'Hin ist alle meine Kraft'. One of the most recent bequests to the Library, from the scholar Alan Tyson, includes one of these cards bearing this touching valediction.[31]

List of manuscript sources in the British Library

This list is an expanded and corrected version of that given in the booklet *Haydn & England* that accompanied the British Library's 1989 exhibition with the same title. Reference is given here to complete pages and details from the manuscripts reproduced in that booklet and in a small number of other sources. Facsimiles of selected autograph pages are almost always to be found in critical editions, notably the complete Haydn edition prepared by the Joseph Haydn-Institut, Cologne, and published by Henle in Munich. These are not cited here. Reference is also made to the translations of the letters published by Landon.

Abbreviations used in the list:

Gerstenberg	Walter Gerstenberg, *Musikerhandschriften von Palestrina bis Beethoven* (Zurich: Atlantis, 1960)
Landon	*The Collected Correspondence and London Notebooks of Joseph Haydn*, ed. by H. C. Robbins Landon (London: Barrie and Rockcliff, 1959)
Rosenthal	Albi Rosenthal, 'The contract between Joseph Haydn and Frederick Augustus Hyde (1796)' in *Studies in Music History Presented to H. C. Robbins Landon on his Seventieth Birthday*, ed. by Otto Biba and David Wyn Jones (London: Thames and Hudson, 1996), pp. 72–81
Searle, *Haydn*	Arthur Searle, *Haydn & England* (London: British Library, 1989)
Searle, *Zweig*	Arthur Searle, *The British Library Stefan Zweig Collection: Catalogue of the Music Manuscripts* (London: British Library, 1999)

Music scores, parts, sketches, etc

Symphony no. 40, 1763. *Autograph* full score. Add. MS 47849. 16 fols.

Piano Sonata in E flat (Hob.XVI:45), 1766. *Autograph.* Add. MS 32173, fols 33–38. *Reproduced:* fol. 34v, Searle, *Haydn*, p. 12.

---

31. British Library, Tyson MS 25, fol. 1.

Song 'Beim Schmerz der dieses Herz' (Hob.XXVIa:37). *Autograph*, [*c.* 1765–75?]. Add. MS 32173, fols 1–2v.

Opera *Orlando Paladino* (Hob.XXVIII:11), 1782. *Autograph* full score. Act I and greater part of Act II. Add. MS 32172. 244 fols. *Reproduced:* fol. 228, Searle, *Haydn*, p. 13.

Copyists' parts sent to Forster, 1780s:
    Symphonies 77, 78. Egerton MS 2335. 35 fols.
    Symphonies and Overture, *Armida*. Egerton MS 2379, fols 191–386.
    String Quartets, op. 50. Egerton MS 2379, fols 1–54.
    Piano Trios. Egerton MS 2379, fols 55–124.
    Divertimenti. Egerton MS 2379, fols 125–48.
    Seven Last Words. Egerton MS 2379, fols 150–89.
    Reproduced: Egerton MS 2379, fol. 319, Searle, 1989, p. 15.

Copyists' parts from the Hummel Collection, [1780s?]:
    Six Overtures: Hob.Ia:1, 2 (*Il ritorno di Tobia*), 6, 10, 13 (*L'isola disabitata*) and 15 (*La vera costanza*). Add. MS 32174, fols 33–79.
    Symphony no. 84. Add. MS 32174, fols 80–101.
    String Quartets, op. 50, nos 1, 2, 4–6. Add. MS 32174, fols 102–47.

Trio 'Pieta di me' (Hob.XXVb:5*), [1791]. Vocal score and copyist's parts, Add. MS 34073, fols 8–40, Novello's full score, ibid., fols 41–66ᵛ.

The 'London' Symphonies, set of full scores, two *autograph*, ten contemporary copies, made for and owned by Johann Peter Salomon, 1791–[1795]. Bound into four volumes:
    Symphony no. 97. *Copy*, [1792]. Add. MS 64931. 52 fols.
    Symphony no. 93. *Copy*, [1791]. Add. MS 64932. 40 fols.
    Symphony no. 94. *Copy*, [1791]. Add. MS 64933. 42 fols.

    Symphony no. 98. *Copy*, [1792]. Add. MS 64934. 48 fols.
    Symphony no. 95. *Autograph*, 1791. Add. MS 64935. 29 fols.
    Symphony no. 96. *Autograph*, 1791. Add. MS 64936. 32 fols.

    Symphony no. 104. *Copy*, [1795]. Add. MS 64937. 75 fols.
    Symphony no. 103. *Copy*, [1795]. Add MS 64938. 78 fols. [See also autograph below.]
    Symphony no. 102. *Copy*, [1794]. Add. MS 64939. 71 fols.

    Symphony no. 99. *Copy*, [1793?]. Add. MS 64940. 54 fols.
    Symphony no. 101. *Copy*, [1793/4]. Add. MS 64941. 85 fols.
    Symphony no. 100. *Copy*, [1793/4]. Add. MS 64942. 74 fols.

Reproduced: Add. MS 64936, fol. 1r, Gerstenberg no. 92 and also in the Haydn article in *The New Grove Dictionary of Music and Musicians*, ed. by Stanley Sadie, 20 vols (London: Macmillan, 1980), VIII, 345.

Symphony no. 97, 1792. *Autograph* full score. Zweig MS 39. 43 fols. *Reproduced*: fols 1r, 30r, Searle, *Zweig*, pl. XL, XLI; fol. 30r (detail only), Searle, *Haydn*, p. 23.

March for the Prince of Wales (Hob.VII:3), [1792]. Copyist's parts. R.M. 21.c.26–31.

Notturni (Hob.II:27*, 28*, 31*), 1792. Copyist's parts. R.M. 21.a.27.(1–3). 38, 36, 21 fols.

Der Sturm (Hob.XXIVa:8). Partly *autograph* full score, [1793]. Add. MS 32173, fols 7–24.

Neptune to the Commonwealth of England. Autograph full score, [1794]. Add. MS 9284. 16 fols.

Symphony no. 103, the 'Drum Roll'. *Autograph* full score, 1795. Add MS 31707. 40 fols. *Reproduced*: fol. 2v (detail only), Searle, *Haydn*, p. 22.

Three songs from second set of Original Canzonettas (Hob.XXVIa:34, 33, 31), published 1795. Copy by Johann Elssler, with words for third song *autograph*. Add. MS 32173, fols 25–32v.

Piano Trio in E flat minor (Hob.XV:31). *Autograph*, 1795. Zweig MS 40. 9 fols. *Reproduced*: fol. 6r (detail only), Searle, *Haydn*, p. 28, and (complete page), Searle, *Zweig*, pl. XLI.

Duet 'Nisa e Tirsi' (Hob.XXVa:1). *Autograph*, 1796. Add. MS 32173, fols 3–6v.

Variations in G on the anthem 'Gott erhalte Franz den Kaiser', for keyboard (Hob.III:77). *Autograph*, [1797–99]. Zweig MS 41.1 fol. *Reproduced* Searle, *Zweig*, pl. XLII.

Sketches for choruses from *The Creation* (Hob.XXI:2). *Autograph*, [1796–98]. Add. MS 28613, fols 2–3v.

Settings of Scottish and Welsh folk songs [1802–05]

Autograph (signed and dated): 'The blue bell[s of Scotland]', 1805. Add. MS 35275, fols 28–29r. *Reproduced*: Searle, *Haydn*, p. 18.

Autographs (unsigned and undated, nos from the list in *The New Grove Dictionary* (1980)): nos 51, 50, 291, 358, 294, 349, 188, 204, [1802–03]. Add. MS 35275, fols 4–11.

Partial *autographs* (introductory and concluding piano parts): nos 110, 11, 387, 271, 77, 232. Add. MS 35272, fols 21–22v.

Signed copyists' MSS: Add. MS 35274, 1804. 44 fols. Signed fols 1 and 44r, the first as 'Harmonisiert by Dr Haydn', and dated 1804.

Copyists' MSS. (including settings incorrectly ascribed to Haydn; all sent to Thomson): Add. MS 35272, fols 1–20v; Add. MS 35273 (partly by Sigismund Neukomm). 92 ff.; Add. MS 35275, fols 1–26v, 30–42v.

Letters and papers

Forster papers:
Contract, 1786, signed by Haydn. Egerton MS 2380, fol. 12. (printed Landon, pp. 53–56).
Letters from Haydn, all in Egerton MS 2380: fols 1–2, 8 April 1787 (Landon, pp. 59–60); fols 3–4, 28 June 1787 (Landon, pp. 65–66, *reproduced* pl. XVII); fols 5–6, 8 Aug. 1787 (Landon, p. 69); fols 7–8, 20 Sept. 1787 (Landon, p. 70); fols 9–10, 28 Feb. 1788 (Landon, p. 76).

Letter to Artaria, 17 Aug. 1788, Add. MS 29804, fol. 1 (Landon, pp. 77–78 and *reproduced* pl. XVIII).

Agreement with Johann Peter Salomon, 13 Aug. 1795, Add. MS 38071, fol. 5 (last page only *reproduced* Searle, *Haydn*, p. 9).

Contract with Augustus Frederick Hyde, 1796. MS Mus. 1713/1. *Reproduced* and transcribed in Rosenthal.

Handbill giving the programme for Haydn's benefit concert on 4 May 1795, annotated by someone present. Music Deposit 1998/04. *Reproduced* in Searle, *Haydn*, p. 10.

Thomson papers:
Letters (except where stated) and receipts to George Thomson, all in Add. MS 35263: fol. 130, 27 Oct. 1801, in Haydn's hand, but not signed (Landon, p. 194); fols 136–37, 5 Dec. 1801, with wrapper for packet it accompanied (Landon, pp. 194–95); fols 138–39, 2 Jan. 1802 (Landon, pp. 198–99); fols 140–41, 29 Jan. 1802 (Landon, pp. 200–01); fol. 142, receipt 12 Feb. 1802; fols 164–65,

wrapper and receipt, 8 June 1803 (see Landon p. 219, not transcribed in full); fol. 170, 30 June 1803 (Landon, pp. 218–19); fol. 171, 1 July 1803 (Landon, p. 219); fols 172–73, 6 July 1803 (Landon, pp. 219–20); fols 196–97, 18 Dec. 1803, with receipt on conjoint fol. 197 (Landon, pp. 222–23 and pl. XXII), with related wrapper fol. 209; fols 225–26, 6 April 1804 (Landon, pp. 228–29 and pl. XXIII); fol. 233, 10 May 1804 (Landon, p. 229); fol. 234, receipt 11 May 1804, signed only by Haydn for money received from Viennese bankers Fries by way of Coutts in London (fol. 235 is Thomson's office wrapper for receipts from Haydn, 12 Feb. 1802–11 May 1804); fol. 238, receipt and declaration of Thomson's ownership, signed only, 11 June 1804; fols 244–45, 30 Oct. 1804 (Landon, pp. 235–36); fol. 246, receipt, signed only, 30 Aug. 1804.

Receipt to William Whyte, 3 Feb. 1804 (Landon, pl. X).

Index